무문관 강론

영어 번역 수록

이 책은 2010.1부터 2011.2까지 불교신문에 격주로 실렸던 '우학 스님의 무문관'을 모아 엮었습니다. 또한, 최근에까지 미국 뉴욕의 〈미주현대불교(월간지)〉에도 연재되었던바, 미주 불자들로부터 큰 반향을 불러일으켰습니다. 영어번역은 미국인 명행 스님께서 해 주셨습니다.

無一 우학 스님의

무문관 강론
영어번역수록

한국불교
감포도

머릿말을 대신하여…

〈천일 무문관 청정결사〉 중이신 우학 스님을 대신하여 평소 즐겨 치시던 일원상을 머릿말에 대신합니다.

차례

8
머릿말을 대신하여

무문자서_ 17
無門自序, 무문혜개 스님의 서문

차례

제1칙_ 29
趙州狗子, 조주 큰스님의 무자 화두

제2칙_ 39
百丈野狐, 백장 큰스님과 여우 이야기

제3칙_ 49
俱胝竪指, 구지 큰스님 손가락을 세우다

제4칙_ 59
胡子無鬚, 달마대사는 수염이 없다

제5칙_ 69
香嚴上樹, 향엄 큰스님 나무에 오르다

제6칙_ 79
世尊拈花, 부처님 꽃을 드시다

제7칙_ 89
趙州洗鉢, 조주 큰스님 발우 씻으라고 하시다

제8칙_ 99
奚仲造車, 해중의 수레 만들기

제9칙_ 109
大通智勝, 대통지승 부처님

제10칙_ 119
清稅孤貧, 청세의 가난

차례

제11칙_ 129
州勘庵主, 조주 큰스님 암주를 간파하다

제12칙_ 139
巖喚主人, 서암 큰스님 주인공을 부르다

제13칙_ 149
德山托鉢, 덕산 큰스님의 탁발

제14칙_ 159
南泉斬貓, 남전 큰스님 고양이를 베다

제15칙_ 169
洞山三頓, 동산 스님 세 차례 몽둥이를 맞다

제16칙_ 181
鐘聲七條, 종소리에 7조 가사를 수하다

제17칙_ 191
國師三喚, 국사가 세 번 부르다

제18칙_ 201
洞山三斤, 동산 큰스님의 마삼근

제19칙_ 211
平常是道, 평상심이 도이다

제20칙_ 221
大力量人, 큰 힘을 갖춘 사람

차례

제21칙_ 231
雲門屎橛, 운문의 똥 막대기

제22칙_ 241
迦葉刹竿, 가섭존자의 찰간

제23칙_ 251
不思善惡, 선도 악도 생각마라

제24칙_ 261
離却語言, 말을 끊고서

제25칙_ 271
三座說法, 삼좌가 설법함

제26칙_ 281
二僧卷簾, 두 스님이 발을 걷어 올리다

제27칙_ 291
不是心佛, 마음도 아니요 부처도 아니다

제28칙_ 301
久響龍潭, 오랫동안 용담의 소문을 듣다

제29칙_ 317
非風非幡, 바람도 아니요 깃발도 아니다

제30칙_ 327
卽心卽佛, 이 마음이 곧 부처이다

차례

제31칙_ 337
趙州勘婆, 조주 큰스님 노파를 점검하다

제32칙_ 349
外道問佛, 외도가 부처님께 여쭙다

제33칙_ 359
非心非佛, 마음도 아니고 부처도 아니다

제34칙_ 371
智不是道, 지혜는 도가 아니다

제35칙_ 381
倩女離魂, 천녀의 혼이 나가다

제36칙_ 391
路逢達道, 길에서 도인을 만나면

제37칙_ 403
庭前柏樹, 뜰 앞의 측백나무

제38칙_ 415
牛過窓櫺, 소가 창틀을 빠져 나가다

제39칙_ 425
雲門話墮, 말에 떨어지다

제40칙_ 435
趯倒淨甁, 정병을 넘어 뜨리다

차례

제41칙_ 445
達磨安心, 달마가 마음을 편안하게 해주다

제42칙_ 455
女子出定, 여인을 삼매에서 깨우다

제43칙_ 465
首山竹篦, 수산의 죽비

제44칙_ 475
芭蕉拄杖, 파초의 주장자

제45칙_ 485
他是阿誰, 그 사람이 누구인가

제46칙_ 495
竿頭進步, 장대 끝에서 한걸음 내딛어라

제47칙_ 505
兜率三關, 도솔의 세 가지 관문

제48칙_ 515
乾峯一路, 열반으로 가는 한 길

무문자서(無門自序)

Preface by Venerable Mu-Mun Hye-Gae

무문혜개(無門慧開) 스님의 서문

禪宗無門關

佛語心爲宗, 無門爲法門. 旣是無門, 且作麽生透. 豈不見道, 從門入者不是家珍, 從緣得者始終成壞, 恁麽說話, 大似無風起浪, 好肉剜瘡. 何況滯言句, 覓解會. 掉棒打月, 隔靴爬痒, 有甚交涉. 慧開, 紹定戊子夏, 首衆于東嘉龍翔. 因衲子請益, 遂將古人公案, 作敲門瓦子, 隨機引導學者. 竟爾抄錄, 不覺成集. 初不以前後敍列, 共成四十八則. 通曰無門關. 若是箇漢, 不顧危亡, 單刀直入. 八臂那吒, 攔他不住. 縱使西天四七, 東土二三, 只得望風乞命. 設或躊躇, 也似隔窓看馬騎, 貶得眼來, 早已蹉過.

선종의 문이 없는 관문이란?

부처님께서 말씀하신 가르침은 마음을 으뜸으로 삼고 문 없는 문을 법문으로 삼는다. 그러니 이에 문이 없다면, 어떻게 뚫고 나가겠는가?

"문을 통해 들어오는 것은 집안의 보배가 될 수 없고 인연을 따라 얻은 것은 시작과 끝이 있어, 이루어지면 무너진다."라는 말을 들어보지 못했는가?

　이렇게 말하는 것조차 바람 없는데 파도를 일으키는 격이며, 멀쩡한 살을 찔러서 상처를 내는 것과 같다. 그러니 어찌 언어나 문자에 매달려 알음알이로 구하리요, 이는 막대기를 휘둘러 달을 치며, 신발을 신고 가려운 데를 긁는 것과 같은 꼴이니 무슨 좋은 결과가 있겠는가?

　본인, 혜개(慧開)가 소정 무자년(1228년) 여름, 동가에 있는 용상사에서 대중들의 수좌로 있을 때, 법을 물어오는 납자들의 청에 따라 옛사람들의 공안을 '문을 두드리는 기왓조각'으로 삼아 각자 근기에 따라 공부하는 이들을 인도하였다. 마침내 간추려 기록하다 보니 어느새 책 한 권이 되었다. 애초부터 앞뒤 순서를 고려한 것은 아니었으며, 모아보니 48칙이 되었다. 이것을 통틀어 『무문관』이라고 이름을 붙였다.

　만약에 어떤 사람이 목숨을 돌보지 아니하고 칼 한 자루 들고 곧바로 뛰어든다면, 팔이 여덟 개나 되는 신장도 그를 막아 붙잡아 두지 못할 것이며, 설령 서천의 스물여덟 조사와 동토의 여섯 조사라도 그 위풍을 바라보며 그저 목숨을 구걸할 것이다. 만약 주저하고 머뭇거린다면 달리는 말을, 창을 통해 보는 것처럼, 눈 깜빡할 사이에 놓치고 말 것이다.

頌曰. 大道無門, 千差有路. 透得此關, 乾坤獨步.

게송으로 읊노니,
　　"대도에는 문이 없도다.
　　천 갈래 길은 있으니
　　이 관문을 뚫고 나아가면
　　온 천지 당당히 활보하리라."

강론(講論)

『무문관(無門關)』은 선가(禪家)에서 간화선의 기본 텍스트로 널리 사용되어 왔다. 『벽암록』, 『종용록』 등의 선서(禪書)가 이미 편찬되어 있었지만, 간화선의 종지를 결론적으로 더욱 굳건히 제시한 공안집은 무문혜개 스님의 이 무문관이다. 무문관에서 제시한 48칙의 공안마다 화두참구하는 방법과 정법의 안목을 열어 주는 자비방편이 가득하다.

　무문혜개(1183~1260) 스님은 출가 후 월림사관(月林師觀) 선사의 문하에 들어가 조주 큰스님의 무자(無字) 화두와 씨름하였다. 6년이 지난 어느 날 점심공양을 알리는 북소리를 듣고 불법의 대의를 깨달았다. 스님의 오도송이다.

"맑은 날에 한소리 큰 우뢰
대지의 중생들 눈 활짝 열었도다.
삼라만상이 한결같이 머리 조아리니
수미산을 뛰어넘어 덩실덩실 춤추도다."

스님은 월림사관 선사로부터 법을 계승한 이후 세상에 나와 중생을 구제하였다. 보인사를 비롯 여러 사찰의 주지직을 역임하였으니 이(理)·사(事)를 종횡무진하는 대선지식의 행적이라 아니할 수 없다. 어록에 의하면 스님은 자기가 들어갈 탑을 만들고 곧바로 열반에 들었다. 스님의 임종게이다.

"허공은 남도 없고
허공은 멸함도 없는 것
이러한 허공의 경지를 증득하면
허공과 다름없으리."

무문혜개 스님은 자신의 화두였던 무(無)에 대한 확신을 특이한 게송으로 읊기도 하였다.

"無無無無無 無無無無無 無無無無無 無無無無無"

현재 '무문관'이란 특수선방도 『무문관』 책으로부터 그 이름이 비롯되었다고 본다면 스님의 법력은 시공을 초월하고 있다.

Preface by Venerable Mu-Mun Hye-Gae

What is the gateless gate of the Seon sect?

Buddha taught that mind is the principle, and the gateless gate is the teaching. But if there is no gate, how can you pass through it?

Haven't you heard the saying which says "That which passes through a gate can never be your own treasure. That is to say, anything which is achieved by following your karmic inclinations has a beginning and an end, and thus will fade away."

Even speaking like this is making waves when there is no wind; it's like slicing unblemished flesh. If you try to seek the way while clinging to the words of others, it's swinging a stick and trying to hit the moon, or like trying to scratch an itch after putting on your shoes. What's the use of that?

In the summer of 1228 C.E., Ven. Hye Gae was the head monk of the monastic community at the temple Yong Sang Sa in Dongga(China). Whenever the practitioners requested Dharma teachings, he used the cases of the ancients as "tile fragments beating on their doors." and instructed them, each according to their respective abilities. Eventually he summarized and recorded the cases into a single volume. The book was not organized in any particular order at first, but a total of 48 cases were collected and the text was called The Gateless Gate.

If someone takes hold of a sword and dashes forward without regard for his own life, then even an eight-armed demon who grabs him cannot stop him. Even the twenty-eight patriarchs from India and the six patriarchs from China would beg for their lives before his stately demeanor. If one hesitates or wavers, then it's like seeing a galloping horse passing by a window; it's gone in the blink of an eye.

A verse:
    The Great Way has no gate.
    Though the path has a thousand branches,
    Once you pass through this barrier,
    You confidently stride across the universe.

Commentary

The Gateless Gate is a basic text widely used for Hwadu(Great Doubt) practice in the Seon sect. Other Seon texts such as the Blue Cliff Record and the Book of Equanimity had already been compiled, but Ven. Mu Mun published this collection, which more strongly emphasized the teachings of the Seon sect. Each of the 48 selected Gongan cases in The Gateless Gate compassionately offers a way to thoroughly investigate the Great Doubt and open one's true Dharma eye.

After Ven. Mu Mun(1183-1260) was ordained, he went to study under the great Seon Master Wol-Rim Sa-Gwan. He wrestled with the question "Mu" for six years, until one day he heard the sound of the temple drum calling everyone to the formal meal and attained the deep meaning of Buddha-Dharma.

Ven. Mu Mun's enlightenment poem:
    A great thunderclap on a clear day;
    All beings on earth open their eyes.
    Everything under heaven bows together,

Leaping over Mt. Sumeru, I dance merrily.

After receiving Dharma transmission from Seon Master Wol-Rim Sa-Gwan, he reentered the world to help sentient beings. He became the abbot of the temple Bo In Sa, as well as many other temples, and did not distinguish between administrative duties and formal meditation practice, which is the mark of a true Seon practitioner. According to records, as soon as he had constructed the pagoda his relics were to be enshrined in, he entered Nirvana right away.

Ven. Mu Mun's Nirvana poem:
    In emptiness there is no appearing,
    In emptiness there is no disappearing.
    If you attain this level of emptiness,
    You and emptiness are not different.

Ven. Mu Mun wrote a rather unique poetic verse concerning the Hwadu "Mu", which he used personally:

"Mu-mu-mu-mu Mu-mu-mu-mu Mu-mu-mu-mu Mu-mu-mu-

mu"

These days some special Seon rooms are called "Gateless Gate", which shows that Ven. Mu Mun's Dharma power stretches beyond time and space.

제 1 칙
趙州狗子(조주구자)

조주 큰스님의 무자(無字) 화두
Case1: Seon Master Jo Ju's "Mu"

가. 본칙(本則)

趙州和尙. 因僧問. 狗子還有佛性也無. 州云. 無.

조주 큰스님께 한 스님이 물었다.
"저 개에게도 불성(佛性)이 있습니까?"
큰스님께서 대답하였다.
"없다(無)."

나. 평창(評唱) 및 송(頌)

無門曰. 參禪須透祖師關, 妙悟要窮心路絶. 祖關不透, 心路不絶, 盡是依草附木精靈. 且道, 如何是祖師關. 只者一箇無字, 乃宗門一關也. 遂目之曰, 禪宗無門關. 透得過者, 非但親見趙州, 便可與歷代祖師, 把手共行, 眉毛廝結, 同一眼見, 同一耳聞. 豈不慶快. 莫有要透關底麽. 將三百六十骨節, 八萬四千毫竅, 通身起箇疑團, 參箇無字. 晝夜提撕. 莫作虛無會, 莫作有無會. 如吞了箇熱鐵丸相似, 吐又吐不出. 蕩盡從前惡知惡覺, 久久純熟, 自然內外打成一片. 如啞子得夢, 只許自知. 驀然打發, 驚天動地.

如奪得關將軍大刀入手, 逢佛殺佛, 逢祖殺祖, 於生死岸頭, 得大自在, 向六道四生中, 遊戱三昧. 且作麼生提撕. 盡平生氣力, 擧箇無字. 若不間斷, 好似法燭一點便著.

무문 스님이 평하여 말하였다. 선(禪) 수행을 하고자 하면 반드시 조사의 관문을 뚫어야 하고, 오묘한 깨달음을 얻고자 하면 마음길이 끊어지는 경험을 궁구하지 않으면 안 된다. 조사의 관문을 뚫지 못하고 마음길을 끊지 못하는 이는 모두 풀잎이나 나무에 달라붙어 사는 정령(精靈)과도 같다.

자, 말해 보라. 도대체 어떤 것이 조사의 관문인가?

이 한 가지, 무자(無字) 화두만이 선종의 제일관문이다. 그래서 이를 일러 선종무문관(禪宗無門關)이라고 하는 것이다. 이 관문을 꿰뚫고 통과한다면 조주 큰스님을 친견할 수 있을 것이다. 뿐만 아니라 역대의 조사들과 함께 손잡고 같이 다니며, 눈썹과 눈이 맞닿아 있듯이, 같은 눈으로 보고 같은 귀로 듣게 될 것이다. 어찌 경사스럽고 유쾌한 일이 아니겠는가. 이 관문을 꿰뚫고 싶지 않은가?

삼백육십 개의 뼈마디와 팔만 사천의 털구멍을 가진 온몸 그 자체가 의심덩어리가 되어 이 한 가지 '무자(無字)' 화두를 들되 낮이고 밤이고 잡도리해야 한다. 그렇지만, 이 무(無)를 허무(虛無)

의 무로 여기거나, 유(有)·무(無)의 무라고 여기지는 말라. 꼭, 시뻘겋게 단 쇳덩이를 삼켜 버려 토해 내려고 하여도 토해 낼 수 없는 것과 같이 하여야 한다. 이제까지의 그릇된 지식과 잘못된 견해를 다 떨쳐 버리고 오래오래 잘 익히면 저절로 안과 밖이 하나가 될 것이다. 그것은 마치 벙어리가 꿈을 꾼 것처럼 스스로만 알고 다른 사람에게는 말해주지 못하는 것과 같은 체험이다. 갑자기 의정이 타파되면 하늘이 놀라고 땅이 진동할 것이다. 꼭 관우 장군의 큰 칼을 빼앗아 자신이 쥔 듯, 부처를 만나면 부처를 죽이고 조사를 만나면 조사를 죽인다. 생사의 갈림길에서 대자유를 얻고 육도와 사생의 세상에 있으면서도 유희삼매를 만끽한다.

이제, 어떻게 공부를 지어갈 것인가? 평생의 기력을 다하여 이 무자(無字) 화두를 들어라. 만일 끊어지지 않는다면, 법의 등불에 한번 '확' 하고 불이 붙어서 환한 경지가 될 것이다.

頌曰. 狗子佛性, 全提正令. 纔涉有無, 喪身失命.

무문 스님이 다시 게송으로 말하였다.
　"개의 불성에 대한 큰스님의 한마디는
　온전하게 제시된 바른 가르침이네.

어리석게, 있고 없고를 따지면
몸도 버리고 목숨도 잃게 되리라."

다. 강론(講論)

무자(無字) 화두는 1700공안의 결정판이다.

어느 화두라도 깨치면 '무' 자 화두는 저절로 알게 된다는 사람들도 있지만, 그것은 화두수행을 철저히 해보지 않은 미숙에서 비롯된 망발이다. 무자 화두야말로 가장 난이도가 높으며 공부의 결론이다. 그렇다면 이 중요한 무자화두의 핵심이 어디에 있는가?

분별심(分別心)의 제거이다. '불성이 있다, 불성이 없다' 라는 견해는 분별이다. 분별은 사고의 체계이므로 다분히 주관적 인식이다. 주관적 인식의 본질은 욕망이므로 분별심은 결국 욕망을 가져오고 중생고를 초래할 수밖에 없다.

분별과 사량을 모두 놓아버리고 무고안온의 절대경지에 들어가려면 대신근, 대분지, 대의정을 일으켜 밀어붙여야 한다.

'개에게 왜 불성이 없는가?'

이 무(無)는 이미 유·무를 초월해 버렸다.

Case 1
Seon Master Jo Ju's "Mu"

A. Original Case

A monk asked Seon Master Jo Ju:

"Does a dog also have Buddha nature?"

Ven. Jo Ju answered "Mu(not)"

B. Commentary and Verse

Ven. Mu Mun commented: If you want to practice Seon meditation, then you must pass through the gateway of the patriarchs. In order to attain this subtle and mysterious enlightenment, you must completely cut off your thinking. If you don't pass through the gateway of the patriarchs and cut off all thinking, then you are like a spirit clinging to blades of grass and trees. So tell me: What in the world is the gateway of the patriarchs? This question "Mu" is the main gate to the Seon sect. Therefore it's called the "The Gateless Gate of the Seon sect". If you pass through this gateway, then you can meet Seon Master Jo

Ju face-to-face. Not only that, but you will walk hand in hand with the patriarchs, and it will be like your eyes and eyebrows merge with each other. You will see with the same eyes and hear with the same ears. Would it not be a joyous and wonderful event! Wouldn't you like to pass through this gateway?

Let your entire body with its three hundred and sixty joints and eighty-four thousand pores become a ball of Great Doubt, and take hold of this question "Mu" continuously day or night. However, do not think of this "Mu" as empty, or in relative terms of "has" or "has not". It would be just as if you had swallowed a red-hot iron ball that you cannot spit out, no matter how hard you try. You should throw away all the deluded concepts and false ideas you have accumulated until now, and if you continue to practice for a very long time, then inside and outside will spontaneously become one. You alone will understand this by yourself. However, it's like a mute who has had a dream; you can't explain the experience to somebody else. All of a sudden, such a dramatic shift will occur that the heavens will reel and the earth will tremble. It will be as if you have snatched away the great sword from General Gwan Wu and are grasping it. When you meet the Buddha, you kill him; when you meet the patriarchs, you kill them. You attain great freedom at the crossroads of life and death; even while living in the world of life and death and the six realms, you enjoy the bliss of Samadhi.

So now, how are you going to carry out this kind of practice? Grasp the Great Question "Mu" tightly, using every bit of energy in your life. If you don't stop, then your Dharma lamp will suddenly become lit, and you will radiate forth the truth.

Ven. Mu Mun's Verse:

    The Master spoke about a dog's Buddha nature;

    Correct teaching, perfectly expressed.

    If you ignorantly judge that it "has" or "has not",

    You throw away your body and lose your life too.

C. Explanation

The Hwadu(Great Doubt) "Mu" is the definitive from the collection of 1700 cases. There are those who say that if you have a breakthrough with any Hwadu, that the question "Mu" will become clear byitself. But this is merely ridiculous speech born from the inexperience of those who have not thoroughly completed their own Hwadu training. Indeed, the Hwadu "Mu" has the highest level of difficulty, so it is the conclusion of one's practice. But what is the key point of this important Hwadu? The point is how to take away one's discriminating consciousness, because the idea that "there is Buddha nature" or "there is no Buddha nature" is based on dualistic thinking. A system of thought based on dualistic concepts is full of subjective perceptions. As the very essence of subjective perceptions is desire, the dualistic mind carries this kind of craving along with it, and cannot help but bring about suffering for sentient beings. If you want to enter an absolute state of equanimity, free from suffering, you must discard all discrimination and conceptualization, raise up your Great Faith, Great Resolve and Great Doubt, and steadfastly push forward.

"Why does a dog not have Buddha nature?"

This "Mu" (not) has already transcended "has" or "has not".

제 2 칙
百丈野狐(백장야호)

백장 큰스님과 여우 이야기
Case 2: Master Baek Jang and the Fox

가. 본칙(本則)

百丈和尙, 凡參次, 有一老人, 常隨衆聽法. 衆人退, 老人亦退. 忽一日不退. 師遂問, 面前立者, 復是何人. 老人云, 諾, 某甲非人也. 於過去迦葉佛時, 曾住此山. 因學人問, 大修行底人, 還落因果也無. 某甲對云, 不落因果. 五百生墮野狐身. 今請, 和尙代一轉語, 貴脫野狐. 遂問, 大修行底人, 還落因果也無. 師云, 不昧因果. 老人於言下大悟, 作禮云, 某甲已脫野狐身, 住在山後. 敢告和尙. 乞依亡僧事例. 師令維那白槌告衆, 食後送亡僧. 大衆言議, 一衆皆安, 涅槃堂又無人病. 何故如是. 食後只見師領衆, 至山後巖下, 以杖挑出一死野狐, 乃依火葬. 師至晚上堂, 擧前因緣. 黃檗便問, 古人錯祇對一轉語, 墮五百生野狐身, 轉轉不錯, 合作箇甚麼. 師云, 近前來, 與伊道. 黃檗遂近前, 與師一掌. 師拍手笑云, 將謂胡鬚赤, 更有赤鬚胡.

백장 큰스님이 설법할 때마다 한 노인이 대중과 함께 법문을 들었다. 그는 대중이 물러가면 같이 물러가곤 하였는데 어느 날은 물러가지 않았다.

그래서 큰스님이 그 노인에게 물었다.

"내 앞에 서 있는 그대는 누구시오?"

노인이 대답하였다.

"예, 저는 사람이 아닙니다. 옛날 가섭불 시대에 이 절의 주지였습니다. 당시 어떤 학인이 '훌륭한 수행자도 인과(因果)에 떨어집니까, 떨어지지 않습니까?' 하고 묻기에 저는 '인과에 떨어지지 않는다' 라고 대답했습니다. 그 때문에 오백생 동안이나 여우의 몸을 받게 되었습니다. 지금 큰스님께 간청하오니 저를 대신하여 딱 옳은 한 말씀을 해 주십시오. 그리하여 이 여우의 몸을 벗게 해 주십시오."

그리고는 그는 여쭈었다.

"훌륭한 수행자도 인과에 떨어집니까, 떨어지지 않습니까?"

이에 큰스님은 대답했다.

"인과에 어둡지 않느니라."

노인은 이 말이 떨어지자마자 크게 깨달았다. 그는 곧 예를 올리면서 말했다.

"저는 이제 여우의 몸을 벗게 되었습니다. 저의 껍데기는 뒷산에 남길 것입니다. 큰스님께 말씀드리기 죄송하오나 저를 돌아가신 스님들 장례 치르는 방식으로 해주십시오."

이에 큰스님이 유나 스님을 시켜 추를 쳐 대중을 모이게 한 뒤

"공양 후에 어떤 돌아가신 스님의 장례가 있다."고 일렀다. 대중 스님들은 서로 "온 대중들은 모두 건강하고 열반당에도 아픈 스님이 없는데 무슨 까닭으로 저런 말씀을 하실까?"하며 수군댔다. 공양이 끝나자 큰스님은 대중을 이끌고 뒷산 바위 밑에 이르러 지팡이로 죽은 여우 한 마리를 끄집어 내었다. 그리고 스님 장례 하듯 다비해 주었다. 큰스님은 그날 저녁 법상에 올라 지금까지 있었던 일을 말씀하셨다. 이때 황벽 스님이 여쭈었다.

"그 노인은 한마디 대답을 잘못하여 오백생 동안 여우의 몸을 받았다고 했습니다. 그렇다면, 만약 한마디 어긋나지 않게 말했다면 어떻게 되었겠습니까?"

그러자 큰스님께서, "이리 가까이 오너라, 일러주리라."라고 말씀하셨다. 그 말에 황벽 스님이 가까이 다가가더니 손바닥을 한 번 '탁' 쳐 보였다. 그러자 백장 큰스님은 박수를 치며 웃으면서 말씀하셨다.

"달마의 수염은 붉다고 말하려 했더니 여기에 또 붉은 수염의 달마가 있구나."

나. 평창(評唱) 및 송(頌)

無門曰. 不落因果, 爲甚墮野狐. 不昧因果, 爲甚脫野狐. 若向者裏著得一隻眼, 便知得前百丈贏得風流五百生.

무문 스님이 평하여 말하였다.
'인과에 떨어지지 않는다.'고 말했는데 어찌하여 여우의 몸을 받게 되었는가? '인과에 어둡지 않다.'라는 말은 어찌하여 여우의 몸을 벗게 하였는가?
만약 이것을 알아차릴 수 있는 지혜로운 눈을 갖춘 자라면, 백장 큰스님 앞의 그 노인이 오백생 동안 풍류를 누리고 있었음을 알 수 있으리라.

頌曰. 不落不昧, 兩彩一賽. 不昧不落, 千錯萬錯.

무문 스님이 다시 게송으로 말하였다.
　　"불락(不落)과 불매(不昧)여
　　두 가지가 한바탕이네.
　　불락(不落)과 불매(不昧)여
　　천만 번 틀렸도다."

다. 강론(講論)

　인과법과 해탈의 절묘한 조화를 보여주는 상황 전개이다. 각자(覺者)에게는 불락(不落)이 들어맞지만 깨닫지 못하였으니 불매(不昧)라도 과분하다. 반야와 무명이 한 공간이듯 깨달음과 미혹 또한 한 뿌리이다. 부처가 곧 중생이라지만 어느 쪽에서 보느냐에 따라 십만 팔천리 거리가 생긴다. 선화(禪話)는 논리를 초월할 뿐 비논리적이지는 않다.

Case 2
Master Baek Jang and the Fox

A. Original Case

Whenever Seon Master Baek Jang gave a Dharma speech, an old man would sit with the community of monks and listen to his lecture. The old man would normally leave with the assembly at the end of the lecture, but one day he remained behind, so the Seon Master asked him:

"Who is the one who stands before me?"

The old man answered, "I am not a human being. A long time ago, in the era of Kashyapa Buddha, I was abbot of this temple. One disciple at the time asked me 'Does an enlightened person also fall into cause and effect, or does he not?'

I answered 'He does not.' As a result, I received a fox's body for five-hundred lifetimes. I now beseech you, master, please give me the correct answer and liberate me from this fox's body."

Whereupon the old man asked the master, "Does an enlightened person also fall into cause and effect, or does he not?"

"Do not ignore cause and effect."

As soon as the old man heard this speech, he attained great enlightenment. As he was prostrating himself before the master he said,

"I am now liberated from this fox's form. My lifeless corpse still remains on the mountain behind this temple. Master, I am sorry to ask you this, but could you please hold a funeral for me the way you would for a deceased monk?"

The Seon Master then had the monk in charge of ceremonies strike the gavel to assemble the community and inform them that after lunch there would be a funeral ceremony for a monk who had died. The monks whispered among themselves, "Everyone in our community is healthy, moreover there isn't anybody sick in the infirmary, so why is he saying that?"

When the midday meal had finished, the master led the members of the community to a rock on the mountain, where he uncovered the body of a dead fox with his staff. He then cremated the body as if performing the funeral ceremony for a monk.

That evening the Seon Master ascended the high rostrum and

told the assembly of the events that had unfolded that day. At this time the Ven. Hwang Byeok asked him:

"You told us that the old man gave the wrong answer and was reborn a fox for five-hundred lifetimes. But what would have happened if he had spoken correctly?"

The Seon Master said, "Come closer and I'll tell you." As Ven. Hwang Byeok approached, he slapped the master once with his palm.

Seon Master Baek Jang clapped his hands and laughed, exclaiming: "I was about to say that Bodhidharma's beard is red, but a red-bearded Bodhidharma is also right here."

B. Commentary and Verse

Ven. Mu Mun commented:

The old monk said, "He does not fall into cause and effect." Why did he receive the body of a fox? Moreover the phrase, "Do not ignore cause and effect." Why did this liberate him from a fox's body? If you come to understand this, then you can also understand how the old man in front of Seon Master Baek Jang would have enjoyed those five-hundred lifetimes.

Ven. Mu Mun's verse:

> Not falling into and not ignoring:
> Two sides of the same coin.
> Not falling into and not ignoring:
> Both are gigantic mistakes.

C. Explanation

The development of this situation shows us the delicate balance between the law of causation and ultimate liberation. It is correct that an enlightened person does not fall into causation; but when you haven't attained enlightenment, even not ignoring causation is beyond your capacity. Just as wisdom and ignorance coexist, so enlightenment and delusion are also of the same root.

Although a Buddha is none other than a sentient being, there is a huge difference between a Buddha and a sentient being, depending on the point of view. Seon speech merely transcends logic, but it is never illogical.

제 3 칙
俱胝竪指(구지수지)

구지 큰스님, 손가락을 세우다
Case3: Master Gu-Ji Raises a Finger

가. 본칙(本則)

俱胝和尙, 凡有詰問, 唯擧一指. 後有童子. 因外人問, 和尙說何法要. 童子亦竪指頭. 胝聞遂以刃斷其指. 童子負痛號哭而去, 胝復召之. 童子廻首, 胝却竪起指. 童子忽然領悟. 胝將順世, 謂衆曰, 吾得天龍一指頭禪, 一生受用不盡. 言訖示滅.

　구지 큰스님은 언제나 누구의 질문을 받으면 오직 손가락 하나만을 세워 보였다. 어느 날 그 절 방문객이 "너희 큰스님께서는 어떻게 법을 설하시는가?" 하고 묻자 동자 역시 손가락 하나를 세워 보였다. 구지 큰스님은 이 이야기를 듣고 동자의 그 손가락을 날카로운 칼로 잘라버렸다. 동자는 아픔을 못 이겨 울부짖으며 달아났다. 구지 큰스님이 다시 동자를 불렀다. 동자가 고개를 돌리자 큰스님은 바로 손가락을 세워 보였다. 동자는 홀연히 깨달았다.

　구지 큰스님은 임종에 이르러 대중들에게 말했다.

　"내가 천룡(天龍) 선사로부터 일지두선(一指頭禪)을 배운 뒤 일생 동안 써먹었지만 다 쓰질 못하였다."

　그러고는 곧 입적했다.

나. 평창(評唱) 및 송(頌)

無門曰. 俱胝幷童子, 悟處不在指頭上. 若向者裏見得, 天龍同俱胝幷童子, 與自己一串穿却.

　무문 스님이 평하여 말하였다.
　구지 큰스님과 동자가 그 깨달은 곳이 손가락 끝에 있지 않다. 만약 이것을 안다면 천룡 선사와 구지 큰스님과 동자, 그리고 자기 자신도 한 꼬챙이에 꿰는 것이 된다.

頌曰. 俱胝鈍置老天龍, 利刃單提勘小童. 巨靈擡手無多子, 分破華山千萬重.

　무문 스님이 다시 게송으로 말하였다.
　　"구지 큰스님은 천룡 노선사를 적당히 얕보고
　　날카로운 칼로 동자를 시험하였네.
　　거령신이 별 조작도 안 하고 손을 들어
　　천만 겹의 화산을 쪼개 버렸듯이."

다. 강론(講論)

　구지 큰스님이 작은 암자에 살고 있을 때에 실제(實際)라는 비구니가 찾아와서 삿갓을 쓰고 지팡이를 짚은 채 스님의 선상을 세 바퀴나 돌고는 석장을 우뚝 스님 앞에 세우고 서서 말하였다.
　"큰스님께서 저의 질문에 대답을 하시면 삿갓을 벗겠습니다."
　스님께서 대답을 하지 못하니 비구니는 그냥 떠나려고 하였다. 이에 스님은 말씀하셨다.
　"날이 이미 저물었으니 하루 저녁 묵어가도록 하시오."
　비구니가 다시 말했다.
　"제 질문에 대답을 하시면 묵어가겠지만 대답을 하지 못하시면 이대로 떠나겠습니다." 하고는 잠시 후 가버렸다.
　이에 스님은 혼자 탄식하였다.
　"나는 명색이 사문이라고 하면서 비구니의 웃음거리가 되었다. 외람되이 장부의 형상을 갖추었으나 장부의 작용이 없구나! 이 산을 떠나 선지식을 두루 친견하리라."
　그리고 조용히 사색에 드니 갑자기 어떤 신인(神人)이 나타나 이렇게 말했다.
　"보름 안에 큰 보살이 오셔서 화상께 설법해 드릴 것이오."

그런지 열흘이 지나지 않아 천룡 노선사가 왔거늘 스님은 뛰어나가 발에 절을 하고 맞아들여, 모시고 서서 오전의 일을 자세히 이야기한즉 천룡 노선사가 손가락 하나를 보이니 당장에 활짝 깨달았다. 그 뒤 구지 큰스님 또한 스승 천룡 노선사처럼 손가락을 세워 보이는 일지선(一指禪)으로 수좌들을 제접하였다. 이상은 『조당집(祖堂集)』에 나오는 이야기이다.

삼라만상의 근원자리는 청정하고 본연(本然) 하다. 그리하여 있지 않은 곳이 없으며 또한 작용하지 않는 곳이 없다. 곡식 한 알, 꽃 한 송이에 온 우주가 들어가 있듯이 한 손가락 속에 만고의 진리가 갖추어져 있다. 한마디로 만법귀일(萬法歸一)이다. 손가락을 세우는 것은 연꽃이나 불자(拂子)를 드는 것과 같은 맥락이다. 작위(作爲)를 쓰지 않고 무심(無心)의 경지에서 행해진다면 그 어떤 수작도 기연(機緣)이 된다. 그렇지만 언어문자나 행위를 흉내 내는 것은 단호히 거부한다. 모방이나 가식의 허물은 칼로써 손가락이 잘리는 수모도 부족하다.

실참실오(實參實悟)만이 살길이다.

Case 3
Master Gu-Ji Raises a Finger

A. Original Case

Whenever Seon Master Gu-Ji was asked a question by anyone, he only raised one finger. One day a visitor to the temple asked his young attendant, "How does your master teach the Dharma?" The boy also raised one finger in response. When Master Gu-Ji heard about this, he cut off the boy's finger with a sharp knife. The boy couldn't endure the pain and ran away screaming. Master Gu-Ji called out to him, and as the boy turned his head, Gu-Ji raised one finger. His attendant saw this and suddenly got enlightenment.

When Master Gu-Ji was about to pass away, he spoke to the assembly "I inherited this One-Finger Seon teaching from Master Cheon Ryong. Though I used it my whole life I still did not exhaust it." Having said this he entered into Nirvana.

B. Commentary and Verse

Ven. Mu Mun commented: The enlightenment of Master Gu-Ji and his attendant is not in the finger tip. If you understand this point, then Master Cheon Ryong, Master Gu-Ji, his attendant and even you are all pierced with one skewer.

Ven. Mu Mun's verse:
    Master Gu-Ji looked down on old Master Cheon Ryong
    And tested the boy with a sharp knife;
    Just like when the patron spirit lifted his hand
    And split the great mountain in half.

C. Explanation

When Master Gu-Ji was staying at a small hermitage, a nun named Shil Jae came to visit him. She circled around his Dharma seat three times, wearing a broad hat and carrying a walking staff. Finally she placed the staff before the master and spoke:

"Great Master, if you can answer my question correctly, I will remove my hat."

As the master couldn't answer her question, she was about to leave. At which Master Gu-Ji said, "Since it's already dark out, you should spend the night here."

The nun spoke to him again, "I'll spend the night if you can answer my question correctly, but if you cannot, I'll just leave." A little while later she left.

Master Gu-Ji moaned to himself, "Even though I'm a so-called monk, that nun has made a fool out of me. I presumptuously wear the clothes of a master, and yet I can't even behave like one. I should leave this mountain and look everywhere to meet a true man of the way."

As he sat there, quietly lost in thought, a divine man suddenly appeared and spoke to him: "Within the next two weeks a great Bodhisattva will come and teach you the Dharma."

Not even ten days had passed when the elderly Seon Master Cheon Ryong came to see him. Gu-Ji rushed out, bowed at his feet, and then escorted the master into the temple, where he told him in detail of the events that had transpired that morning. Master Cheon Ryong showed him one finger, and Gu-Ji suddenly became completely enlightened. Just like the old Master Cheon Ryong, Master Gu-Ji later used this "One-finger Seon" teaching to instruct practitioners. This story is recorded in the ancient book of the patriarchs.

Universal substance is originally pure and just as it is. There is no place that lacks this original nature, also nowhere that it doesn't function. Just as a single grain or a flower contains the entire universe, eternal truth is also contained in one finger. As the saying goes, "The ten thousand Dharmas return to one." Raising a finger can be taken in the same context as holding up a lotus flower or a horsehair whisk. If your actions come from a mind of true emptiness, without making something special, then whatever appears will be as it should be. However, it is absolutely forbidden to merely copy someone else's speech or behavior. Even having one's finger sliced off is insufficient humiliation for the grievous error of imitation or false pretense. One should live by the principle "Seek the truth and be enlightened to the truth."

제 4 칙
胡子無鬚(호자무수)

※

달마대사는 수염이 없다
Case4: Bodhidharma Has No Beard

가. 본칙(本則)

或庵曰, 西天胡子, 因甚無鬚.

혹암 큰스님이 말씀하셨다.
"서천의 오랑캐, 달마대사는 어찌하여 수염이 없는가?"

나. 평창(評唱) 및 송(頌)

無門曰. 參須實參, 悟須實悟. 者箇胡子, 直須親見一回始得. 說親見, 早成兩箇.

무문 스님이 평하여 말하였다.
참선은 반드시 실다운 참선이어야 하고 깨달음 또한 실다운 깨달음이어야 한다. 이 오랑캐는 꼭 한번은 친견하지 않으면 안 된다. 그런데 친견했다고 말한다면 이미 두 명이 되고 말리라.

頌曰. 癡人面前, 不可說夢. 胡子無鬚, 惺惺添懵.

무문 스님이 다시 게송으로 말하였다.

"어리석은 사람 앞에서

꿈 이야기를 하지 말라.

달마대사가 수염이 없다함은

밝고 밝은 것에 흐린 것을 덧씌우는 꼴."

다. 강론(講論)

달마대사는 언제부터인가 우리 불자들에게 텁석부리 수염의 인물로 각인되어 왔다. 스님들이나 화가들이 달마대사를 그릴 때에는 으레 빽빽한 수염을 턱 전체에 갖다 붙인다. 그래서 수염이 없는 달마대사는 아예 생각할 수가 없게 된 것이다. 그런데 이러한 턱수염의 이미지가 가득한 달마대사를 두고 혹암 큰스님은 다짜고짜 달마대사가 왜 수염이 없느냐고 생뚱맞은 말씀을 하시니 기가 찰 노릇이다. 이는 마치 나는 새를 쳐다보고 '어찌하여 날개가 없는가?' 하고 묻는 것이나 다를 바가 없다.

그리고 보면 화두는 지천에 깔렸다.

자아정체성을 부정하는 모든 말들이 화두가 된다. 그렇지만 이러한 류의 화두가 그리 쉽게 해결되지는 않는다.

그래서 옛사람들은 '달마대사가 왜 수염이 없는가?' 라는 화두를 두고 '수천 선지식의 말을 합친 만큼의 가치가 있다' 고 칭송해 마지않았다.

'달마대사는 어찌하여 수염이 없는가?'

참으로 말 길이 끊어져서 사량분별(思量分別)이 들어설 틈이 없다. 수염이 없다고 해도 걸림이 되고 또한 있다고 해도 걸림이 된다.

걸림은 진성(眞性)의 자유와 위배된다. 없다는 말에 걸리면 수염이 있는 것이 되고, 있다는 말에 걸리면 애시당초 없다는 전제를 무시하고 만다. 이런 모순이 또 어디 있겠는가.

있고 없음에 끄달리지 말고 닥치는 경계를 초월해서 살아가라는 노파심의 메시지가 담겨져 있음을 엿볼 수 있다. 그러한 힘을 기르기 위해 선(禪)이 필요하다. 따라서 선은 학문이 아니고 실재적 수행이다. 즉, 실참이다. 실참함으로써 실오가 있게 되는 것은 당연하다. 실참실오의 자리는 본래적인 마음자리이다. 상대적인 분별과 대립이 쉰 곳에는 버려야 할 망념도, 돌아가야 할 진성도 없다.

육조혜능 스님은 신수 스님의 게송 '부지런히 털고 닦아서 먼지 앉고 때묻지 않도록 하라.' 는 말에 대해서 "본래 한 물건도 없는데 어느 곳에 먼지 앉고 때가 끼겠는가?"하고 근원적인 가르침을 제시한 적이 있다.

본래 성품은 청정무구한 하늘과 같아서 그 어떤 망상의 구름에도 초연할 뿐이다.

달마대사의 진신(眞身)은 무상(無相)이다. 유(有)·무(無)의 차별경계에 떨어진 무상이 아닌 즉, 유·무를 초월하면서도 유·무를 포용하는 실상(實相)의 무상을 말한다. 이 무상의 달마대사를 친견하는 자리는 능견(能見)과 소견(所見)이 하나 된 곳이다. 참된 친견은 자신이 그렇게 되는 방법 외에는 달리 묘수가 없다.

직접 확인하여 추호도 의심이 없으려면 달마대사의 본래면목과 계합하면 된다. 그때 우리는 분명히 말할 수 있다.

달마대사는 왜 수염이 없는가를.

Case 4
Bodhidharma Has No Beard

A. Original Case

Master Hok Am asked, "Why doesn't the western barbarian Bodhidharma have a beard?"

B. Commentary and Verse

Ven. Mu Mun commented:

Your Seon practice should be sincere, and your enlightenment must also be genuine; you must meet this barbarian one time face-to-face. But if you say that you have met him face-to-face, then the two of you have already become separate.

Ven. Mu Mun's verse:

    Don't speak of your dream

    Before a fool.

    Bodhidharma without a beard

    Obscures that which is perfectly clear.

C. Explanation

For some time Bodhidharma has been portrayed as a figure with a bushy beard. When monks and artists draw Bodhidharma, they invariably portray him with a thick beard covering his entire chin, so Bodhidharma without a beard is unimaginable.

However, Master Hok Am does away with this image of a fully-bearded Bodhidharma and abruptly asks us the peculiar question, "Why does Bodhidharma have no beard?" This is as if I have just looked at a bird and then asked "Why doesn't the bird have wings?" If we look at it this way, we can find a Great Question everywhere; all speech that negates one's idea of self becomes a Great Question.

However, this kind of problem cannot be solved so easily. Therefore the people of olden times could not praise this question enough, saying "It has the value of thousands of other sayings of the masters put together!"

"Why does Bodhidharma have no beard?"

When speech has truly been cut off, there is no chance for relative views to enter the mind. It's a hindrance whether you said there is a beard or there isn't one, which runs counter to the freedom of our true-nature. If you are attached to "not," then there is a beard, but if you are attached to "is," then it ignores the original premise. What a contradiction this is!

Don't get caught in existence or nonexistence, but transcend that boundary, and you can live with a sense of the compassionate message that is contained within this question. One must do Seon practice in order to gather that kind of energy. Seon is not academic study, but true practice, in other words, genuine cultivation of the mind. Through this genuine cultivation, one will naturally have an authentic experience of awakening to our original mind. At this point where relative distinctions and opposition have ceased, there are no delusory thoughts to be discarded, nor is there a true nature that one must return to. Ven. Shin Su once wrote a verse that said, "Diligently polish(cultivate) so that no dust remains." The Sixth Patriarch Hye Neung was pointing to this fundamental teaching when he responded, "Originally there is not even one thing. Where will dust abide?"

Our original nature is like the pure, clear, untainted sky, which is unaffected by clouds of delusion. Bodhidharma's true body does not have any relative idea. This is not talking about the relative stage of "is" or "is not," but it means an absolute truth that transcends and includes both of these at the same time. When you come face-to-face with Bodhidharma at this point, all relative views and opinions become one. This is no other way to have a true encounter with him except to become him.

If you confirm it for yourself and remove even the least bit of doubt, then you will see Bodhidharma's original face. At that time we can clearly state "why Bodhidharma has no beard."

제 5 칙
香嚴上樹(향엄상수)

향엄 큰스님, 나무에 오르다
Case5: Hyang Eom is up in a tree

가. 본칙(本則)

香嚴和尙云, 如人上樹, 口啣樹枝, 手不攀枝, 脚不踏樹. 樹下有人, 問西來意, 不對卽違他所問, 若對又喪身失命. 正恁麽時, 作麽生對.

향엄 큰스님이 말씀하셨다.

"어떤 사람이 나무 위에 올라가서 입으로 나뭇가지를 문 채 손으로는 나뭇가지를 잡지 않고, 발로도 나뭇가지를 딛지 않고 있었다. 그때 나무 아래서 어떤 사람이 '달마대사가 서쪽에서 온 뜻이 무엇인가?' 하고 물었다. 만약 대답하지 않는다면 질문을 피하는 것이 될 것이고, 대답하면 몸을 상하고 목숨을 잃게 될 것이다. 그야말로 이와 같을 때에는 어떻게 해야 할 것인가?"

나. 평창(評唱) 및 송(頌)

無門曰. 縱有懸河之辨, 總用不著. 說得一大藏敎, 亦用不著. 若向者裏對得著. 活却從前死路頭, 死却從前活路頭. 其或未然, 直待當來問彌勒.

무문 스님이 평하여 말하였다.

설령 폭포수가 떨어지는 듯한 달변이라도 다 소용없다. 또 대장경의 가르침을 모두 설할 수 있어도 역시 소용없다. 만일 여기서 딱 알맞게 대응할 수 있다면 지금까지 죽어있던 것을 살리고, 지금까지 살아있던 것을 죽일 수도 있다.

혹시 그게 잘 안 된다면 그대로 먼 훗날을 기다렸다가 미륵 부처님에게나 물어보아야 하리라.

頌曰. 香嚴眞杜撰, 惡毒無盡限. 啞却衲僧口, 通身迸鬼眼.

무문 스님이 다시 게송으로 말하였다.
　　"향엄 큰스님은 참으로 황당무계한 사람.
　　그가 퍼붓는 독설은 끝이 없다네.
　　납승의 입을 벙어리로 만들어 놓고
　　온몸으로 신통의 눈을 뜨도록 하네."

다. 강론(講論)

입을 열어도 낭패고, 입을 다물고 있어도 낭패다. 입열음(開口)

과 입닫음(閉口) 사이의 틈새를 공략해야 살길이 있다. 목숨이 경각에 달렸으니 부귀영화인들 무슨 소용이 있겠는가! 탐낼 일도, 성낼 일도 깡그리 없어졌다. 입을 열어도 그르치고 입을 닫아도 그르치니 어느 한 쪽을 택한다면 그것은 망심(妄心)에 기인한 분별(分別)이다.

양비(兩非) 즉, 둘 다 아니다. 선택을 용납지 않는다. 불개불폐(不開不閉)의 중도(中道)의 자리라야 무분별지(無分別智)가 된다. 무분별지에서는 죽음과 삶이 함께하고 순간과 영원히 함께한다. 용과 이무기가 뒤섞여도 관계없고, 중생과 부처가 같이 놀아도 간섭하지 않는다. 화두가 제대로 잡히면 무의식(無意識) 너머의 소식 즉, 무분별지의 땅에 이르게 되는데 그곳이 진정 살길이다.

발도 떼고 손도 놓은 상태에서 입으로 나뭇가지를 물었다는 것은 입은 아예 닫고 대답하라는 뜻이다. 이쯤 되면 일체의 언어 문자는 소용없게 되었다. 사구(四句)와 백비(百非)를 죄다 끊어버린 상태라야 한다.

만일, 백번 양보하여 나뭇가지를 물지 않고 멀쩡한 상태에서 '달마대사가 서쪽에서 온 뜻이 무엇인가?' 하고 묻는 말에 대답할 인물이라면 진퇴유곡(進退維谷)의 이러한 급박한 상황을 무난히 타개할 수 있는 유력인(有力人)이다. 이럴 수도 저럴 수도 없는 궁지에 처했을 때 어리석은 자는 포기해서 나락에 떨어지고 지혜 있는 자는 전혀 새로운 세상을 열어나간다.

향엄 큰스님이 대중에게 본칙(本則)의 화두를 던졌을 때 초(招) 상좌가 여쭈었다.

"나무 위에 오른 일은 묻지 않겠습니다. 나무에 오르기 이전은 어떻습니까?"

그러자 큰스님은 '허허' 하고 웃으시며 게송을 읊으셨다.

"병아리는 안쪽에서, 어미 닭은 바깥쪽에서 쪼으니
병아리가 어미 닭의 껍질을 깨쳤다.
병아리와 어미 닭 모두 함께 없으니
인연따라 한 치의 오차도 없구나.
한 가지 길을 조화로이 노래하니
묘한 구름 홀로 그윽하구나."

문제의 해결은 문제가 일어나기 이전의 근원으로 되돌아가는 것이 유일하고도 완전한 해결방법이다. 온갖 망상으로 비롯된 병마를 치료한다는 것은 본래의 건강한 상태로 되돌아가는 것을 의미한다. 초(招) 상좌의 대꾸가 기발하다 아니할 수 없다.

Case 5
Hyang Eom is up in a tree

A. Original Case

Master Hyang Eom said, "Someone is up in a tree, hanging from a branch by his mouth. He doesn't grasp the limb with his hands; his feet don't rest on a branch. At that time someone under the tree asks him, 'Why did Bodhidharma come from the West(India)?' If he doesn't answer, he avoids the question, but if he does answer, then he will be injured and lose his life. What would you do in such a situation?"

B. Commentary and Verse

Ven. Mu Mun commented:

Even if your eloquence flows like a waterfall, it is of no use. Though you may be able to expound all of the Buddhist sutras, it is still of no avail. If you can answer correctly, then that which has been dead until now comes alive, and that which has been alive until now can be destroyed. Otherwise you must wait for a day in the distant future and ask Maitreya Buddha.

Ven. Mu Mun's verse:
Master Hyang Eom is truly foolish.
His scathing remarks have no end.
He stops up the mouths of the monks,
So that mystical eyes open up all over their bodies.

C. Explanation

If you open your mouth, you're in trouble, but if you don't open it, you're still lost. Only by pointing to the space between the "open" and "closed" mouth is there a way to live. What's the use of wealth and honor when your life is at risk! Desire and anger have completely disappeared. You'll be wrong whether you open or close your mouth, since whichever way you choose will only be a relative view arising from a deluded mind.

There aren't actually two ways at all; in other words it's impossible to make a choice. This middle way, which is neither open nor closed, is none other than our non-discriminating awareness in which life and death, moment and eternity, all coexist. Even though dragons and serpents are intertwined, it is of no consequence; even though Buddha and sentient beings frolic about, it does not cause any interference. If you properly keep the Great Question, you pass beyond the unconscious, and reach this realm of non-discriminating awareness. This is the true way to stay alive.

Since both your hands and feet are bound, and your mouth grasps the branch, you must answer without opening your mouth. When you reach this point, speech and words are of no use; all teachings and relative concepts must be severed. Even if you were not in this kind of extreme situation, and under ordinary circumstances someone were to ask you this question, you would still need to be a powerful person in order to easily resolve the dilemma. When encountering this kind of predicament where there is no way out, the foolish man avoids it and falls into a bottomless pit, whereas a wise man opens up a totally new world.

When Master Hyang Eom put this case before the community as a question for their practice, disciple Cho asked him:

"One should not ask about being up a tree. How about asking

before ascending the tree?"

Whereupon the master chuckled and composed the following verse:

> The baby chick is pecking from inside, the mother hen is pecking from outside,
> So the baby chick breaks through the mother hen's shell.
> Since the mother hen and baby chick both do not exist,
> There is not even the slightest error according to causality.
> As I sing harmoniously of one path,
> The mysterious cloud exists alone.

The only way to completely resolve this problem is to return to the root, before the situation even arises. This means returning to the original state of health, which cures all the various diseases of delusion. Disciple Cho's answer was brilliant, wasn't it?

제 6 칙
世尊拈花(세존염화)

❦

부처님, 꽃을 드시다
Case6: Buddha Holds Up a Flower

가. 본칙(本則)

世尊, 昔在靈山會上, 拈花示衆. 是時衆皆默然, 惟迦葉尊者, 破顏微笑. 世尊云, 吾有正法眼藏, 涅槃妙心, 實相無相, 微妙法門. 不立文字, 敎外別傳, 付囑摩訶迦葉.

    옛날, 부처님께서 영산회상에서 설법하실 때 꽃 한 송이를 들어 대중에게 보이셨다. 그때 모든 대중은 다 침묵한 채 아무 말이 없었는데, 오직 가섭 존자만이 얼굴에 밝은 표정을 지으며 미소를 띠었다. 이에 세존께서 말씀하셨다.
  "나에게 정법안장(正法眼藏)이 있는데,
  열반의 묘한 마음이며, 참모습이되 모습이 없다.
  미묘한 법문이라 문자를 세우지 않고 따로 전하려 한다.
  이것을 마하가섭에게 부촉하노라."

나. 평창(評唱) 및 송(頌)

無門曰. 黃面瞿曇, 傍若無人, 壓良爲賤, 懸羊頭賣狗肉. 將謂多少奇特, 只如當時大衆都笑, 正法眼藏, 作麽生傳. 設使迦葉不

笑, 正法眼藏, 又作麽生傳. 若道正法眼藏有傳授, 黃面老子, 誑
諄閭閻. 若道無傳授, 爲甚麽獨許迦葉.

 누런 얼굴을 한 붓다가 방약무인(傍若無人)하게 양민을 억지로 노예로 만드는가 하면, 양의 대가리를 내걸어 놓고 개고기를 팔고 있다. 다소 기특하다고는 말할 수 있다. 하지만 그때에 대중 모두가 빙그레 웃었다면 정법안장은 어떻게 전수되었을까?

 만일 가섭이 웃지 않았다면 정법안장은 또 어떻게 전수되었을까?

 만약 정법안장이란 것이 전수되는 것이라고 말한다면 황면노자(黃面老子)가 촌사람들을 속인 것이 되고, 또 만약 전수되지 않는 것이라고 말한다면 어찌하여 가섭 한 사람에게만큼은 허락하였을까?

頌曰. 拈起花來, 尾巴已露. 迦葉破顏, 人天罔措.

 무문 스님이 다시 게송으로 말하였다.
  "꽃을 들어 올렸을 때
  이미 꼬리가 드러났다.

가섭은 빙그레 웃었으나
인간과 천인은 어쩔 줄 몰라 하네."

다. 강론(講論)

  정법의 안목을 갖춘 제자를 인가하는 성스러운 정법안장의 부촉 현장을 본다. 이른바, 삼처전심(三處傳心)의 하나이다. 삼처전심이라 하면 영산회상거염화(靈山會上擧拈花), 다자탑전분반좌(多子塔前分半座), 사라쌍수곽시쌍부(沙羅雙樹槨示雙趺)인데 특히 여기서 소개되는 '세존염화'의 전체 줄거리는 다음과 같다.

  "세존께서 영축산에 법단을 마련하고 팔만 사천 대중을 모이게 하였다. 세존께서 단에 오르기 직전 대범천왕이 금파라(金波羅)라는 꽃가지 하나를 부처님께 올렸다. 대중들은 세존의 설법을 기대하며 묵묵히 기다리고 있었던 상황인데 세존께서는 금파라를 들고 법단에 오르자마자 그 꽃가지를 번쩍 들어 대중에게 보일뿐 일언반구 한 말씀도 없으셨다. 이때 대중들은 그것이 무슨 영문인지 몰라 그저 묵묵히 지켜볼 뿐이었다. 그런데 단 한 사람, 가섭 존자만이 의미를 알아차리고 빙그레 웃었다. 그때 세존께서 '대중 가운데 가섭 한 사람만이 나의 뜻을 알았도다' 하시며 정법안장(正

法眼藏), 열반묘심(涅槃妙心), 실상무상(實相無相)의 미묘한 법문을 마하가섭에게 부촉하셨다."

세존께서 꽃을 들어 보이시는 격외(格外)의 몸짓으로 무분별한 본래의 자리를 보이셨다. 가섭은 이에 딱 맞게 줄탁동시(啐啄同時)로 계합한 것이다. 여기에는 언어 문자가 이르지 못할뿐더러 오히려 언어 문자가 소용없다.

"세존께서 왜 꽃을 들어 보이실까?"

대사일번(大死一番)이 요구된다. 사무치고 사무쳐서 나를 완전히 매몰시킨 무아(無我)의 경지에 들면 천사량만계교(千思量萬計較)의 분별심이 쉬고 어느 순간 밝은 소식을 접할 수 있다. 부처님께서는 열반에 드시기 직전 이미 팔만 사천 법문을 하셨음에도 불구하고 '나는 한마디도 설한 바가 없다'고 말씀하셨는데 여기 '세존염화'의 이야기가 그 말씀을 대변하고 있다.

기실 꽃가지를 번쩍 들어 올린 것은 만고불역(萬古不易)의 진리의 표상이 아닐 수 없다. 이는 사고(思考)라는 분별의식 이전의 소식이며 본래의 마음바탕 그대로를 보여주신 모습이다. 자신의 참면목을 보려고 하는 수행자들은 이 같은 전혀 새로운 방식의 가르침을 거부하지 않아야 한다.

Case 6
Buddha Holds Up a Flower

A. Original Case

Long ago, when the Buddha gave a Dharma speech for the assembly on Vulture Peak, he held up a single flower and showed it to the community. Everyone in the assembly was silent, no one said anything- only Mahakashyapa smiled brightly.

Then the World-Honored One spoke, "I have the Treasury of the True Dharma Eye, the Mystical Mind of Nirvana, the True Form of the Formless, this subtle Dharma speech; I transmit this separately, without depending on speech. This I have entrusted to Mahakashyapa."

B. Commentary and Verse

The Golden-faced Buddha disregarded his listeners and intentionally made them into slaves; he promised them a ram's head but sold dog meat. We might even say it was praiseworthy.

However, if everyone in the assembly at that time had

smiled, how could he have transmitted his True Dharma Eye? And also, if Mahakashyapa had not smiled, how could he have transmitted it? If you say that the True Dharma Eye can be transmitted, then the golden-faced old man(Buddha) fools a country bumpkin. If you say it cannot be transmitted, then how could he have approved of Mahakashyapa?

Ven. Mu Mun's verse:
   Holding up a flower,
   His tail was already revealed;
   Mahakashyapa smiled,
   Heavenly beings and men were bewildered.

C. Explanation

This case concerns the approval of a disciple who possesses the sacred True Dharma Eye; it is one of the three so-called instances of mind-to-mind transmission(by the Buddha to Mahakashyapa). The three cases of mind-to-mind transmission are: through a smile, when Buddha held up a flower on Vulture Peak; at the Stupa of Many Children, when Buddha shared his seat with Mahakashyapa; when Buddha put his feet through the coffin after entering Nirvana. Here is a summary of the entire story of Buddha holding up a flower:

"The World-honored One prepared his Dharma seat, and eighty-four thousand members of the community assembled. Just before the Buddha ascended the high rostrum, the king of the Brahman heaven offered him a lotus flower. Though the members of the assembly were waiting quietly for the Buddha's Dharma speech, as soon as he ascended the rostrum carrying the flower, he simply picked it up for all to see, without a single word. The assembly didn't know what the reason was for this, and only watched in silence. Only one person, Mahakashyapa, realized the meaning and smiled. At that moment, the World-Honored One said, 'Only one person in the assembly has understood my true meaning.' I have entrusted the subtle Dharma speech of the Treasury of the True Dharma Eye, the Mystical Mind of Nirvana, and the True Form of the Formless to Mahakashyapa."

Through the uncharacteristic action of holding up a flower, the Buddha demonstrated the original point of no relative distinction;

this was fitting for Mahakashyapa, like the mother hen and the baby chick pecking through the shell of the egg at the same time. Speech and words are of no use, as they cannot even reach this point.

"Why did the World-honored One hold up a flower?"

One needs to die the "great death" once(i.e. completely lose the egocentric self). When you enter the realm of selflessness and completely bury your ego, as the death has pierced you, the infinite minds of relative discrimination are at rest. At any time you can encounter enlightened wisdom.

Just before the Buddha entered Nirvana, he said that though he had already given eighty-four thousand Dharma speeches, that "he never spoke a single word." This story of him picking up a flower represents that kind of wordless speech. Actually, picking up the flower stem is a symbol of eternal, unchanging truth; he is showing us the original mind-essence, just as it is, before any discriminating consciousness or conceptual thought. Those practitioners who would like to see Buddha's true face should never reject this new method of teaching.

제 7 칙
趙州洗鉢(조주세발)

❦

조주 큰스님,
발우 씻으라고 하시다

Case7:
Seon Master Joju's Wash Your Bowls

가. 본칙(本則)

趙州, 因僧問, 某甲乍入叢林, 乞師指示. 州云, 喫粥了也未. 僧云, 喫粥了也. 州云, 洗鉢盂去. 其僧有省.

    조주 큰스님에게 한 스님이 찾아와 말했다.
    "저는 이제 막 총림에 들어왔습니다. 부디 큰스님께서 가르침을 주십시오."
    큰스님이 말씀하셨다.
    "아침 죽은 먹었는가?"
    스님이 대답했다.
    "먹었습니다."
    큰스님이 다시 말씀하셨다.
    "그럼, 발우는 씻었는가?"
    이 말씀에 찾아온 스님은 깨달은 바가 있었다.

나. 평창(評唱) 및 송(頌)

無門曰. 趙州開口見膽, 露出心肝. 者僧聽事不眞, 喚鐘作甕.

무문 스님이 평하여 말하였다.

조주 큰스님은 입을 열어 쓸개를 내보이고 심장과 간까지 밖으로 드러내었다. 그런데도 저 스님은 진짜 사실은 알아듣지 못하고, 종을 항아리라고 하고 있다.

頌曰. 只爲分明極, 翻令所得遲. 早知燈是火, 飯熟已多時.

무문 스님이 다시 게송으로 말하였다.
　　"너무나도 분명하기 때문에
　　도리어 알아듣는데 더디다.
　　일찌감치 등불이 곧 불인 줄 알았다면
　　밥 지은 지 이미 오래되었을 것을."

다. 강론(講論)

『조주록(趙州錄)』에 실린 이야기이다.

조주 스님이 처음 남전보원(南泉普願) 대선사(大禪師)를 찾아갔다. 그때 남전 대선사는 방장실에 누워서 쉬고 있었는데 조주 스님이 오자 불쑥 물었다.

"어느 곳에서 왔는가?"

조주 스님은 답했다.

"서상원(瑞像院)에서 왔습니다."

남전 대선사가 다시,

"상서로운 모습을 보았는가?"라고 묻자

조주 스님은 "서상은 보지 못하고 누워있는 여래는 보았습니다."라고 대답했다.

남전 대선사는 벌떡 일어나서, "그대는 주인이 있는 사미냐? 주인이 없는 사미냐?"라고 물었다. 이에 조주 스님은 "주인이 있는 사미입니다."라고 대답했다.

남전 대선사는 또 "주인이 누구인가?"라고 물었다. 조주 스님은 몸을 굽히며, "동짓달은 매우 춥습니다. 바라옵건대 큰스님께서는 기거하심에 존체(尊體)만복하십시오."라고 답했다.

남전 대선사는 기특하게 생각하고 입실(入室)을 허락하였다. 두 분의 대화는 애초부터 어렵지도 않거니와 다분히 현실적이다. 오가는 문답(問答)이 곱씹을수록 재미가 난다. 여기서 소개되는 '조주세발'의 화두 또한 조주 큰스님이 남전 대선사를 처음 뵈었을 때의 대화처럼 할(喝)을 한다거나 방(棒)을 휘두르는 과격함이 전혀 없이 일상언어 속에서 조용한 깨우침을 제시하고 있다.

우리는 日用而不知(일용이부지)를 염두에 둘 필요가 있다. 행·주·좌·와·어·묵·동·정(行·住·坐·臥·語·默·動·靜)의 일상사(日常事)가 도행(道行)아님이 없을 때 살아있는 공부인(工夫人)이다.

생사대사(生死大事)의 해결도 결국은 조고각하(照顧脚下)에서 비롯된다는 사실을 깨닫지 않으면 안 된다.

일상의 모든 일을 마음으로 자각하고 생활 가운데 자기 자신을 잃어버리지 않는다면 진리, 깨달음이라는 거창한 말들이 굳이 소용없다. 저 『금강경』의 서분(序分)에서 보이는 내용도 이런 점에서 재미있다. 부처님의 극히 일상적 행위에 대해서 수보리가 찬탄해 마지않는 장면은 가히 충격적이다. 어떠한 진리나 도(道)도 일상성을 떠나서는 아무런 의미가 없음을 금강경은 직접적으로 보여주고 있다.

현성공안(現成公案)이란 말이 있듯이 '지금 바로', '여기 이곳'에서 자기의 일상생활을 잘 펼쳐나가는 사람이 진실한 깨달음의 구현자이다.

공양을 하였으면 발우를 씻는 일이 당연하지 않은가!

Case 7

Seon Master Joju's Wash Your Bowls

A. Original Case

A monk came to see Seon Master Joju and said, "I have just now entered the monastery. Please teach me, great master."

The Seon Master asked him, "Did you eat your breakfast?"

The monk answered, "Yes, I did."

The Seon Master replied again, "Well, did you wash your bowls?"

When the monk heard this, he attained something.

B. Commentary and Verse

Ven. Mu Mun commented: When Seon Master Joju opens his mouth, he displays his gall bladder; he reveals his heart and liver. However, that monk couldn't really understand the truth-he mistook a bell for a jar.

Ven. Mu Mun's verse:

> Since it's too clear,
>
> One is slow to understand it.
>
> If early on you realize that a lamp is a flame,
>
> Then your rice has already been done for a long time.

C. Explanation

There is a story mentioned in the Record of Joju:

When Joju first went to visit Seon Master Nam-Jeon Bo-Won, the master was lying down in his room resting; as soon as Joju entered the room, Nam Jeon unexpectedly asked him, "Where have you come from?"

Joju answered, "I came from the Holy-Image temple."

Nam Jeon then asked him, "Have you seen the holy image?"

Joju answered, "I couldn't see the holy image, but I have seen the Tathagata lying down."

Nam Jeon abruptly stood up and asked him, "Do you have a master or not, baby monk?"

At this Joju answered, "I have a master."

Nam Jeon continued, "Who is your master?"

Joju bowed and said, "December is very cold. I wish you great happiness in your life, Seon Master."

Seon Master Nam Jeon thought highly of him, so he let him enter the room. From the beginning, their conversation was not complicated and quite down-to-earth. The more one looks at their back and forth exchange, the more fascinating it is. This episode of Joju telling the monk to wash his bowls, as well as the case of Joju meeting Nam Jeon for the first time, point to the silent awakening within everyday speech, without any radical actions such as giving a strong shout or waving a stick. We should remember to keep a "not-knowing mind," even in the midst of our daily lives.

A true living practitioner is one who, while going about daily business, whether working, resting, sitting, lying down, speaking, keeping silence, moving or being still, takes nothing to be less than the practice of Dharma. Even to resolve the great matter of life and death, we must ultimately reflect on the truth that's right under our feet. Though one may be aware of all daily affairs, if you don't lose yourself in daily life, then grandiose words such as truth and enlightenment are really of no use at all.

It is also interesting that the preface of the Diamond Sutra can be seen from this point of view; the scene of Subhuti marveling at the Buddha's common daily activities is really shocking. The Diamond Sutra shows us directly that any truth or practice which is separate from daily life has no meaning at all. Someone who realizes true enlightenment is one who manifests their practice in daily life, right here and now. So it's only natural that you wash your bowls after a meal!

제 8 칙

奚仲造車(해중조차)

❦

해중의 수레 만들기
Case8: Hae Jung Makes a Cart

가. 본칙(本則)

月庵和尙問僧. 奚仲造車一百輻. 拈却兩頭, 去却軸. 明甚麽邊事.

    월암 큰스님이 어느 스님에게 물었다.
    "해중이라는 사람이 백 개의 바퀴살이 들어가는 수레를 만들면서 두 바퀴를 지탱하는 굴대를 빼버렸다. 이는 도대체 무엇을 밝히고자 한 것이겠는가?"

나. 평창(評唱) 및 송(頌)

無門曰. 若也直下明得, 眼似流星, 機如掣電.

    만약 이것을 바로 깨달을 수 있다면 눈은 유성(流星)과 같고 기(機)는 섬광과 같을 것이다.

頌曰. 機輪轉處, 達者猶迷. 四維上下, 南北東西.

무문 스님이 다시 게송으로 말하였다.

　"수레바퀴가 굴러가는 곳에서는

　뛰어난 사람도 어리둥절하게 된다.

　동서남북과 사유상하(四維上下)를

　자유로이 돌아다니게 될 것이다."

다. 강론(講論)

　해중(奚仲)은 중국의 상고시대인 하(夏)나라 사람으로 소나 말이 끄는 수레를 처음 고안한 발명가이다. 수레 만들기 1인자인 셈이다. 그런데, 해중은 괴각을 부리듯 바퀴살이 백 개나 되는 훌륭한 수레를 만들면서 양쪽의 바퀴를 꿰고 있는 굴대를 빼버렸다. 수레의 가장 중심축인 굴대를 뽑아버렸으니 어쩌자는 것인가? 즉, 양쪽 바퀴를 꿰고 있는 굴대를 제거하면 어떤 현상이 일어날 것인가를 묻고 있다. 무문혜개 스님은 굴대를 제거한 수레바퀴가 굴러가는 곳에서는 뛰어난 사람도 어리둥절하게 된다고 자기 의견을 피력하고 있다. 오히려 한술 더 떠서 동서남북과 사유상하를 자유로이 돌아다니게 될 것이라고까지 말한다. 여기서 굴대는 우리들의 삶의 현실을 꿰고 있는 업보의 축(軸), 인과의 축이라고 볼 수 있다. 중생이 중생일 수밖에 없는 것은 이 때문이다.

그것은 결국 현실적으로는 고정관념이나 틀, 집착의 굴대이다. 참으로 허망하기 짝이 없고 오히려 괴로움의 원인이 될 그런 쓰잘데 없는 것에 범부중생들은 목숨을 건다. 굴대를 제거하면 금방이라도 모든 것을 잃을 것 같지만, 오히려 빼버리고 나면 온 천하는 자기 것이 된다.

살활자재(殺活自在)하는 대기대용(大機大用)은 상식과 인식의 범위를 초월하지 않으면 안 된다. 즉, 무심(無心)의 지혜작용은 굴대 빠진 수레바퀴가 자유롭게 시방세계를 구르듯 우리들을 자유자재하게 살도록 한다.

그러한 면에서 '제8칙의 해중조차'는 차사문의(借事問義)의 논법이 특출한 공안이다. 자아의식을 완전히 날려 보내고 그저 텅 비워 버리려면 사상(四相)을 수행의 금강방망이로 여지없이 깨부수어야 한다. 아상, 인상, 중생상, 수자상은 차별과 분별이라는 번뇌, 망심(妄心)일 뿐이다.

망념(妄念)의 자기 자신이 없어지고 나면 본래의 참된 모습인 진실의 자기가 드러난다. 전도된 생각을 초월하고 깨달음에라도 집착하지 않아야 자기 스스로가 굴대 빠진 수레가 되어 시방세계를 무애자재하게 활보할 수 있다.

정반성(定盤星)을 인정하지 말라는 말이 있다. 정반성이란 천칭 저울의 중앙막대기 기점에 있는 별 표시(星印)를 말하는데 이것은 물건의 무게 경중(輕重)에는 아무런 관계가 없다. 저울대의 중앙을 표시하는 것일 뿐인데 수준이 낮은 사람들은 여기에 신경 쓴다. 참선에서 이 비유를 쓰는 것은 언어, 문자에 집착하지 말라는 경고이다.

생각의 담을 허물고 인식의 카테고리를 벗길 일이다. 무심(無心)의 작용(作用), 공(空)의 실천적인 중도(中道)의 묘용(妙用)을 살려낼 때 마음의 수레는 사방천지 종횡무진 할 수 있다.

대자유의 삶에는 굴대가 필요치 않다.

Case 8
Hae Jung Makes a Cart

A. Original Case

Seon Master Wol Am asked a monk,

"A man named Hae Jung made a cart with one-hundred spokes, but removed the axle which supported both wheels. What became clear?"

B. Commentary and Verse

If someone can directly attain this, his eye will be like a shooting star, and his wit will be like a flash of light.

Ven. Mu Mun's verse:
>Even an accomplished person is confused
>At the point where the wheels spin;
>Traveling freely in four directions-above and below,
>North, south, east, and west.

C. Explanation

Hae Jung was a man in ancient China who invented the first horse/ox-drawn cart; he was the top cart-maker. Oddly enough, Hae-Jung made an excellent cart with one-hundred spokes, yet removed the axle that transfixed the wheels on both sides. Why did he take away the main axle-the cart's central axis? In other words, it is asking what happens if you eliminate the central axle that runs through the wheels on both sides. Ven. Mu Mun frankly states his opinion that if you remove the point where the wheels rotate, even an accomplished person is at a loss. Furthermore, he says that you can wander freely in the four directions, above and below, north, south, east and west.

In this case, the axle is the karmic fruit of our actions which runs through our present lives-in other words, the results of cause and effect. This is the reason that sentient beings cannot help but just be sentient beings. Ultimately, in a practical sense this axle refers to our fixed ideas, concepts and attachments. It is truly for naught that ordinary sentient beings stake their lives on useless things which cause suffering. If you take away this axle, it seems like at any moment you could lose everything; actually if you take it away the whole universe becomes yours.

This great faculty, which is liberated from life and death, must transcend the scope of mere common sense and knowledge. That is to say, just as the wheel with no axle freely rolls in all directions, the wise functioning of no-mind allows us to live freely and independently.

Seen from this standpoint, the episode of Hae Jung's making a cart is an exceptional case that uses a metaphor to pierce through to the truth. If you want to completely discard any sense of self, then you have to thoroughly flatten the four marks of existent phenomena with the diamond club of practice. These four marks(concept of self, concept of individual personality, notion that all beings have reality, concept of existence) are merely delusory thoughts and relative distinctions. When the deluded concept of self disappears, then the original true-self is revealed. When you transcend perverted thoughts and don't attach even to enlightenment, then you yourself become the cart with no axle and can stride freely anywhere, without hindrance.

There is an expression which says, "Don't pay attention to the fulcrum star." which refers to the star at the fulcrum of the beam supporting the two scales in the constellation Libra. This has nothing to do with the relative weight of material objects-it merely indicates the center of the beam, but people of low capacity put their attention here. In Seon this metaphor is used as a warning not to attach to speech and words. Tear down the wall of thought, and the framework of intellectual understanding is cast away. When the function of no-mind and the mystic usage of the practical, middle-way of emptiness are brought to life, then the cart of the mind can go anywhere in the universe. An axle is not needed for a life of great liberation.

제 9 칙
大通智勝(대통지승)

❦

대통지승 부처님

Case9:
The Buddha of Supreme
Penetration and Superior Wisdom

가. 본칙(本則)

興陽讓和尙, 因僧問, 大通智勝佛, 十劫坐道場, 佛法不現前, 不得成佛道時如何. 讓曰, 其問甚諦當. 僧云, 旣是坐道場, 爲甚麽不得成佛道. 讓曰, 爲伊不成佛.

    홍양(興陽)의 청양(淸讓) 큰스님께 어느 스님이 여쭈었다.
    "대통지승불은 십겁(十劫)이라는 오랜 세월을 도량에서 좌선했지만, 불법(佛法)이 나타나지 않아 불도(佛道)를 이루지 못했다고 합니다. 이것은 도대체 무슨 의미입니까?"
    그러자 청양 큰스님이 대답하셨다.
    "그 질문이 제법 이치에 맞구나."
    그 스님은 거듭 여쭈었다.
    "이미 그렇게 도량에서 좌선을 하고 있었는데, 어째서 불도를 이루지 못했는지요?"
    청양 큰스님이 대답하셨다.
    "그가 성불하지 않았으니까 그렇지."

나. 평창(評唱) 및 송(頌)

無門曰. 只許老胡知, 不許老胡會. 凡夫若知卽是聖人, 聖人若會卽是凡夫.

다만 늙은 부처가 지혜로써 아는 것은 인정하지만, 알음알이로써 이해하는 것은 용납할 수 없다. 범부도 지혜를 얻으면 바로 성인이라 하고, 성인이라도 분별심을 내면 바로 범부인 것이다.

頌曰. 了身何似了心休, 了得心兮身不愁. 若也身心俱了了, 神仙何必更封侯.

무문 스님이 다시 게송으로 말하였다.
　　"몸을 닦는 것이 어찌 마음 닦아 쉬는 것만 할까?
　　마음을 닦아내 버리면 몸은 근심 없어지는 것을
　　만약 몸과 마음 둘 다 닦아졌다면
　　신선에게 다시 작위를 줄 필요가 있겠는가?"

다. 강론(講論)

본 화두에서 인용되는 대통지승불의 이야기는 『법화경』 화성유품(化城喩品)에 근거한다.

"대통지승불이 보리도량에 앉아서 온갖 마구니를 항복 받고 무상정등정각을 이루려 할 때 불법(佛法)이 앞에 나타나지 않았다. 그래서 십소겁까지 가부좌를 틀고 앉아 몸과 마음을 움직이지 않았는데도 역시 불법이 현현하지 않았다."

참선은 마음을 다스리는 공부이지 몸을 훈련시키는 공부가 아니다.

수레를 끄는 소가 그 수레를 잘 끌지 못하면 '소를 때려야 하느냐, 수레를 때려야 하느냐?' 하는 말이 있다. 소에 매질을 해야지 수레에 매질해서야 무슨 소용이 있겠는가! 제대로 가부좌를 틀고 앉아있지 못하면 십겁이 아니라 백천 겁이라도 아무 소용없다. 외형만의 좌선을 고집하다 보면 평생을 해도 깨치지 못한다. 끽반운작(喫飯運作)중에서도 선(禪)이 되어야 공부라 할 수 있다. 즉, 동중지공부(動中之工夫)까지 되어야 하는데 그냥 앉아있는 흉내만으로는 어림없다. 이쯤되면 정중지공부(靜中之工夫)의 요체가 분명해진다. 마음공부가 순숙(順熟)해지면 직심시도량(直心是道場)이 결코 건방진 말이 아니다. 운시급수(運柴汲水)가 모두 선(禪)이 되었을 때 활선(活禪)이라 할 수 있다. '제9칙 대통지승'에 대한 전혀 빛깔이 다른 답이 『임제록』에 나오고 있다.

자칫 잘못 생각하면 다기망양의 헝클어진 사상이 선(禪)인듯 하여 혼돈스러울 수도 있으나 열린 사고, 자유의지를 존중하는 것이 선의 큰 특징임을 확인할 수 있다.

임제의현의 말씀이다.

"대통이란 바로 자기 자신이니, 어디서나 만법의 무성(無性)과 무상(無相)을 통달하는 것을 말한다. 지승이란 일체의 모든 곳에서 한 법도 얻을 것이 없음을 의심하지 않는 것을 말한다. 부처란 청정하고 밝은 마음이 시방법계를 사무쳐 비추는 것을 이름 한다. '10겁 동안 도량에 앉았다.' 하는 것은 십바라밀을 닦은 것이다. '불법이 나타나지 않았다' 고 하는 것은 부처는 본래 나지 않고(佛本不生), 법은 본래 없어지지 않는 것(法本不滅)인데, 거기서 무엇이 나타나겠는가?

'불도를 이루지 못했다.' 고 하는 것은 부처가 다시 부처가 되지는 않는다(佛不能更作佛)는 뜻이다. 그러므로 옛사람이 이르기를, '부처는 항상 세간에 계시면서도 세간법에 물들지 않는다.' 고 하셨다."

수증일여(修證一如)라!

불도를 이루려는 마음 또한 번뇌임을 자각해야 한다.

Case 9

The Buddha of Supreme Penetration and Superior Wisdom

A. Original Case

A monk asked Seon Master Cheong Yang of Heung Yang, "The Buddha of Supreme Penetration and Superior Wisdom sat meditation on the seat of Bodhi for ten kalpas(a very long time), and yet the Buddha-Dharma did not appear-he did not attain Buddhahood. What is the meaning of this?"

Seon Master Cheong Yang answered, "Your question is quite reasonable."

The monk asked again, "He already practiced meditation on the seat of Bodhi, how could he not attain Buddhahood?"

The Master answered, "Because he did not become Buddha."

B. Commentary and Verse

That which the ancient Buddha realizes with wisdom is

acknowledged, but that which is comprehended through intellectual understanding is not permitted. When even an ordinary man attains wisdom, he is a sage; though one is a sage, if he forms distinctions he is just an ordinary man.

Ven. Mu Mun's verse:
    It is better to cultivate the mind than the body;
    If one cultivates the mind, then the body's troubles disappear.
    If both body and mind are cultivated together,
    Then does one need give another title to a sage?

C. Explanation

The story of the Buddha of Supreme Penetration and Superior Wisdom quoted in the original case is based on the seventh chapter of the Lotus Sutra(the Parable of the Conjured City).

"The Buddha of Supreme Penetration and Superior Wisdom sat on the seat of Bodhi and overcame all sorts of demons in order to attain supreme perfect enlightenment, but the Buddha-Dharma did not appear before him. Though he sat for ten kalpas in the full-lotus position, without moving either body or mind, Buddhahood still did not manifest."

Seon meditation is the practice of controlling the mind, not of disciplining the body. There's an expression that says, if the ox pulling the cart falters, "Do you hit the cart or the ox?" Of course you whip the ox-what's the use of whipping the cart! If you don't sit meditation correctly, then even if you sit for infinite kalpas, it is of no use. If you merely cling to the outside form of sitting meditation, then even you practice your entire life, you won't attain it. Only when Seon becomes part of your daily life can it be called cultivation. In other words, one has to be able to practice even while being active; just sitting as a form of imitation is far from it. If you achieve this, then the key point of cultivating through stillness becomes clear. When the cultivation of the mind matures, then it's never arrogant to say that the pure mind is the seat of Bodhi. When carrying wood and drawing water have all become Seon practice, it can be called "living Seon." A completely different interpretation of this episode is found in the Record of Linchi.

If you give rise to even the slightest delusory thought, you can become confused, taking some twisted, dead-end philosophy to be Seon; one can recognize this outstanding and unique aspect of Seon, which respects open-mindedness and spontaneity.

According to Lin-chi I-hsuan:

Supreme penetration is none other than your true-self; it means that one perceives that everywhere, the ten-thousand Dharmas have no substance and no form. Superior wisdom means having complete confidence that there is no attainment with nothing to attain anywhere. Buddha is the name of the pure, clear, radiant mind which thoroughly illuminates the Dharma realms in all directions. The phrase "sat for ten kalpas" refers to the cultivation of the ten Paramitas(perfections). "Buddha-Dharma did not appear" means that originally Buddha does not appear and Dharma does not disappear. So what became clear? The phrase "Could not attain Buddhahood" means that Buddha does not become Buddha again. Therefore, the people of olden times said "A Buddha is always living in the world and yet not affected by the ways of the world."

Practice is in itself awakening! One should realize that the very mind that one would attain Buddahood is itself delusion.

제 10 칙
清稅孤貧(청세고빈)

※

청세의 가난
Case10: Cheong Sae's Poverty

가. 본칙(本則)

曹山和尙, 因僧問云, 淸稅孤貧, 乞師賑濟. 山云, 稅闍梨. 稅應諾. 山曰, 靑原白家酒, 三盞喫了, 猶道未沾脣.

　　조산(曹山) 큰스님께 청세(淸稅) 스님이 물었다.
　　"저, 청세는 몹시 외롭고 가난합니다. 큰스님께서 은혜를 베풀어 구제하여 주십시오!"
　　큰스님은 이에 "청세 스님!"하고 불렀다.
　　스님은 "예!"하고 대답하였다.
　　큰스님께서 다시 말씀하셨다.
　　"그대는 청원 땅의 백씨네 술을 이미 석 잔이나 마셨으면서도, 아직 입술도 적시지 않았다고 하는구나!"

나. 평창(評唱) 및 송(頌)

無門曰. 淸稅輸機, 是何心行. 曹山具眼, 深辨來機. 然雖如是, 且道, 那裏是稅闍梨喫酒處.

청세의 매끄럽지 못한 행동은 어떤 마음에서 나온 것일까?

조산 큰스님은 이미 안목을 다 갖추고 있어서 찾아온 사람의 근기를 꿰뚫어보고 있다.

비록 그렇다 할지라도 한번 말해보라. 도대체 어느 곳이 청세가 술을 마신 자리인가?

頌曰. 貧似范丹, 氣如項羽. 活計雖無, 敢與鬪富

무문 스님이 다시 게송으로 말하였다.
　"가난하기는 고결한 선비, 범단(范丹)을 닮았고
　기세는 저 항우(項羽)와도 같구나.
　한 푼도 없어 생계도 못 이끌어 가면서,
　감히 조산 큰스님과 더불어 부(富)를 다투다니."

다. 강론(講論)

청세 스님이 고빈(孤貧)하다는 마음을 갖고 조산 큰스님께 법거량을 요청하는 장면이다. 가난하다고 말하지만 아직 마음에 잔상이 많음을 스스로 드러내는 실수를 하고 있다. 청세 스님 자신은 반야(般若)의 진공무상(眞空無相)의 경계를 터득했다고 자부하지만, 본래무일물(本來無一物)의 필경공(畢竟空)에는 계합하지 못함이 보인다.

조산 큰스님은 밑천이 부족한 청세 스님이 자기의 가난을 인정해 달라는 말에 단 한마디로 시험하면서 훈계하신다.

"청세 스님"하고 부르자 "예"하는 순간에 상황은 끝났다. 텅 비워 잘났다는 사람이 명상(名相)에 사로잡혀 곤혹을 치르고 있는 것이다.

천하의 명주라는 백씨네 술을 석 잔이나 마시고도 입술을 적시지 않았다고 겸손한 척하는 청세 스님은 아직 공부가 덜된 것이 분명하다.

수행자에게 있어서 가난은 미덕이다.

그 가난은 물질적 가난이 아니라 마음의 가난이어야 한다. 아무 데도 집착할 것이 없고 그 어떤 상황에도 분별심이 일어나지 않아야 가난하다고 할 수 있다.

저 유명한 한산자(寒山子)는 정신의 가난이 정말 가난한 것(神貧始是貧)이라고 읊은 적도 있다. 탐·진·치 삼독심으로 가득차 있어서는 제아무리 물질적으로 적게 가지고 있다손 치더라도 마음의 가난은 아니다. 마음의 가난은 끊임없는 자기 성찰에 근거한 철저한 수행에서 비롯된다. 공부가 익고 익어서 지난해에는 하도 가난하여 송곳 꽂을 땅이 없다 하였는데 올해는 더욱 가난하여 꽂을 송곳마저 없다고 한 옛 스님의 행적을 귀감 삼지 않으면 안 된다.

그런데 이 가난이 가난해졌다는 마음까지 없어졌을 때 참가난이라 할 수 있다. 가난의 뿌리조차 파헤쳐졌을 때 가식도 체면도 죄다 날아가고 텅 빈, 오롯한 자신이 존재한다. 청세 스님은 그런 점에서 미흡했다. 고빈(孤貧)하다면 그뿐이지 무엇 때문에 구걸하듯 인정을 받으려 하였는지….

그러니 조산 큰스님은 "청세 스님" 하고 그의 이름을 불러 상(相)을 부수는 자비를 보여주는 것이다.

진실로 그 마음이 무상(無相)하였을 때 무생(無生)이 되는데 청세 스님의 부족함이 여기에 있다.

아집의 본질은 늘 갈등과 모순을 동반한다는 사실을 놓쳐서는 안 된다는 메시지를 던지고 있다. 무일물(無一物)하여야 무진장(無盡藏)한 세상을 자유로이 노닐 수 있다.

무일물(無一物)! 참으로 쉽고도 어려운 말이다.

Case 10
Cheong Sae's Poverty

A. Original Case

The Ven. Cheong Sae asked Seon Master Jo San, "I, Cheong Sae, am very lonely and destitute. Master, I would be so grateful if you helped me."

The Master called out "Cheong Sae!"

The monk replied, "Yes!"

The Master spoke again, "Even though you have already drunk three cups of the finest wine in China, you say that you have not yet wet your lips!"

B. Commentary and Verse

What was the reason for Cheong Sae's unskillful behavior? Since Master Jo San had already attained the eye of discernment, he penetrated his visitor's capacity. But though that may have been the case, please tell me: at what point did Cheong Sae drink the wine?

Ven. Mu Mun's verse:

> Poverty like the high-minded scholar Beom Dan;
>
> Spirit like the nobleman Hang Wu.
>
> Without a single penny for his livelihood,
>
> Master Jo San dares to rival the wealthy.

C. Explanation

This is the scene of Ven. Cheong Sae, with his mind of loneliness and poverty, requesting Dharma combat with Master Jo San. He said that he was destitute, but made the mistake of revealing that there were still many delusions in his mind. Cheong Sae was proud that he had attained the level of wisdom wherein true emptiness has no form, but he seems not to have encountered the absolute emptiness of "originally not even one thing." With a single phrase Master Jo San tested and admonished Ven. Cheong Sae, who asked for confirmation of his poverty while lacking even seed money.

The moment when the Master called out "Cheong Sae" and the monk answered "yes," the situation was already finished; the great man of emptiness was still caught in name and form, so he was at a loss. By saying he had already drunk three cups of fine wine but had not yet wet his lips, the Master demonstrated that Ven. Cheong Sae was just feigning humility and that his practice was not complete. Poverty is a virtue to a practitioner - however this does not refer to material poverty, but poverty of mind. We can call it poverty when one does not attach to anything at all, but also when the mind of relative distinctions does not appear in any situation whatsoever. The famous lay practitioner Han San once recited a verse which said that "Poverty of the spirit is truly poverty." Not matter how few material possessions one may own, it is not poverty of spirit if one's mind is still full of the three poisons of desire, anger and ignorance. Poverty of the spirit begins with the fundamental, thorough practice of ceaseless self-reflection. Practitioners should follow the example of a monk from ancient times, who stated that as his practice continued to mature, "though in years past I was so poor I didn't even have a bit of earth to dig with an awl, this year I became poorer and don't even have an awl."

However, when even this mind of poverty disappears, it can be termed true poverty. When the root of poverty is dug up, any pretense and sense of reputation also vanish entirely? only the complete, empty self exists. The Ven. Cheong Sae was lacking in this respect. If one is lonely and destitute, it's just that; why try to get confirmation, as if begging for it….

Therefore, when Master Jo San called out his name, "Cheong Sae," he was showing the compassion which smashes through appearances. Cheong Sae's shortcoming was that when mind truly has no form, it does not exist at all. This is telling us we should not forget that the nature of obstinacy always carries with it contradictions and conflict. If there is not even one thing, then one can stroll freely in the limitless world.

Not even one thing! This is something which is both easy(to say) yet difficult(to do).

제 11 칙
州勘庵主(주감암주)

~~~

조주 큰스님, 암주를 간파하다
Case11: Joju Sees Through the Hermits

가. 본칙(本則)

趙州, 到一庵主處問, 有麼有麼. 主竪起拳頭. 州云, 水淺不是泊舡處, 便行. 又到一庵主處云, 有麼有麼. 主亦竪起拳頭. 州云, 能縱能奪, 能殺能活, 便作禮.

조주 큰스님이 한 암주(庵主)의 처소에 이르러 물었다.

"누구 계시는가? 누구 계시는가?"

암주가 주먹을 세워 보였다.

이에 조주 큰스님은 '물이 얕아서 배를 댈 곳이 못 된다.' 하고 떠났다.

그리고는 다른 암주의 처소에 이르러 물었다.

"누구 계시는가? 누구 계시는가?"

그 암주도 역시 주먹을 세워 보였다.

조주 큰스님은 '능히 놓아주기도 하고 능히 빼앗기도 하고 능히 죽이기도 하고 능히 살리기도 하는구나.' 하고 얼른 절하였다.

나. 평창(評唱) 및 송(頌)

無門曰. 一般竪起拳頭, 爲甚麼肯一箇, 不肯一箇. 且道, 誵訛在甚處. 若向者裏下得一轉語, 便見趙州舌頭無骨, 扶起放倒, 得大自在. 雖然如是, 爭奈趙州却被二庵主勘破. 若道二庵主有優劣, 未具參學眼. 若道無優劣, 亦未具參學眼.

주먹을 세워 보이기는 똑같은데, 어찌하여 한 쪽은 긍정하고 다른 쪽은 부정하였을까? 일러보라. 이렇게 말이 어긋나는 까닭이 어디에 있을까?

만약 그 속사정에 대해서 한마디 할 수 있다면, 곧 조주 큰스님의 혓바닥에 뼈가 없어 부축해 일으켜 세우고, 밀어서 넘어뜨리는 것을 마음대로 한 것임을 알게 된다. 비록 그러하나, 조주 큰스님께서 도리어 두 암자의 주인들에게 시험당했다는 사실을 어찌할 것인가? 만약, 두 암주에게 우열이 있다고 말한다면 아직 공부의 안목을 갖췄다고 하지 못할 것이고, 반대로 우열이 없다고 말한다 해도 또한 공부의 안목을 갖추지 못했다.

頌曰. 眼流星, 機掣電. 殺人刀, 活人劍.

무문 스님이 다시 게송으로 말하였다.

"안목(眼)은 유성(流星)과 같고,

지혜작용(機)은 번개와 같으니

사람을 죽이는 칼도 되고

사람을 살리는 검도 된다."

다. 강론(講論)

두 암주는 똑같이 주먹을 세워 보였다. 그런데 첫째 암주는 조주 큰스님의 눈 밖에 났고, 둘째 암주는 조주 큰스님으로부터 인정을 받았다.

과연 그랬을까?

무슨 연유일까?

무엇 때문일까?

왜일까?

은산철벽(銀山鐵壁)이라 도무지 진척이 없다. 눈구멍도, 콧구멍도, 귓구멍도 없는 수수께끼이다. 막다른 궁지에 쳐 넣어 놓고 죽겠느냐 사느냐의 극한 상황에서 입을 떼보라는 식이다. 귀머거리가 되고 장님이 되어 궁구하지 않으면 접근조차 힘들다. 더 이상 마음 쓸 곳이 없어서 초승달 그림자가 물소 뿔에 각인(刻印)되는 경지에 이르러야 늙은 쥐가 소뿔 속에 덜컥 걸려들어 가듯 할 것이다. 순일무잡의 자리에서 더욱 밀치고 들어가야 조금 화두 맛을 보았다 하리라.

상황은 같은데 정반대의 판정을 받은 이 사건은 결코 만만치 않다. 이유나 근거도 없이 어째서 하나는 부정하고 하나는 긍정하였을까? 그렇지 않다. 이유, 근거가 반드시 있다. 단지 감추어져 있을 뿐이다. 분명히 속셈이 있다는 말이다. 그러한 깊은 믿음이라야 분별 망상의 산을 넘는 불가사의한 의정(疑情) 덩어리가 생긴다. 대신근(大信根), 대분지(大憤志), 대의정(大疑情)의 에너지가 융합하고 용솟음쳐 곧 큰일을 낸다. 무의식(無意識)의 경계마저 허물고 체험 이전의 세상을 관통한다.

한편, 두 암주 사이에 우열(優劣)이 있다는 생각이나 주먹(拳頭)에 무엇이 있다는 생각은 다 분별의식이다. 또한 조주 큰스님이 학인(學人)의 공부를 시험(試驗)하려는 수작이 아닌가 하는 태도도 금물이다. 아무튼, 죽든가 살든가, 살인도(殺人刀)를 잡든가 활인검(活人劍)을 잡든가하는 기로에 서 있다. 여기에서는 조주 큰스님의 평가(評價) 마저도 아무 소용없어야 한다. 자칫 잘못하면 우리 자신도 조주 큰스님의 시험에 걸려들 것이므로 함부로 딴전을 피워서는 안 된다. 바짝 정신을 차릴 일이다.

Case 11
Joju Sees Through the Hermits

A. Original Case

Seon Master Joju went to a hermitage and asked, "Who is there? Who is there?"

The hermit raised his fist.

To this Joju replied, "The water is too shallow to anchor the boat here." and left.

Joju went to another hermitage and asked again, "Who is there? Who is there?"

That hermit also raised his fist. Master Joju said, "Free to give, free to take, free to kill, free to save." and immediately bowed.

B. Commentary and Verse

They both raised their fists; why was one accepted and the other rejected? Tell me: What is the reason for this contradictory speech? If one can say something about the deep meaning, you'll realize that Master Joju's tongue has no bone; he both helps others stand up and knocks them over as he pleases. Though that is the case, could it rather be true that Master Joju was tested by the two hermits? If you say that one is superior and the other inferior, then you have no eye of realization. On the other hand, if you say there is no difference, then you also have no eye of discernment.

Ven. Mu Mun's verse:
    An eye like a shooting star,
    Wisdom that functions like lightning.
    Both a knife which kills,
    And a sword which gives life.

C. Explanation

The two hermits raised their fists identically. However, the first hermit was rejected by Master Joju, whereas the second hermit received his approval.

Was it really so?

What was the reason?

For what?

Why?

This is an unsolvable situation; it's a riddle without an eye, nose, or ear hole. Caught in this hopeless predicament, try and give an answer to this kind of extreme, life or death situation. Unless you become blind and deaf and thoroughly investigate it, it's hard to even come close. When there's no place any more for conceptual thought, and you reach the level where the shadow of the new moon leaves its mark on the horn of the water buffalo, then it's as if an old mouse has suddenly entered the horn and gotten stuck. If you push forth from this state of complete purity, without any delusion at all, you can taste the Great Question a little bit. The same situation, but the two episodes get completely opposite responses? it's really tough!

How could it be that one was approved and the other rejected without any reason or grounds? It's not like that - there is a definite reason and basis, it's only hidden. In other words, there is a clear intention. If you have that kind of deep faith, then the inconceivable ball of doubt which transcends the mountain of relative distinctions and delusions arises. The energy of the Great Faith, Great Courage, and Great Doubt fuse together and surge up, and soon the great matter is settled. Even the boundary of thoughtlessness is torn down, and one penetrates the realm before experience.

On the one hand, believing that one hermit is superior while the other is inferior, or wondering about the meaning of the raised fist, is all conceptual thought based on relative distinctions. It's also not the case that Joju merely had the attitude of testing the hermits' practice. At any rate, one is standing at a crossroads - live or die, holding the knife that kills, or the sword that gives life. At this point, even the opinion of Master Joju is of no use at all. If we make even the slightest mistake, we are also caught by Master Joju's test, so we should not get too easily distracted? just keep your mind clear.

제 12 칙
巖喚主人(암환주인)

❦

서암 큰스님, 주인공을 부르다
Case12: Master Seo Am calls 'Master'

가. 본칙(本則)

瑞巖彥和尙, 每日自喚主人公, 復自應諾. 乃云, 惺惺著, 喏. 他時異日, 莫受人瞞, 喏喏.

　서암사언(瑞巖師彦) 큰스님은 매일 자기 스스로를 '주인공'하고 부르고는 또 스스로 '예.'하고 대답했다.
　그리고 또 말하기를 '깨어 있거라.' 한 뒤 다시 '예.' 하고 대답했다. 또 '언제 어느 때든지 다른 사람에게 속아서는 안 되네.' 라고 한 뒤 '예, 예.' 하고 혼자 대답했다.

나. 평창(評唱) 및 송(頌)

無門曰. 瑞巖老子, 自買自賣, 弄出許多神頭鬼面. 何故. 聻. 一箇喚底, 一箇應底. 一箇惺惺底, 一箇不受人瞞底. 認著依前還不是. 若也傚他, 總是野狐見解.

　서암 노스님은 자신이 사고 자신이 팔면서 장난치듯 수많은 귀신이나 도깨비 얼굴을 내보였다. 왜 그랬을까? 저것 좀 보게. 하나는 부르고 하나는 대답한다. 하나는 '깨어 있거라.' 하고 다른 하나는 '다른 사람에게 속지 말라.'고 하네. 그러한 것을 인정하면 앞서처럼 또한 옳지 않다. 만일 서암 큰스님을 흉내라도 낸다면 그것이야말로 들여우의 견해가 될 것이다.

頌曰. 學道之人不識眞, 只爲從前認識神. 無量劫來生死本, 癡人喚作本來人.

무문 스님이 다시 게송으로 말하였다.
　　"도를 배우는 사람들이 진실을 알지 못하는 것은
　　다만 종전의 식신(識神)이 본래 자기인 줄 알기 때문.
　　무량겁 이래로 나고 죽는 근본이 되어온 것을
　　어리석은 사람은 본래의 자기라 부르고 있네."

다. 강론(講論)

본칙, 주인공(主人公) 화두의 서암 큰스님은 덕산(德山), 암두(巖頭)의 법맥을 잇고 있다. 스승 암두 선사로부터 '들숨·날숨과 대·소변 누는 곳에 본래 자연히 영원불멸의 진리가 나타나고 있는 것이다. 모두 각자 자기 발밑을 잘 살피고 회광반조(廻光返照)하여라.' 라는 가르침을 잘 계승하고 있다.

　서암 큰스님은 모자라는 사람처럼 반석위에 앉아서 스스로 '주인공' 하고 부르고, 또 스스로 '예.' 하고 대답하였다고 하니 이는 위에서 말한 스승, 암두 선사의 기백(氣魄)과 맥을 같이한다.

　주인공(主人公)이란 무위(無爲)의 진인(眞人), 무상(無相)의 자기본래면목(自己本來面目)으로서 자각의 주체인 불성(佛性)을 스스로 지칭하여 말할 때 쓰여진다. '주인공'이 지혜와 인격을 형성하는 주체라고 하지만 아트만(atman) 같이 불변(不變)하는 실체는 결코 아니다.

　아무튼, 여기 서암 큰스님의 자문자답(自問自答)적인 수행은 번뇌 망념의 분별심적 작용을 근원적으로 봉쇄하는 장치가 된다. 그럼에도 불구하고 주인공이니 불성(佛性)이니 하는 지엽적인 개념 파악에만 치중한다면 공부의 진척은 전혀 없게 된다. 생사윤회의 근본인 분별심, 식신(識神)을 쉬라고 주인공을 들먹거렸더니 오히려 그 글자에 매달려 헤매는 사람들이 없지 않아서 하는 말이다. 공부인(工夫人)은 진실한 참구(參究)로서 무아(無我) 무심(無心)의 경지가 되어야 만법(萬法)의 소유자며, 만물(萬物)의 초월자라고 할 수 있다.

주인공! 저 임제(臨濟) 선사는 수처작주입처개진(隨處作主立處皆眞)을 말씀하셨다. 중국 선종(禪宗)에서는 불성, 여래장(如來藏), 진여(眞如) 등과 같은 불교경전의 언어를 사용하는 대신 주인(主), 주인공, 본래인(本來人), 무사인(無事人) 등 싱그럽고 풋풋한 현실 언어를 적절하게 잘 활용하고 있다.

주인공이란 도대체 무엇일까?

마음과 주인공은 둘인가, 하나인가?

절대 경계할 것은 주인공을 찾는 공부가 형식적이거나 모방적이어서는 안 된다. 그것을 무문 스님은 당부하고 있다. 무문 스님의 평창과 송을 자칫 오해하면 서암 큰스님의 공부를 저울질하는 것처럼 보이나 사실은 후학들의 공부를 염려한 노파심의 발로임을 간과해서는 안 된다.

주인공을 찾던 서암 큰스님은 이미 열반에 들었는데 지금 '주인공아!' 하고 부르면 누가 대답할 것인가?

Case 12
Master Seo Am calls 'Master'

A. Original Case

   Every day Seon Master Seo-Am Sa-Eon used to call to himself, "Master!" and then answer, "Yes!"
   He would then say, "Wake up!" and reply "Yes!"
   "Never be deceived by others at any time!"
   "No, I won't!"

B. Commentary and Verse

   The old monk Seo Am both buys and sells himself; he shows the faces of many ghosts and goblins, as if playing a game. Why does he do that? Let's take a look. One calls and the other answers; one is wide awake, and the other one is saying he will never be deceived by others. If you acknowledge either of them, as mentioned earlier, it's not correct. But also, if you imitate Master Seo Am, you play the wild fox.

Ven. Mu Mun's verse:

> Those who study the Way cannot realize the truth;
>
> By taking only manifestations of consciousness to be the original-mind
>
> The root of birth and death for countless eons -
>
> A foolish person calls it the original-self.

C. Explanation

Master Seo Am, with his dilemma of calling his master, follows the Dharma lineage of Seon Masters Deok Sahn and Am Du. He truly inherited the Dharma of his teacher, Master Am Du, who said "The original, naturally eternal and undying truth appears at the place of inhalation and exhalation and of urination and defecation. Each and every one of you, look closely beneath your feet, turn the mind's light inward and illuminate within." Like a fool, Master Seo Am sits on the cushion and calls himself "Master!" then answers himself "Yes!" This is in the same spirit as his teacher, Master Am Du's lineage. "Master" refers to an effortless, true man of the Way, and is also used to refer to realization of the independent Buddha-nature, which is one's original face of formlessness. Though this "master" is said to be independent, manifesting as wisdom and characteristics, it is not an immutable essence, like atman is. Anyway, at this point Master Seo Am's practice of asking himself and then answering becomes a technique that fundamentally blocks the defilements and delusions of the discriminating consciousness. Nevertheless, if you only put emphasis on grasping such trivial concepts as "master" or "Buddha nature," your practice will not make any progress. This is pointed out because when the concept of "master" is mentioned to put to rest the mind of discriminating consciousness, the root of birth and death, many people instead get caught by the word itself and become lost. A practitioner who truly investigates and attains the level of selflessness and no-mind can be called one who possesses the ten thousand Dharmas while transcending all things.

"Master!" Seon Master Linchi said, "When you are your own master, wherever you are, then everything is truth." In the Chinese Seon sect, instead of using words from the scriptures, such as Buddha-nature, womb of the Tathagata and true-suchness, they appropriately utilized original terms such as owner, master, original-person, and man of no affair. What is this master? Is mind the same as the master or different? Any practice is not permitted that seeks the master while setting absolute limits of formality or imitation.

This is what Ven. Mu Mun was trying to say. If you misunderstand Ven. Mu Mun's commentary or verse even a bit, then you appear to be judging Master Seo Am's practice; actually you have to keep in mind his sincere concern for the practice of future generations. Master Seo Am, who was seeking his master, has already entered Nirvana; so right now if you call "Master!" who will answer?

제 13 칙
德山托鉢(덕산탁발)

덕산 큰스님의 탁발

Case13:
Seon Master Deok Sahn Carries His Bowls

가. 본칙(本則)

德山, 一日托鉢下堂. 見雪峰問, 者老漢, 鐘未鳴鼓未響, 托鉢向甚處去, 山便回方丈. 峰擧似巖頭. 頭云, 大小德山, 未會末後句. 山聞, 令侍者喚巖頭來, 問曰, 汝不肯老僧那. 巖頭密啓其意. 山乃休去. 明日陞座, 果與尋常不同. 巖頭至僧堂前, 拊掌大笑云, 且喜得老漢會末後句. 他後天下人, 不奈伊何.

　덕산 큰스님은 어느 날 발우를 받쳐 들고 식당으로 가고 있었다. 그런데 설봉(雪峰) 스님이 "노스님, 종도 아직 안 울렸고, 아직 북도 치지 않았는데 발우를 가지고 어디로 가시는 겁니까?"하고 물으니 그대로 거처하는 방장실(方丈室)로 휙 돌아가 버렸다.
　설봉 스님은 이 일을 암두(巖頭) 스님에게 전하였다. 암두 스님은 말했다.
　"덕산 노스님같이 대단한 분이 아직 '말후(末後)의 구(句)'를 알지 못하시는군!"
　덕산 큰스님은 이 이야기를 듣고, 시자에게 암두를 불러오게 해서 물었다.
　"너는 이 노승(老僧)을 수긍하지 않는다는 것이냐!"

암두 스님은 무엇인가 비밀스럽게 덕산 큰스님에게 말씀드렸다. 그러자 큰스님은 더 이상 아무 말씀도 하지 않았다. 그 다음날 법좌에 오른 덕산 큰스님은 과연 보통 때와는 달랐다. 암두 스님은 승당(僧堂) 앞에 와서 손뼉을 치고 크게 웃으며 말했다.

"야아, 기뻐해야 할 일이다. 노스님께서도 '말후(末後)의 구(句)'를 터득하셨다. 이제 앞으로는 천하의 어떤 사람도 저분을 어쩌지 못하리라."

나. 평창(評唱) 및 송(頌)

無門曰. 若是末後句, 巖頭德山俱未夢見在. 撿點將來, 好似一棚傀儡.

만일 이것이 '말후(末後)의 구(句)'라면, 암두 스님과 덕산 큰스님 모두 꿈에도 보지 못한 것이다.

잘 살펴보면, 마치 한바탕 꼭두각시 인형 그대로이다.

頌曰. 識得最初句, 便會末後句. 末後與最初, 不是者一句.

무문 스님이 다시 게송으로 말하였다.

"최초(最初)의 구(句)를 알면

바로 말후(末後)의 구(句)도 안다.

말후의 구와 최초의 구는

이 '일구(一句)'가 아니다."

다. 강론(講論)

여기 덕산탁발 공안의 핵심은 암두 스님이 말하는 말후구이다. 아울러 암두 스님이 덕산 큰스님의 귓전에다 대고 무엇을 수근 거렸다는데 그것이 말후구와 무슨 관계가 있느냐는 것이다. 말후(末後)의 구(句) 즉, 최후의 한마디가 도대체 뭘까?

말도 안 되는 소리들 같지만 이런 화두를 잡고 스스로와 철저히 싸우다 보면 생각이 절대 미칠 수 없는 무분별지(無分別智)의 세계에 침잠하게 된다.

옛사람들의 말처럼 문으로 들어온 것은 집안의 참된 보배가 될 수 없다(從門入者 不是家珍). 물이 차가운지 따뜻한지는 스스로가 알 수밖에 없다(冷暖自知). 그러기 위해서는 본인 자신이 이 이야기의 주인공이 되어야 한다.

말후일구는 모든 지혜를 응집한 전생명(全生命)이며 불법(佛法)의 대의를 체득한 자내증(自內證)의 일목요연한 표출이다. 즉, 자기 향상(向上)의 외침이며 근원적인 본래심의 경지에서 토해지는 법음(法音)이다. 그렇다면 과연 덕산 큰스님은, 본문에서 보여지는 것처럼, 암두 스님의 견해대로 말후일구를 몰랐다고 하는 말이 타당성이 있는가? 아마도 덕산방(德山棒)으로 서슬이 퍼런 대선지식이 이런 수모를 당할 만큼 나약하지는 않았을 것이다.

분명 무슨 속셈이 있었다. 이 사건은 덕산 큰스님의 입적 3년 전에 이루어졌는데 당시 설봉 스님은 공양을 책임지고 있는 반두(飯頭)였다. 사실 덕산 큰스님이 설봉 스님 앞에 발우를 들고 나타난 것 자체가 말후구의 법문(法門)이다. 설봉 스님이 스승의 가르침을 놓친 것이다. 그래서 덕산 큰스님은 암두까지 끌어들여 꼭두각시놀이까지 해 보였다. 이쯤 돼야 말후의 구를 몰랐다는 암두 스님의 의사가 무엇인지 눈치챌 수 있다.

덕산탁발! 무연중생(無緣衆生)은 천불(千佛)이 출세해도 제도할 수 없다 하였지만 스승의 자비방편은 끝 간 데 없다.

Case 13

Seon Master Deok Sahn Carries His Bowls

A. Original Case

One day Seon Master Deok Sahn went to the dining room, carrying his bowls. However, Ven. Seol Bong asked him "Old master, the bell has not yet been rung and the drum has not yet been struck? where are you going carrying your bowls?" The old monk simply turned and went straight back to his room.

Seol Bong mentioned this to Ven. Am Du, who commented, "Even a great monk like Master Deok Sahn doesn't understand the last word."

Master Deok Sahn heard of this exchange and asked his attendant to call Am Du to him.

"Do you not approve of me?"

Am Du whispered something privately to Master Deok Sahn, who did not say anything else. The next day, when Deok Sahn ascended the high rostrum, sure enough he was different than before.

Am Du went to the front of the hall, clapped his hands, and laughed loudly, saying, "Wonderful! Our old master has realized the last word. From now on, no one anywhere can outdo him!"

B. Commentary and Verse

If you call this the last word, then neither Am Du nor Deok Sahn have even seen it in a dream. Look at it closely, it's just like a scene of two puppets.

Ven Mu Mun's verse:
    If you realize the first word,
    Then you also understand the last.
    The first and last word
    Are not the same word.

C. Explanation

Am Du mentioning the "last word" is the main point of this story of Deok Sahn carrying his bowls. But also, what did Am Du secretly whisper into Master Deok Sahn's ear, and what connection does that have with the last word? What is the last word?

Though it sounds ludicrous, if you grab hold of this question and thoroughly wrestle with it yourself, you'll become absorbed in the realm of non-discriminating awareness, which thinking can't touch at all. Like the saying of the ancients, "That which comes in through the door cannot be your family's true treasure." Only you can know for yourself whether the water is hot or cold. In order to do this, you must become the master of this story yourself.

The last word is the omnipresent wisdom that connects all sentient beings, a clear expression of one's attainment of the deep meaning of the Buddha-Dharma. In other words, an exclamation of one's progress, a Dharma speech emitted from the level of the fundamental, original mind. If that is the case, then is it appropriate that Am Du said, like we saw in the original story, that in his view Master Deok Sahn didn't understand the last word? We might even say that this keen-eyed, great Seon teacher, known for the sharpness of his blows, could never be weakened, no matter how great the humiliation.

However, he did have a clear intention. This episode took place three years before Master Deok Sahn entered Nirvana, and at that time Seol Bong was the kitchen master, responsible for preparing the temple meals. Actually, when Master Deok Sahn appeared in front of Seol Bong carrying his bowls, this in itself was his Dharma teaching on the last word; however, Seol Bong couldn't grasp his teacher's teaching. Therefore, Master Deok Sahn intentionally took part in this puppet show with Am Du; at this point we can realize what Am Du's mind was, though he didn't understand the last word. Master Deok Sahn carrying his bowls! Though a thousand Buddha's may appear in the world, they cannot save beings with whom they have no affinity; however, the teacher's compassionate methods have no end.

제 14 칙
南泉斬貓(남전참묘)

남전 큰스님, 고양이를 베다

Case14:
Master Nam Jeon Cuts the Cat in Two

가. 본칙(本則)

南泉和尙, 因東西兩堂爭貓兒. 泉乃提起云, 大衆道得卽救, 道不得卽斬却也. 衆無對. 泉遂斬之. 晚趙州外歸. 泉擧似州. 州乃脫履, 安頭上而出. 泉云, 子若在, 卽救得貓兒.

　남전 큰스님이 동당, 서당의 스님들이 고양이 한 마리 때문에 다투는 것을 보았다.

　큰스님이 이에 고양이를 잡아들고 말했다.

　"대중들이여! 한마디 일러볼 수 있다면 이 고양이를 살려줄 것이고, 한마디 이를 수 없다면 당장 목을 베어버리겠다."

　대중들은 아무도 답하지 못했다. 남전 큰스님은 즉시 고양이를 베어 버렸다.

　저녁때가 되어 조주 스님이 밖에서 돌아왔다. 남전 큰스님은 조주 스님에게 이 이야기를 하였다.

　그러자 조주 스님은 신발을 벗어 머리에 이고 나가버렸다. 남전 큰스님이 말했다.

　"만약 자네가 있었다면 그 고양이를 살릴 수 있었을 텐데……."

나. 평창(評唱) 및 송(頌)

無門曰. 且道, 趙州頂草鞋, 意作麽生. 若向者裏下得一轉語, 便見南泉令不虛行. 其或未然, 險.

    자아, 일러보아라. 조주 스님이 짚신짝을 머리에 올려놓은 뜻은 무엇인가?
    만약 여기에서 제대로 한마디 이를 수 있다면 남전 큰스님의 명령이 쓸데없는 짓이 아님을 알 수 있을 것이다.
    아직 그렇지 못하다면 위험하도다.

頌曰. 趙州若在, 倒行此令. 奪却刀子, 南泉乞命.

    무문 스님이 다시 게송으로 말하였다.
        "조주 스님이 만약 그 자리에 있었다면,
        명령을 거꾸로 받들었겠지.
        그 칼을 빼앗아버렸다면
        남전 큰스님도 목숨을 구걸했을걸."

다. 강론(講論)

　고양이가 도대체 누구의 고양이인가 하고 판단하는 것은 다분히 주관적이다. 고양이 자신이 스스로 누구의 것이라고 하지 않았기 때문이다. 즉, 판단의식(判斷意識) 자체가 문제이다. 판단의식은 분별(分別), 계교(計較)이다. 그런데, 주관적 판단으로는 사물의 실상(實相)과 만날 수 없다. 즉, 동당 서당의 스님들은 공부하고는 십만 팔천 리 떨어진 헛짓거리를 하고 있었던 것이다.
　남전 큰스님이 고양이 목을 벤 것은 스님들이 전도몽상에 허덕이고 생사망념(生死妄念)에 사로잡혀 있었기 때문이다. 그래서 남전 큰스님의 칼은 살인도(殺人刀)가 아니라 활인검(活人劍)인 것이다.
　생사대사 일대사(生死大事 一大事)를 해결하기 위하여 신명(身命)을 내걸고 수행해야 하는 스님들이 자신들의 본분사(本分事)를 망각하고 한낱 고양이에 끄달려 밖을 향해 내달리는 모습은 가히 꼴불견이다. 스승은 차마 그것을 용납할 수 없었던 것이다. 그래서 제자의 공부를 위해서는 살생(殺生)의 중죄(重罪)마저 자행하는 큰스님의 기행(奇行)이야말로 스스로 축생도에 떨어져 불도(佛道)를 행하는 이류중행(異類中行)의 모습 그대로이다.

한편, 조주 스님이 짚신을 머리에 이고 문밖으로 나간 것은 본말전도의 극치이다. 발에 신어야 할 신을 머리에 이는 것은 시비(是非)의 표본으로써 조주 스님 자신은 그런 쓸데없는 것에 개입할 이유가 없다는 의사표시이다.

한마디로 방하착(放下着)을 주문하고 있다. 삶과 죽음, 옳고 그름, 고통과 즐거움, 나와 남이라는 상대적 분별과 집착을 버리지 않는 한 공부의 성취는 요원하다. 그리고 공부의 끝은 그러한 분별의 세계를 넘어서 있는 무분별지(無分別智)라야 한다.

다툼과 시비가 사라진 진정한 평화는 천지미분전(天地未分前), 부모미생전(父母未生前)의 소식에서 얻어진다.

요약하면, 고양이 한 마리 때문에 스님들이 패거리 지어 싸우고 또 그들의 스승은 논쟁의 씨앗을 없앤다는 핑계로 그 고양이 목을 친 것은 소가 다 웃을 일이다. 조주가 짚신을 머리에 이고 문밖으로 나간 것은 당연하다.

Case 14

Master Nam Jeon Cuts the Cat in Two

A. Original Case

Seon Master Nam Jeon saw that the monks of the eastern and western halls were arguing over a single cat. The Master held up the cat and said, "All of you! If anyone among you can give me one word, you can save this cat - if you cannot, I will kill it right now!"

Nobody in the assembly could say a word, so Master Nam Jeon immediately cut the cat in two.

That evening, when Ven. Joju returned to the temple, Master Nam Jeon related the day's events to him. Whereupon Joju took off his shoe, put it on his head and left the room.

Nam Jeon then said, "If you had been here, you could have saved that cat."

B. Commentary and Verse

You there, tell me! What did Joju mean when he put his sandal on his head? If you can speak properly at this point, then you'll realize that Master Nam Jeon's demand was not without reason.

If you can't do that, then you're in danger!

Ven. Mu Mun said it again with a verse:
　If Joju had been there,
　He would have done the opposite;
　If the knife had been taken away,
　Then even Master Nam Jeon would have begged for his life.

C. Explanation

Deciding who the cat belongs to is subjective, for the most part, since the cat is not able to say for itself whose cat it is. In other words, the problem is with this judgmental consciousness itself, this mind of relative distinctions and comparisons. However, one cannot encounter the true aspect of all things with this selective consciousness. That is to say, the monks of the eastern and western halls were acting foolishly, a million miles away from their true practice. Master Nam Jeon cut the cat in two, since the monks were all floundering in their collective dream, caught by their deluded thoughts of life and death. Therefore, Master Nam Jeon's knife is not the blade that kills, but the sword that restores life.

It was really a horrible sight to see monks who should practice by risking their very lives in order to resolve the great matter of life and death, this one great affair, instead forsaking their original jobs and getting caught by a mere cat. This was something their teacher could not tolerate at all. Therefore, the master committed a grave sin in order to benefit his disciples' practice; this kind of strange action is in itself a perfect example of a Seon Master using various expedient means in order to enlighten people, even falling into the animal realm himself.

In the same way, Joju putting his sandal on his head and leaving the room was the perfect example of one manipulating the original meaning of words. By putting on his head a sandal that should have been worn on his foot, Joju's intention was to do something that had no relevance at all in a situation that was totally useless, in order to make a point about this argument over right and wrong. In a nutshell, he was telling them put down all their attachments. Practice that is still based on relative distinctions of life & death, right & wrong, suffering & pleasure, and self & other is still far from complete.

The completion of one's practice means that one must have non-discriminating awareness which transcends the world of relative distinctions. True peace, wherein all conflict and ideas of right and wrong have vanished, can be found within the realms "before heaven and earth were separated" and "before your parents were born." To sum it up, monks ganging up and fighting over a cat, and also their teacher killing this cat to get rid of the root of the conflict, were both quite ridiculous situations? enough to even make a cow laugh! Therefore, rather appropriately, Joju put his shoe on his head and left the room.

제 15 칙
洞山三頓(동산삼돈)

동산 스님,
세 차례 몽둥이 맞다

Case15:
Dong Sahn's Three Rounds of Blows

가. 본칙(本則)

雲門因洞山參次, 門問曰, 近離甚處. 山云, 查渡. 門曰, 夏在甚處. 山云, 湖南報慈. 門曰, 幾時離彼. 山云, 八月二十五. 門曰, 放汝三頓棒. 山至明日却上問訊, 昨日蒙和尙放三頓棒, 不知過在甚麼處. 門曰, 飯袋子, 江西湖南, 便恁麼去. 山於此大悟.

운문(雲門) 큰스님께서 동산(洞山) 스님이 참선하러 왔을 때 물었다.
"최근 어디에 있다가 왔느냐?"
동산 스님이 대답했다.
"사도(查渡)에 있다가 왔습니다."
운문 큰스님이 또 물었다.
"하안거(夏安居)는 어디에서 났느냐?"
동산 스님이 대답했다.
"호남의 보자사(報慈寺)에서 났습니다."
운문 큰스님이 다시 또 물었다.
"언제 거기에서 떠났느냐?"
동산 스님이 대답했다.

"8월 25일입니다."

운문 큰스님이 말했다.

"네게 몽둥이로 세 차례 때려야겠지만 용서하리라."

다음 날 동산 스님이 다시 운문 큰스님께 가서 여쭈었다.

"어제 큰스님께서 몽둥이로 세 차례 때릴 것을 용서한다고 하셨는데, 도대체 저 자신 어디에 허물이 있었는지 모르겠습니다."

운문 큰스님이 말씀하셨다.

"이 밥통아, 강서와 호남을 그런 식으로 왔다 갔다 했느냐?"

동산 스님이 이 말에 크게 깨쳤다.

나. 평창(評唱) 및 송(頌)

無門曰. 雲門當時, 便與本分草料, 使洞山別有生機一路, 家門不致寂寥. 一夜在是非海裏著倒, 直待天明再來, 又與他注破. 洞山直下悟去, 未是性燥. 且問諸人, 洞山三頓棒合喫不合喫. 若道合喫, 草木叢林皆合喫棒. 若道不合喫, 雲門又成誑語. 向者裏明得, 方與洞山出一口氣.

운문 큰스님이 그때 곧바로 꼭 알맞은 먹이를 주어서 동산 스님으로 하여금 생기 넘치는 살길을 마련해 주었다.

그래서 가문의 쇠퇴함을 면했다. 밤새도록 시비의 바닷속에 빠뜨렸다가 다음 날 하늘이 밝아지는 것을 기다려 다시 그에게 가르쳐 주었다. 동산 스님이 그 자리에서 깨달았다고 하더라도 아직 완전하지는 못하다.

그렇다면 여러 사람들에게 묻겠다. 동산 스님이 세 차례 몽둥이를 맞아야 했을까, 맞지 않아도 되었을까?

만약 맞을 만하다고 한다면 초목총림(草木叢林)의 모든 이들이 맞아야 할 것이고 만약 맞지 않아도 된다면 운문 큰스님이 또 허튼소리를 한 셈이 되리라. 이 말뜻을 분명히 알게 된다면 바야흐로 동산 스님에게 울분을 풀도록 해줄 수 있을 것이다.

頌曰. 獅子教兒迷子訣, 擬前跳躑早翻身. 無端再敍當頭著, 前箭猶輕後箭深.

무문 스님이 다시 게송으로 말하였다.

"사자가 새끼를 가르칠 때 어리석은 새끼를 인도하는 비결이 있으니, 앞에다 내던져 버리려 하면 어느새 몸을 뒤집어 날려 되돌아온다. 뜻밖에도 운문의 두 번째 설명이 동산에게 정통으로 명중했으니, 처음의 화살은 오히려 가벼우나 두 번째 화살은 깊게 꽂혔구나!"

다. 강론(講論)

'최근, 어디 있었나?'
'마음공부는 어디서 했나?'
'언제 그곳을 떠났나?'

자기 정체성을 확인시키려는 스승의 자상한 배려이다. '자기 자신'에 대한 물음인 금강왕보검(金剛王寶劍)으로 생사(生死)의 길, 범성(凡聖)의 길을 끊어야 한다. 그래서 사량분별, 시비득실이 없어진 채 벌거벗은 그대로 서 있어야 한다.

업식(業識)에 이끌려 악취에 떨어지지 않으려면 끊임없는 자기 탐구만이 살길이다. 선(禪)은 도리(道理)를 이해하는 수준이 아니라 직접 체험하는 것이다. 오온(五蘊)의 전부를 내던져 법신화(法身化)하려는 몸부림이 선(禪)이다.

운문 큰스님의 세 가지 물음은 겉으로는 분별의 차원 같으나 그 속뜻은 무분별한 반야, 공의 자리를 요구하고 있다. 그러므로 분별로써 답할 일이 아니다.

세 차례 몽둥이 세례를 받을 만한 이유가 있다. 차별계(差別界)니 평등체(平等體)니 하는 한계를 넘어서서 종횡무진하지 못하면 집착이라는 허물 때문에 오히려 대선지식을 원망하게 된다. 스승은 그를 이 '밥통아(飯袋子)' 하고 야단치고 있는 것이다.

Case 15

Dong Sahn's Three Rounds of Blows

A. Original Case

Ven. Dong Sahn came to practice Seon with Master Un Mun, who asked him,

"Where have you come from recently?"

Dong Sahn answered,

"I came from the village of Sa Do."

Master Un Mun asked him again,

"Where did you spend the summer retreat season?"

Dong Sahn replied,

"I was at the temple Boja-sa, south of the lake."

Master Un Mun asked once more,

"When did you leave that place?"

Dong Sahn answered, "On August 25."

Master Un Mun then said,

"I should give you three rounds of blows with my staff, but I'll spare you."

The next day, Ven. Dong Sahn came to the Seon Master's room and asked him,

"Yesterday you said that you spared me three rounds of blows - I just don't understand where I was at fault!"

Master Un Mun replied,

"You idiot! Why do you wander about in this way, now west of the river, now south of the lake?"

Ven. Dong Sahn was greatly enlightened by these words.

B. Commentary and Verse

Master Un Mun gave Dong Sahn some fitting(Seon) food at the time and encouraged him to gather up his vital spirit; he thereby avoided the decline of his tradition. Un Mun trapped Dong Sahn all night long in the sea of right and wrong - he waited for dawn to break the next day, and then gave him another teaching. Though Dong Sahn attained enlightenment at that point, he was not yet complete.

Therefore, I'd like to ask everyone, "Should Dong Sahn have received three rounds of blows or not?" If you say yes, then you are saying that all the grasses, trees, weeds and shrubs(i.e. the whole universe) also deserve to be beaten; if you say no, then Master Un Mun was just speaking nonsense. If you clearly understand the meaning of these words, then you can almost relieve Dong Sahn's pent-up frustration.

   Ven. Mu Mun said it again with a verse:
>When the lioness teaches her cubs, she has a trick for guiding a dim-witted cub;
>If she flings him out ahead of her, he'll flip over immediately and come right back.
>Unexpectedly, Master Un Mun's second answer hit Dong Sahn right on the head.
>He was barely struck by the first arrow, but the second one pierced him deeply.

C. Explanation

   "Where have you been recently?"
   "Where did you do your practice?"
   "When did you leave that place?"

This is the careful attention of a teacher, encouraging a disciple to examine his sense of self. One must sever the path of life and death, the ways of ordinary men, by questioning "the self" with the treasured sword of the Vajra-king. Once all thoughts of logical discrimination, right and wrong, gain and loss have vanished, you should then stand naked, just as you are.

In order to avoid being pulled about by karmic consciousness and falling into filth, one must ceaselessly investigate the self. Seon practice is not about how well one understands theory, but about direct experience. Seon is struggling with the form-body in order to cast away the five skandhas(form, feelings, perceptions, impulses, consciousness) and transform it into the Dharmakaya(the source of enlightenment).

Master Un Mun's three questions may ostensibly seem to be on the level of relative distinctions, but the underlying meaning is this non-discriminating Prajna, the realm of emptiness. Therefore, one cannot answer using relative thought? this is the reason he gets hit repeatedly.

If you cannot completely cross over the limitations of equality and discrimination, you will blame your great Seon teacher, due to your lingering attachments. His teacher thereby scolded him, calling him an idiot.

제 16 칙
鐘聲七條(종성칠조)

※

종소리에 7조 가사를 수하다

Case16:
At the Sound of the Bell,
Put on Your Seven-fold Robe

가. 본칙(本則)

雲門曰, 世界恁麼廣闊, 因甚向鐘聲裏披七條.

   운문(雲門) 큰스님이 말씀하셨다.
   "세상이 이렇게 광활(廣闊)한데, 무엇 때문에 종소리 난다고 칠조 가사를 수하는고?"

나. 평창(評唱) 및 송(頌)

無門曰. 大凡參禪學道, 切忌隨聲逐色. 縱使聞聲悟道, 見色明心, 也是尋常, 殊不知衲僧家騎聲蓋色, 頭頭上明, 著著上妙. 然雖如是. 且道, 聲來耳畔, 耳往聲邊. 直饒響寂雙忘, 到此如何話會. 若將耳聽應難會, 眼處聞聲方始親.

   대체로 선(禪)을 참구하여 도(道)를 배우는 사람은 소리를 따르고 모양을 쫓아가는 것을 절대 꺼린다. 비록 소리를 듣고 도를 깨닫거나, 모양을 보고 마음을 밝혔다 하더라도 그것 또한 대수로운 일이 아니다.

선가(禪家)의 사람들은 소리를 올라타고, 모양을 덮어서 모든 것을 밝게 보고 한 수 한 수 묘한 경지를 연다는 것을 사람들은 알지 못한다.

그것은 그렇다 치고, 일러보라. 소리가 귀 쪽으로 오는 것인가? 귀가 소리 쪽으로 가는 것인가?

가령, 소리와 고요함- 이 둘을 다 잊어버리는 경지가 되었다 하여도, 여기에 이르러 그 경지를 어떻게 설명해서 이해시킬 수 있을까? 만약 귀로써 들으면 아마도 이해하기 어렵겠지만, 눈으로 소리를 들으면 그때 비로소 깨닫게 될 것이다.

頌曰. 會則事同一家, 不會萬別千差. 不會事同一家, 會則萬別千差.

무문 스님이 다시 게송으로 말하였다.
　"깨달으면 모두가 한집안을 이루지만
　깨닫지 못하면 모든 것이 다 천차만별
　깨닫지 못해도 모두가 한집안을 이루지만
　깨닫고 보아도 모든 것이 다 천차만별."

다. 강론(講論)

제13칙에서, 덕산 큰스님은 종도 울리지 않았는데 발우 들고 공양간으로 갔다가 말후구(末後句)를 모른다는 말을 들었는데, 여기 제 16칙에서는 정반대의 상황이 전개되고 있다. 즉, 종소리가 울렸기 때문에 가사를 수하고 법당으로 가려는 것인데 오히려 이것이 문제가 되었다.

무문 스님은 한 수 더 떠서 소리가 귀로 오느냐, 귀가 소리로 오느냐하고 묻고 있다.

세상은 그대로 툭 터진 진리의 세계이다. 귀에 들리는 것은 다 부처님의 음성이요(一切聲是佛聲), 눈에 보이는 것은 다 부처님의 상호이다(一切色是佛色).

깨달음이란 이러한 도리를 곧바로 아는 맛이 아니겠는가. 예를 들자면 향엄(香嚴) 스님은 무심코 던진 돌멩이가 대나무에 부딪치는 소리를 듣고 깨달았고 서산(西山) 스님은 여행길에서 닭 울음소리를 듣고 깨달았다. 즉, 문성오도(問聲梧道)한 것이다.

한편, 영운(靈雲) 스님은 어느 봄날 복사꽃 핀 것을 보고 깨달았고 세존(世尊)께서는 새벽에 뜬 별을 보고 대각(大覺)을 이루셨다. 즉, 견색명심(見色明心)한 것이다. 불신(佛身)은 법계(法界)에 가득 찼으니 온 세월, 온 공간이 환하게 툭 터져 있다. 즉 광활(廣闊)하다.

그에 상응하는 진리적 삶은 소리를 올라타고(騎聲) 모양을 덮어야 한다(蓋色). 이는 주체성, 주체적 자각을 갖고 살아감을 의미한다. 그럼에도 불구하고 도인(道人)이 종소리에 움직임은 무슨 소식인가? 종소리를 듣자 가사를 수하고 법당으로 향하는 것이 오히려 불작(佛作)이요, 불행(佛行)이다. 이는 소리 경계에 속박된 행위가 아니라 깨달음의 생활 속에서 저절로 행위 되어지는, 즉 무심(無心)의 경지에서 발동하는 대자유(大自由)의 흔적이다.

극히 자연스럽고 당연하여 더 할 말이 없다. 도인의 삶은 사사무애(事事無碍)의 경지를 보인다. 선(禪)은 그런 점에서 원융하기 그지없는 일상생활이다. 부단한 정진 끝에는 수성(隨聲)과 기성(騎聲)의 경계가 무너진다. 분별 자체가 무의미하다. 차별계와 평등체는 한바탕이기 때문이다.

Case 16

At the Sound of the Bell, Put on Your Seven-fold Robe

A. Original Case

Seon Master Un Mun said, "As the world is so wide and spacious, why do you put on your seven-fold robe at the sound of the bell?"

B. Commentary and Verse

Generally speaking, a man of the Way who practices Seon should absolutely avoid following form and sound. Though you may attain the Way hearing sounds, or enlighten the mind seeing forms, this is not something special. People don't realize that Seon practitioners are in control of form and sound, see everything clearly, and reach the mystical realms, level by level.

Though that may be true, please tell me: Does sound come to the ear, or does the ear go to the sound? Sound and silence? when you reach the state wherein both are forgotten, tell me, at this point how could you make yourself understood using explanation? If you listen with your ears, it may be difficult to comprehend, but if you listen with your eyes, you will finally attain it.

> Ven. Mu Mun's verse:
> With realization, everything becomes one family;
> Without realization, everything is divided a million ways.
> Even without realization, everything becomes one family;
> Even with realization, everything is divided a million ways.

C. Explanation

Previously in Case 13, we heard the story of Ven. Deok Sahn, who didn't understand the last word and carried his bowls to the dining room, even though the bell had not yet been rung. This case, number 16, presents quite the opposite situation. That is to say, when the bell is rung, one should put on the robe and go to the Buddha Hall-but that is also precisely the problem. Ven. Mu Mun goes one step further and asks, "Does the sound come to the ear, or does the ear go to the sound?"

This world is one in which the truth explodes forth. That which the ears hear is all the Buddha's voice; that which the eyes see is all the Buddha's form-is not enlightenment directly tasting this principle for oneself? For example, Ven. Hyang Eom awakened when he heard the sound of a small stone that had been carelessly kicked and hit some bamboo; Ven. Seo Sahn got enlightenment when he heard the sound of a rooster crowing while on the road. Therefore, it is said that "Sound is a gate to enlightenment."

On the other hand, one spring day Ven. Yeong Wun saw a peach blossom and got enlightenment; the World-honored One(Buddha) himself saw the morning star and attained supreme awakening. Therefore it is said that, "Perceiving form illuminates the mind." As the Buddhakaya(Buddha-body) completely fills the Dharmadhatu(Dharma realm), all time and space burst radiantly forth? it is wide and spacious. That is to say, a life based on truth is one in control of form and sound, which means to live life utilizing this independent, autonomous self-realization. Nevertheless, what does it mean if an enlightened man is moved by the sound of the bell? Hearing the sound of the bell then putting on the robe and going to the Buddha Hall are the movements and actions of a Buddha. His actions are not limited by the bell sound, but appear naturally from an enlightened life; in other words, the mark of great liberation, moving from the level of no-mind. So exceedingly natural and reasonable, there's nothing more to say. The life of an enlightened sage is the level of non-attachment to anything at all; at this point, Seon practice is everyday life that is limitlessly perfect. Upon completion of ceaseless practice, the limitations of both following and controlling sound disappear, as these distinctions have no inherent meaning in themselves? the realms of both discrimination and equality have the same original essence.

제 17 칙
國師三喚(국사삼환)

국사가 세 번 부르다

Case17:
The National Teacher Calls Three Times

가. 본칙(本則)

國師三喚侍者, 侍者三應. 國師云, 將謂吾辜負汝, 元來却是汝辜負吾.

혜충(慧忠) 국사가 세 번 시자(侍者)를 불렀다. 시자는 세 번 대답했다. 국사가 말했다.

"내가 너를 저버리고 있다고 생각하였더니, 도리어 네가 나를 저버리고 있었구나."

나. 평창(評唱) 및 송(頌)

無門曰. 國師三喚, 舌頭墮地. 侍者三應, 和光吐出. 國師年老心孤, 按牛頭喫草. 侍者未肯承當. 美食不中飽人飡. 且道, 那裏是他辜負處. 國淸才子貴, 家富小兒嬌.

국사가 세 번이나 시자를 부르니 혀가 땅에 떨어졌다. 시자는 세 번을 대답하니 마음 빛(和光)이 그대로 드러났다. 국사가 늙어서 마음이 외로워져 소의 머리를 억지로 눌러서 풀을 먹이려 하였다. 그러나 시자는 그것을 받을 기분이 아니어서, 모처럼의 진수성찬도 배가 부른 사람이 먹기에는 맞지 않다.

말해보라. 그 시자가 국사를 저버린 곳은 어디인가?

나라가 맑게 다스려지면 재간이 있는 사람이 귀하게 대접을 받고, 집안이 부유하면 어린아이의 버릇이 나빠진다.

頌曰. 鐵枷無孔要人擔, 累及兒孫不等閑. 欲得撑門幷拄戶, 更須赤脚上刀山.

무문 스님이 다시 게송으로 말하였다.

"구멍 없는 무쇠 큰칼을 사람 목에 채우려하니,
허물이 자손에까지 미쳐 바빠지게 되었구나.
선종(禪宗)의 문호(門戶)를 지키려고 생각한다면
다시 맨발로 칼산을 오르지 않으면 안 된다네."

다. 강론(講論)

국사(國師)는 육조혜능(六祖慧能) 대사의 제자인 남양혜충(南陽慧忠) 선사이고 시자(侍者)는 탐원응진(耽源應眞) 스님이다. 스승과 제자 사이, 세 번 부르고 세 번 답한 사실에 엄청난 비밀이 숨겨져 있다.

스승은 고부(辜負) 즉, '저버렸다'는 말로 제자를 힐책하는 듯하지만 예사롭게 생각할 일이 아니다. 구멍 없는 무쇠 큰칼이 목에 채워질 판에 무슨 분별과 알음알이가 용납되겠는가.

스승이, 혓바닥이 땅에 떨어질 정도의 자비심을 보인 보람이 있었던지 제자 또한 화광(和光) 즉, 마음 빛을 그대로 드러냈다. 텅 비고 텅 비었기 때문이다. 마음의 영주(靈珠)에 비추어진 대역량인(大力量人)들의 교감, 줄탁동시(啐啄同時)의 절묘한 조화가 돋보인다.

일부러 진흙탕 속으로 들어가는 스승의 은혜가 크고 깊으니 제자의 법기(法器)가 운 좋게도 잘 받쳐주고 있다.

억지로 소의 머리를 눌러 풀을 먹으려 하지만 상대는 그러한 배려를 받아야 할 정도의 철부지가 아니다.

배부른 사람에게 진수성찬이 무슨 의미가 있겠는가!

그렇다면 무문 스님의 닦달처럼 어디가 그 시자가 국사를 저버린 곳인가? 집안이 너무 부유하여 어린아이의 버릇이 나빠진 것이다. 그것은 그렇게 보여질 수밖에 없다.

소에게 억지로 풀을 먹여 키우려 하지만 정작 그 소는 먹지 않으려 한다. 시자는 더 이상 스승의 자비를 받아들일 이유가 없다. 밖으로 무엇을 구하지 않아도 될 만큼 자기살림이 이미 튼튼하다는 뜻이다. 득도(得道) 한다는 말이 있지만 사실은 얻는다는 집착이 있는 이상 도는 십만 팔천 리 멀어질 수밖에 없다.

법을 전하는 일은 선종(禪宗)의 문호(門戶)를 지키는 불사(佛事)이다. 그러려면 맨발(赤脚)로 칼산을 오르지 않으면 안 된다. 석가모니 부처님을 비롯, 모든 대선지식(大善知識)들이 그러하셨다. 덕분에, 거울 속의 사람이 자신을 알아보고 빙그레 웃으니 겸연쩍게 같이 웃는 날이 있게 되는 것이다.

날마다 동거(同居)한 보람이 있어서 오늘 지금 하나로 나타난다. 그래서 스승의 은혜는 머리카락을 잘라 신을 삼아 드려도 모자란다. 그 보은(報恩)을 생각하면 후학(後學)으로서 면목이 없다.

Case 17
The National Teacher Calls Three Times

A. Original Case

National Teacher Hye Chung called his attendant three times; the attendant also answered three times.

The National Teacher then said, "I had thought that I was betraying you, but rather it was you who was betraying me."

B. Commentary and Verse

The National Teacher called his attendant three times and his tongue fell to the ground. The attendant answered three times, and revealed his mind's brilliance. The National Teacher was old and lonely? he pushed down the cow's head and forced it to eat grass. However, the attendant was not in the mood to take it; even a long-awaited sumptuous feast is not fitting for a man who is already satiated.

Tell me! When did the attendant betray the National Teacher?

When the nation is well managed, talented people are received as honored guests; when the household is wealthy, the child's manners worsen.

Ven. Mu Mun's verse:
    Placing an iron collar with no holes around a man's neck-
    This mistake affects even one's descendants.
    If you want to defend the gate of the Seon sect
    You must climb the sword mountain again with bare feet.

C. Explanation

The National Teacher in this story was Seon Master Nam-Tang Hye-Chung, who was the disciple of the Sixth Patriarch Hye Neung; the attendant was Ven. Tam-Won Ung-Jin. There are incredible secrets hidden in the story of the teacher and disciple calling and answering each other three times. With the word "betray" the teacher seems to be reproaching his disciple, but it is not as we commonly think of it-having an iron collar with no holes around his neck, some distinctions and cleverness are permitted. As the teacher shows a mind of compassion so great that his tongue is almost drooping on the ground, he reveals the radiance of his disciple's mind, just as it is - because it is completely empty. In this exchange between two men of great power, reflected in the mystic jewel of their minds, the sublime harmony of each simultaneously helping the other to become free really stands out. Since the teacher with his great, profound compassion, intentionally jumps in the mud, his disciple's practice fortunately holds up well.

Though he pushes the cow's head to the grass in order to eat, the other is also not a child, being capable of accepting that kind of attention. What's the use of a sumptuous feast for a man who is already full! Nevertheless, Ven. Mu Mun, as if nagging, asks at what point the attendant betrayed the National Teacher. When the household is too wealthy, the child's manners worsen? it is to be expected.

He wants to make the cow eat grass in order to raise him, but that cow doesn't want to eat. The attendant has no reason to receive any more of his teacher's teaching, which means that the way he is living is already stable to the extent that he doesn't seek anything externally. There is an expression "attain the

Way," but actually if you attach to the idea of attainment, then the Way becomes a million miles further away.

   Defending the gate of the Seon sect means transmitting the Dharma; in order to do that one must climb the sword mountain with bare feet. Starting with Shakyamuni Buddha, all of the great Seon teachers have done so. Thanks to their virtue, when you look at the mirror and realize that the person inside is actually you, you can smile broadly? actually we can all grin sheepishly together when this day comes. There is a value to living together, appearing as one today, in this moment. Therefore, a teacher's kindness is such that, even if one cut off one's hair and made it into shoes, it would be still not be enough to repay it; if you think of this as sufficient repayment for his kindness, then as his disciple you should be ashamed.

제 18 칙
洞山三斤(동산삼근)

❦

동산 큰스님의 마삼근
Case18:
Dong Sahn's Three Pounds of Flax

가. 본칙(本則)

洞山和尙, 因僧問, 如何是佛. 山云, 麻三斤.

　　동산 큰스님께 한 수행자가 여쭈었다.
　　"어떤 것이 부처입니까?"
　　동산 큰스님이 대답하셨다.
　　"마삼근(麻三斤)이니라."

나. 평창(評唱) 및 송(頌)

無門曰. 洞山老人參得些蚌蛤禪, 纔開兩片, 露出肝腸. 然雖如是, 且道, 向甚處見洞山.

　　동산 노스님은 대합조개와 같은 선 즉, 방합선(蚌蛤禪)을 체득한 것처럼, 조개의 두 껍데기를 조금 열었는가 했는데 간장(肝腸)까지 모두 다 드러내 보였다.
　　비록 그렇다고 하지만 말해보라.
　　어디에서 동산의 본래면목을 친견할 수 있는가?

頌曰. 突出麻三斤, 言親意更親. 來說是非者, 便是是非人.

무문 스님이 다시 게송으로 말하였다.
"갑자기 불쑥 마삼근이라고 말하니
말도 친(親)하지만 뜻은 더욱 친하다.
쫓아와서 시비하는 사람 있다면
바로 그 사람이 시비에 떨어진 사람이다."

다. 강론(講論)

억지로 의정을 내려고 안간힘 쓰면서 화두공부를 한다면 그것은 옳지 못하다. 저절로 의정이 돈발되어져야 한다. 그렇지 않으면 그건 화두로써의 생명력이 없다. 화두가 생기게 된 상황을 구체적으로 살펴보는 것이 그래서 중요하다.

여기 18칙도 그렇다. 동산수초(洞山守初) 큰스님이 저울로 삼을 달고 있는데, 한 스님이 찾아와 지극히 예(禮)를 올리고 대뜸 '부처가 무엇인가'를 묻는다. 마침, 저울대의 눈금은 세 근(斤)을 가리키고 있었다. 큰스님은 주저함 없이 "삼이 서 근 이니라."하고 대답하신다. 여기서 의정이 일어나야 한다.

"마삼근이 어찌하여 부처일고?"

"마삼근이 어찌하여?"

"마삼근?"

"?"

마삼근이라는 일상의 언어를 빌려 분별 너머 있는 적멸의 세계로 들어가야 한다. 분명한 사실은 동산 큰스님의 마삼근 빛깔과 일반사람들의 그것과는 아주 다르다.

동산 큰스님의 마삼근은 간장까지 모두 다 드러내 보여주는 진리의 전체 살림살이이다. 법성공(法性空)에서 저절로 튀어나오는 말씀이기 때문에 범부 중생의 언어와는 차원이 다르다. 차라리, 큰스님께서 '부처는 대웅전에 있지 않느냐? 삼십이상을 갖춘 분이지 않느냐.' 하고 말씀하셨다면 그토록 수많은 납자들이 잠 못 자는 고민은 없었을 것이다.

삼 서 근이 부처라니 이 일을 어떻게 하면 좋을고!

이와 비슷한 유형의 화두 몇 개를 더 들자면 다음과 같다.

'어떤 것이 부처입니까?' 라는 물음에 안횡비직(眼橫鼻直)이라고 대답한 이도 있고, 병정동자래구화(丙丁童子來求火)라고 대답한 이도 있고, 심지어는 농적적(膿滴滴)이라고 대답한 이도 있다.

잘 살펴보면 이보다 더 자상할 수는 없다. 핵심은 여기에 있다. 무작정 별 의미 없이 툭툭 던져지는 말씀처럼 보이나 거기에는 분명한 까닭이 있다. 선지식은 절대 무책임하지 않다. 도리(道理)에 어긋나지도 않는다. 화두를 참구하는 사람들은 우선 스승에 대한, 그리고 화두에 대한 철저한 믿음 즉, 대신근(大信根)을 전제로 정진해야 한다.

　'마삼근!' 이 한마디 속에 만고불변의 진리가 들어있다. 시쾌사(是快事), 통쾌한 답변이다. 초논리적(超論理的)이지만 질서가 있다. 물론 이것은 스스로의 체인(體認)이 요구된다. 그렇지 않으면 미륵불이 하생(下生)하더라도 소용없다.

　'마삼근' 이라고 말씀하시는 동산 큰스님의 마음은 부처의 마음이다. 마삼근은 동산이라는 부처와 하나가 되었다. 차별과 분별심을 떠났기 때문에 시비(是非)를 따질 게재가 전혀 없다. 마삼근이 부처일 수밖에 없다.

Case 18
Dong Sahn's Three Pounds of Flax

A. Original Case

A practitioner asked Seon Master Dong Sahn, "What is Buddha?"

Dong Sahn replied, "Three pounds of flax."

B. Commentary and Verse

The old monk Dong Sahn apparently attained something like clam-shell Seon; if the two halves of a clam are opened even a bit, then the liver and intestines are completely exposed. But though that is the case, please tell me:

Where can you find Dong Sahn's original face?

Ven. Mu Mun said it again with a verse:

    He suddenly said 'Three pounds of flax,'

    The words are close, but the meaning is closer.

    Those who chase after right and wrong

Are inevitably those who get caught by right and wrong.

C. Explanation

It is not suitable if you investigate your Great Question, attempting to resolve this dilemma with all your might; the solution must naturally appear by itself. If that doesn't happen, then your Hwadu(Great Question) investigation will not have any vitality. For this reason, it is important to concretely examine the situation in which the Hwadu arose.

This is certainly true in this case 18. Seon Master Dong-Sahn Su-Cho was weighing flax with a balance scales; a monk came to him, formally bowed, and then at once asked him the question "What is Buddha?" The mark on the balance at that moment read 'three pounds.' Without a moment of hesitation, the master answered "Three pounds of flax." The solution should arise from this point….

"How could Buddha be three pounds of flax?"

"Why three pounds of flax?"

"Three pounds of flax?"

"?"

Even though the phrase "three pounds of flax" uses everyday speech, one must enter the realm of extinction, which transcends relative distinctions. To tell the truth, the underlying meaning of Master Dong Sahn's 'three pounds of flax' and that of average people are complete different - his 'three pounds of flax' is a complete life of truth, which reveals everything, down to the liver and intestines. Since this speech naturally arises from the empty nature of Dharma, it is on a completely different level than the language of common sentient beings. If the Master had replied, "Isn't the Buddha in the Buddha Hall?" or if he had said, "Buddha is the one with thirty-two distinguishing marks," then he would have saved a great many practitioners from so much sleepless worry.

How can it be that Buddha is three pounds of flax! Here are some other examples of a similar type of Great Question such as this. To the question "What is Buddha?" someone answered, "Your eyes are horizontal, your nose is vertical," someone else answered, "Fire has come in search of fire" (i.e. once you've become Buddha, no need to cultivate any more), whereas someone else answered "Once you've left the mind of relative distinctions behind, there is no more right and wrong."

If you examine it closely, you'll see that you cannot be more thoughtful than this? the core of the meaning is right here. Though they seem to be meaningless phrases, just thoughtlessly bantered about, there is a clear meaning there. Great Seon teachers never act irresponsibly, and never run contrary to the Dharma. Those who investigate the great question should first practice with unwavering, great faith in their teacher and in their Hwadu(great question). Eternal truth is contained in this one phrase "Three pounds of flax." This is a joyful, yet penetrating answer. Though it is a truth which transcends logic, there is a certain order to it; of course, one must deeply realize it for oneself. If you don't do that, then even if Maitreya Buddha is reborn in this world, it is of no use.

Seon Master Dong Sahn said "Three pounds of flax." His mind was Buddha's mind. This means that three pounds of flax and the Buddha Dong Sahn had become one; since he left relative distinctions and discrimination behind, there was no reason for thoughts of right and wrong. Three pounds of flax cannot be other than Buddha.

제 19 칙
平常是道(평상시도)

평상심이 도이다
Case19: Everyday Mind is the Way

가. 본칙(本則)

南泉, 因趙州問, 如何是道. 泉云, 平常心是道. 州云, 還可趣向否. 泉云, 擬向卽乖. 州云, 不擬爭知是道. 泉云, 道不屬知, 不屬不知. 知是妄覺, 不知是無記. 若眞達不擬之道, 猶如太虛廓然洞豁. 豈可强是非也. 州於言下頓悟.

 남전(南泉) 큰스님께 조주 스님이 "도(道)가 무엇입니까?"하고 여쭈니 남전 큰스님이 대답하셨다.
 "평상심(平常心)이 곧 도(道)이다"
 조주 스님이 남전 큰스님께 다시 여쭈었다.
 "그렇다면 그것을 향해 닦아 나갈 수 있습니까?"
 남전 큰스님이 대답하였다.
 "그것을 향해 헤아리려고 하면 어긋난다."
 조주 스님이 또 여쭈었다.
 "헤아리지 않으면 어찌 도를 알 수 있겠습니까?"
 남전 큰스님이 대답하셨다.
 "도는 아는데 속하지 않고, 모르는데 속하지도 않는다. 안다고 하는 것은 거짓으로 깨닫는 것이요, 모른다는 것은 무기(無記)이다. 만약 참으로 헤아리지 않는 도를 통달하면, 마치 허공과 같아서 확연하게 탁 트이고 넓어진다. 어찌 억지로 옳으니 그르니 할 수 있겠는가?"

조주 스님은 이 말에 문득 깨달았다.

나. 평창(評唱) 및 송(頌)

無門曰. 南泉被趙州發問, 直得瓦解氷消, 分疎不下. 趙州縱饒悟去, 更參三十年始得.

남전 큰스님이 조주 스님의 질문을 받고서는 곧바로 기왓장이 깨지고 얼음이 풀리듯 해서 다시 설명할 필요가 없었다. 설령 조주 스님이 깨달았다고 해도 다시금 30년은 더 닦아야 비로소 알게 될 것이다.

頌曰. 春有百花秋有月, 夏有涼風冬有雪. 若無閑事挂心頭, 便是人間好時節.

무문 스님이 다시 게송으로 말하였다.

"봄에는 온갖 꽃 피고, 가을에는 밝은 달
여름에는 시원한 바람, 겨울에는 하얀 눈
만약 쓸데없는 일에 마음 두지 않는다면
바로 그때가 인간세계의 좋은 시절."

다. 강론(講論)

평상심(平常心)!

평상심이란 말은 남전보원 큰스님의 스승인 마조도일 선사가 가장 먼저 사용하였다.

"도란 닦을 필요가 없다. 단지, 더러움에 물들지 않으면 된다. 곧바로 도를 이루고자 하는가? 평상심이 도이니라.

평상의 마음이란 어떤 것인가? 조작(造作)하지 않고 시비(是非)하지 않으며, 취사(取捨)하지 않고 단견(斷見)과 상견(常見)을 버리며, 평범하다느니 성스럽다느니 하는 생각이 없는 마음이다."

평상심이란 우리가 본래 구족하고 있는 자성청정심(自性淸淨心)이다. 범부의 중생심 그대로가 아니라 즉심즉불(卽心卽佛)의 마음이며 무심(無心) 자체이다.

염두에 두어야 할 것은 평상심시도라 함은 도(道)의 본질을 일걸음이지 도의 실행은 아니다. 도는 움직여야 한다.

즉, 참으로 도행(道行)이 되도록 깨닫고 난 뒤에도 무문 스님의 말대로 익혀가야 한다. 그리하여 그 어떤 경우에도 흔들리지 않고 무심(無心)하게 그리고 평상심으로 살 수 있다면 삶 자체가 호시절(好時節)이 될 수밖에 없다.

어떤 납자가 장사경잠(長沙景岑) 선사를 찾아와 "평상심이 도라 했는데 어떻게 마음 쓰는 것이 평상심입니까?"하고 물었다. 선사는 답하기를 "배고프면 먹고 졸리면 잔다. 이것 외에 따로 도가 있는 것이 아니다."라고 하였다.

납자는 더 구체적인 답변을 원했다. 선사는 또 말했다.

"더울 때는 부채질하고 추울 때는 화로를 가까이 하라."

사람들은 하나같이 도(道) 속에 살면서 도를 모르고 지낼 뿐이다. 봄에는 꽃, 가을에는 달, 여름에는 시원한 바람, 겨울에는 눈이 있지 않는가.

신통묘용(神通妙用)이 따로 있는 것이 아니다. 일체 헤아리지 않고 물 긷고 땔나무 하는 일거수 일투족임을 알아야 한다.

어느 누가 조주 스님에게 도를 물었다.

"무엇이 도입니까?"

"담장 밖에 있느니라."

"그런 도 말고 대도(大道)를 묻고 있습니다."

"대도는 장안으로 가는 길이지."

헤아리려고 하면 어긋난다!

Case 19
Everyday Mind is the Way

A. Original Case

Ven. Joju asked Seon Master Nam Jeon, "What is the Way?"

Master Nam Jeon answered, "Everyday mind is the Way."

Joju asked him again, "So can I try and cultivate it?"

The Seon Master answered, "If you try to comprehend it, you are already separate from it."

Joju asked again, "How can I know the Way if I don't try?"

Nam Jeon replied, "Don't be concerned with knowing or not knowing; knowing is false realization, not knowing is just ignorance. If you truly become master of the inconceivable Way, it's clearly vast and boundless, like empty space. How can you artificially say that it is right or wrong?"

Hearing these words, Joju suddenly attained enlightenment.

B. Commentary and Verse

Seon Master Nam Jeon heard Joju's question, and then

smashed the roof tile right away, like melting ice - further explanation was not necessary. Though Joju had some realization, he had to cultivate for another thirty years in order to finally understand it.

Ven. Mu Mun said it again with a verse:
> In the spring all sorts of flowers bloom, in the autumn the bright moon;
> In the summer the cool breeze, in the winter the white snow;
> If you do not concern yourself with useless matters,
> Then this moment is a good season in the human world.

C. Explanation

Everyday mind!

This teaching phrase was first used by Nam Jeon's teacher, Seon Master Ma-Jo Do-Il. "It's not necessary to cultivate the Way; merely do not become tainted by delusion. How to attain the Way at once? Everyday mind is the Way. What is this everyday mind? The mind that does not make anything, does not attach to right and wrong or make preferences, which discards both nihilism and eternity, without any thoughts of ordinary or holy."

Everyday mind is our originally complete, pure and clear mind of self-nature. Not the common mind of a sentient being, just as it is, but the mind which is actually Buddha, which is itself no-mind. You should remember that simply calling it everyday mind, the Way, or substance is not the actual practice of the Way. The Way itself is always fluctuating.

In other words, according to Ven. Mu Mun, one should continue to cultivate after awakening, in order to truly behave in accordance with the Way. If you do this, then no matter what situation appears, you are not swayed, acting with no thought; if you can live with this everyday mind, then the nature of life itself will certainly be a favorable season.

A practitioner visited Seon Master Jang-Sa Gyeong-Jam and asked him, "You said that everyday mind is the Way? but what does this everyday mind mean?" The master answered, "When you are hungry, eat; when you are tired, sleep. There is no path outside of this." The practitioner wanted a more concrete answer, so the master replied "When you feel hot, fan yourself; when you feel cold, come closer to the heater."

People live in the Way as if they are one with it; without knowing it is the Way, they just live their lives. Are there not flowers in the spring, the moon in the autumn, a cool breeze in the summer, and snow in the winter? The miraculous, mystical functioning is not something special. Don't try to figure it out? you must realize that it is your every action, just draw water and carry firewood.

Someone asked about the Way to Seon Master Joju, "What is the Way?"

Joju answered, "It's outside the wall."

"I don't mean that path! I was asking about the Great Way!"

Joju replied, "The Great Way leads to the capital city."

If you try to figure it out, you are far away from it.

제 20 칙
大力量人(대력량인)

큰 힘을 갖춘 사람

Case20: A Man of Great Strength

가. 본칙(本則)

松源和尙云, 大力量人, 因甚擡脚不起. 又云, 開口不在舌頭上.

  송원 큰스님이 말씀하셨다.
  "어찌하여 큰 힘을 갖춘 사람이 다리를 쳐들고 일어나지 못하는고?"
  또 말씀하셨다.
  "말을 한다는 것이 혓바닥 위에 있지 않다."

나. 평창(評唱) 및 송(頌)

無門曰, 松源可謂, 傾腸倒腹. 只是欠人承當. 縱饒直下承當, 正好來無門處喫痛棒. 何故. 聻. 要識眞金火裏看.

  송원 스님은 배를 갈라 내장까지 모두 끄집어냈다고 할 만한데, 다만 그것을 알아듣고 받아내는 자는 한 사람도 없구나. 설령 곧바로 받아냈다 하더라도, 이 무문(無門)의 처소에 오면 방망이로 호되게 얻어맞을 것이다.

왜 그럴까?

그것!

순금을 가려내려고 하면 불 속에서 시험해 보아야만 한다.

頌曰. 擡脚踏飜香水海, 低頭俯視四禪天. 一箇渾身無處著, 請續一向.

무문 스님이 다시 게송으로 말하였다.
"다리를 쳐들어 향수해(香水海)를 뒤집어엎고
머리를 숙여 사선천(四禪天)을 내려다본다.
이 한 몸뚱이 집착하는 곳이 없으니
어떤가, 결구(結句)를 이어 붙여 봄이."

다. 강론(講論)

송원 큰스님의 삼전어(三轉語)가 있다. 제 일전어, 제 이전어는 위의 본칙에 소개되어 있고 제 삼전어는 다음과 같다.

"명안납승인심마각하홍사선부단(明眼衲僧因甚麽脚下紅絲線不

斷), 선지식이 왜 발에 매인 붉은 실을 끊지 못하는고?"

　큰스님께서 입적하실 때쯤 이 세 가지 문제, 즉, 삼전어(三轉語)를 내놓고 대중에게 물었으나 분명한 대답을 하는 사람이 없었다고 한다. 그러자 큰스님은 크게 탄식하였다고 한다. 그러면 우선 무문관 본칙을 살펴보자.

　큰 힘을 갖춘 사람은 도대체 누구일까? 생명 가진 모든 존재이다. 왜 큰 힘을 갖추었다고 말할 수밖에 없는가? 불성(佛性)이 있기 때문이다.

　일체중생개유불성(一切衆生皆有佛性). 애시당초 모든 사람, 존재는 큰 힘을 갖추고 있다. 그런데 그러한 큰 역량을 가진 사람이 다리를 쳐들고 일어서지 못하는 까닭은 어디에 있는가? 즉, 불성은 있는데 부처가 되지 못하는 이유를 묻고 있다.

　불성(佛性)이란 부처될 가능성이 있다는 것이지 지금이 곧 부처라는 소리는 아니다. 부처될 씨앗을 가지고 있기는 하지만 아직은 잘 가꾸어야 한다는 말이다. 부처될 유전인자가 중생 각자에게 내재하고 있다가 시절인연이 도래하면 언젠가는 부처가 된다.

　그때가 다리를 쳐들고 일어서는 날이다. 그러한 날을 스스로 만들지 못하고 남에게 의지해서 겨우 살아가서는 안 될 일이다. 불성가진 존재로서 그것은 부끄럽기 짝이 없다. 그렇다면 어떻게 해야 이러한 말들이 공염불에 지나지 않고 실속 있는 언어가 될까?

정말 실속 있는 언어는 무엇일까. 그것은 당연히 혓바닥 놀림은 아닐 것이다. 그것은 실참실수(實參實修)이다. 온 몸과 온 마음을 다 던져서 수행하는 일이 중요하다. 그래서 설령 혀를 빌려 온갖 소리를 하더라도 그것이 헛되지 않으려면 혓바닥에 그쳐서는 안 된다는 말이 너무나 당연하다. 그와 같이, 다리를 쳐들고 일어서는 것도 다리에 있지 않음을 알 수 있다.

덧붙여 제 3의 전어(轉語)를 궁구해 보자.

'눈 밝은 도인(道人)이 다리에 매인 붉은 실을 왜 끊지 못하는고?'

철사도 아닌 실을 끊지 못한다니 애들도 아니면서 도인이 그 뭐 하는 짓인가. 그리고 또 하나 의문스러운 것은 왜 하필이면 붉은 실일까? 이런 쓰잘 데 없는 것에 마음 두지 말아야 한다. 언구(言句)에 걸리면 무문(無門) 스님의 몽둥이가 춤출 것이다.

Case 20
A Man of Great Strength

A. Original Case

Seon Master Song Won said, "How is it that a man of great strength can't lift his own leg and stand up?" He also said, "It is not the tongue with which he speaks."

B. Commentary and Verse

It should be said that Master Song Won just opened his stomach and pulled out his stomach and intestines but not a single person understood it. Even if someone says he got it, if he comes to me he'll be severely beaten with my staff. Why is that? If you want to uncover pure gold, you have to test it in fire.

Ven. Mu Mun said it again with a verse:
 Lifting his leg, he knocks over the Fragrant Ocean;
 Lowering his head, he looks down on the Four Meditation Heavens.

This body is not bound anywhere-

Why don't you add the last line yourself!

C. Explanation

These are Seon Master Song Won's so-called three 'turning phrases.' The first and second turning phrases were introduced in the aforementioned case; the third turning phrase is as follows.

"Why can't a clear-eyed Seon practitioner cut the red thread tied to his foot?"

When the Seon Master was about to enter Nirvana, he posed these three questions on these turning phrases, to the members of his community. It is said that not a single practitioner gave a clear answer, so the master sighed deeply. Let's first take a look at the original case in the Gateless Gate.

What in the world is a man of great strength? This refers to all sentient beings which are alive. One cannot help but say they have great strength, because they have Buddha-nature-each and every sentient being has a Buddha-nature. Originally, every being has this great strength. So why can't one with such great capacity even lift his own leg and stand up? In other words, this is asking the reason why one can't become Buddha if we already possess Buddha-nature. But saying that one has Buddha-nature, or the potential to become Buddha, does not imply that you are Buddha right now. This means that we have the seed to become Buddha, but have not yet cultivated it. Each sentient being inherently possesses the genetic nature to become a Buddha, and some day, when the time is right, he or she will become a Buddha. At that time, you can lift your leg and stand up. We must do it ourselves, and not depend on anyone else-as beings with Buddha-nature, we should be quite ashamed to do that!

But then, what can we do so that these are not just empty recitations, but words of real substance? What actually are true words of substance? Naturally this is not just joking and playing around? it's seeking and cultivating the truth. It's important to practice by throwing your whole mind and body into the effort. Therefore, although you use someone else's words and make all kinds of chatter, for it to be of some use it should not just be empty speech. In the same way, you can realize that lifting your leg and standing has nothing to do with the leg. Next, let's take a look at the third 'turning phrase.'

"Why can't a clear-eyed Seon practitioner cut the red thread tied to his foot?"

What does this mean when an enlightened man, who is not a child, can't even cut a thread which is not made of steel? And another dubious point? why is it necessarily a red thread? Don't fixate on this kind of useless thing? if you get caught by this phrase, then Ven. Mu Mun's staff will be dancing.

제 21 칙
雲門屎橛(운문시궐)

운문의 똥 막대기
Case21: Ven. Un Mun's Dry Shit Stick

가. 본칙(本則)

雲門因僧問, 如何是佛. 門云, 乾屎橛.

운문 큰스님에게 어느 스님이 물었다.
"무엇이 부처입니까?"
큰스님은 말했다.
"마른 똥 막대기야!"

나. 평창(評唱) 및 송(頌)

無門曰. 雲門可謂, 家貧難辨素食. 事忙不及草書, 動便將屎橛來, 撑門拄戶. 佛法興衰可見.

　운문 큰스님은 집이 가난하여 소박한 식사를 차리기도 어려웠고, 일이 바빠 글을 흘려 쓸 틈도 없었던가보다. 그러다 보니 똥 막대기나 가지고 나와 선문(禪門)을 지탱하려고 든다.
　불법(佛法)의 흥함과 쇠함을 이로써 가히 알겠구나.

頌曰. 閃電光, 擊石火. 眨得眼, 已蹉過.

운문 스님이 다시 게송으로 말씀하셨다.
"번쩍이는 번개 빛이요
돌이 부딪쳐서 일어나는 불이니
눈을 껌벅거리면
이미 그르치고 마네."

다. 강론(講論)

운문 큰스님은 청빈(淸貧)의 생활을 하였다. 청빈은 본래로 일체의 번뇌 망념을 텅 비우고 무일물(無一物)의 경지, 일체개공(一切皆空)의 경지에 노님을 표현한다. 그렇다고 하여 법을 묻는 객승에게 똥 막대기를 대접한 것은 다들 심했다고 한다.
"부처가 어찌 똥 막대기인가?"
이야기의 줄거리는 이렇다.

운문 큰스님이 보릿골에 똥거름을 주기 위하여 똥통 지게를 지고 보리밭에 막 도착하였다. 보리밭에는 전날 표시 삼아 꽂아둔, 똥 젓는 막대기 하나가 꽂혀 있었다. 막대기에는 말 그대로 똥이 덕찌덕찌 겹겹이 묻어 있었다. 이제 막 똥지게를 내려놓고, 지고 온 똥통을 들여다보면서 가라앉은 똥물을 저을 요량으로 보릿골에 꽂혀있는 마른 똥 막대기를 막 쥐려는 순간에 저 밭고랑 초입에서 한 스님이 나타나더니,

"스님, 무엇이 부처입니까?" 하고 고함지르며 다급하게 묻는다.

큰스님은 조금도 지체하지 않고 마른 똥 막대기를 뽑아 들고는 "간시궐이니라." 하고 소리 질렀다.

찾아온 납자는 그 자리에서 얼어붙듯 하였다.

'간시궐' 화두는 이렇게 해서 탄생되었다. 그런데, 운문 큰스님은 간시궐을 수시로 사용하였다.

"그대들은 여기서 무슨 간시궐을 구하려고 하는가?"

"악업의 중생이 모두 여기서 무슨 간시궐을 찾아서 씹으려고 하는가?" 하는 내용들이 『운문광록』에 소개되고 있다. 간시궐은 운문 큰스님의 전용어이다.

아무튼, '무엇이 부처인가?'의 물음에 간시궐이라 한 것은 큰 사건이었다. 운문 큰스님의 법문은 그렇지 않아도 '일자관(一字

關)'으로 유명하다.

"어떤 것이 정법의 안목입니까?"라는 물음에 "진(晋)!"이라고 대답한 적이 있었고,

"어떤 것이 취모검(吹毛劍) 입니까?"라는 물음에 "조(祖)!"라고 대답한 적이 있다.

"또한 부처와 조사를 죽이면 어디서 참회해야 합니까?"라는 물음에 "로(露)."라고 대답한 적이 있다.

그런데 이 운문 큰스님의 설법 일구(一句)에는 함개건곤(函蓋乾坤) 재단중류(裁斷衆流) 수파축랑(水波逐浪)의 3구(三句)가 갖추어져 있다. 한마디로 요약하자면, 어느 한 말씀도 무심(無心)의 경지에서 설해지지 않는 말씀이 없다는 뜻이다. 무심이라야 지혜의 안목이 열려 진실을 바로 볼 수 있다. 마음눈이 열리면, 보여지는 모든 것은 부처님의 형상이요, 일거수 일투족이 부처님의 자비행이다.

"간시궐!"

눈을 깜박거리는 틈이라도 주변 사람 분별심이 개재된다. 그 순간 본래심(本來心)과 어긋난다. 운문 큰스님이 평생 마른 똥 막대기를 가지고 놀만한 이유가 있다.

Case 21
Ven. Un Mun's Dry Shit Stick

A. Original Case

A monk asked Seon Master Un Mun, "What is Buddha?"
The master replied, "A dry shit stick!"

B. Commentary and Verse

Master Un Mun's household was poor, so it was difficult for him to prepare simple food; he was so hurried that he didn't even have a chance to scribble something down. He brought out the dry shit-stick in order to support his Seon school; thus, the rise and fall of the Buddha-dharma are easily understood.

Ven. Mu Mun said it again with a verse:
> Lightning flashing,
> Striking the stone, the flame appears;
> If you blink,
> It's already ruined.

C. Explanation

Seon Master Un Mun lived a life of honest poverty. Honest poverty is the stage wherein originally all defilements and delusions are empty? there is not even one thing. This is expressed as strolling in the realm where everything is empty. Nevertheless, everyone agrees it's extreme to greet a guest monk who is asking about the Dharma with a dry shit-stick.

"How can Buddha be a dry shit-stick?" A brief synopsis of the story is as follows. Seon Master Un Mun had just come to the barley patch, carrying a bucket of manure on his back in order to fertilize the plants. A stick moist with manure had been stuck in the barley trench the previous day as a marker-as the name would imply, there were many layers of shit completely covering the stick. He put the backpack down, and while looking at the bucket he had brought along, grasped the dry shit-stick in order to stir up the settled manure. At that moment, a monk entered the barley plot and hurriedly cried out to him, "Master, what is Buddha?"

Without missing a beat, the Seon Master took the dry shit-stick out, lifted it up, and yelled, "Dry shit on a stick!"

The practitioner who had come there was almost frozen in his tracks. This is how the question "Dry shit on a stick" first appeared. However, Seon Master Un Mun frequently used it as a teaching phrase, as in "What kind of dry shit-stick are you looking for?" Or "All you beings with bad karma, what kind of dry shit-stick have you come here hoping to nibble on?" These stories are all related in The Record of Un Mun.

The phrase "Dry shit on a stick" was solely used by Seon Master Un Mun. At any rate, answering "Dry shit on a stick" as a response the question "What is Buddha?" was certainly a big deal. But even if that had not been the case, he certainly would have been known for his 'one-word barriers.' As an answer to the question "What is the discerning eye of the True Dharma?" he answered, "Vast." To the question "What is the sharp sword that severs a falling feather?" he answered, "Patriarch." And to the question "If one kills the Buddha and patriarchs, to whom should one repent?" he answered, "Dew."

This one-phrase Dharma speech of Seon Master Un Mun actually consists of three statements:

"Enveloping heaven and earth," "Cutting through myriad streams," and "Following the waves, according to the current." If one were to summarize these in a nutshell, the meaning of each and every word comes from the realm of no-mind; when the discerning eye of wisdom opens, one can see the truth directly. When the mind's eye is open, everything that is seen is the form of the Buddha, and one's every action is the compassionate action of the Buddha.

"Dry shit on a stick!"

If you blink for even a second, the relative distinctions of those around intervene; in that moment you are separate from the original-mind. Seon Master Un Mun has a just reason to play with this dry shit-stick his whole life.

제 22 칙
迦葉刹竿(가섭찰간)

❦

가섭 존자의 찰간
Case22: Mahakasyapa's Flagpole

가. 본칙(本則)

迦葉因阿難問云, 世尊傳金襴袈裟外, 別傳何物. 葉喚云, 阿難. 難應諾. 葉云, 倒却門前刹竿著.

아난 존자가 가섭 존자에게 물었다.
"세존께서 금란가사를 전하신 이외에 따로 무엇을 전하여 주셨습니까?"
가섭은 대답 대신 "아난아!" 하고 불렀다.
아난은 "예." 하고 대답했다.
가섭이 말했다.
"문 앞의 찰간(刹竿)을 넘어뜨려라."

나. 평창(評唱) 및 송(頌)

無門曰. 若向者裏下得一轉語親切, 便見靈山一會儼然未散. 其或未然, 毘婆尸佛早留心, 直至而今不得妙.

만약 여기에서 꼭 들어맞는 한마디의 말을 할 수 있다면, 영산회상의 법회가 산회하지 않고 아직 계속되고 있다는 것을 금방 알 것이다. 만일 그렇지 않다면, 과거 비바시불이 일찍부터 마음을 기울여 수행하여 왔음에도 불구하고 현재에 이르러서도 깨달음의 묘경을 얻지 못했다고 하는 것이 되리라.

頌曰. 問處何如答處親, 幾人於此眼生筋. 兄呼弟應揚家醜, 不屬陰陽別是春.

무문 스님이 다시 게송으로 말하였다.
"질문은 그 답이 친절한 것에 비하여 어떠한가,
몇 사람이나 여기에서 눈을 부릅뜰까!
형이 묻고 아우가 대답하여 집안의 추태를 보이니
이것은 음양(陰陽)과 관계없는 별도의 봄소식일세."

다. 강론(講論)

아난 존자는 25년간 부처님을 시봉하면서 다문제일(多聞第一)의 명성을 얻었다. 그렇지만 부처님의 정법안장(正法眼藏), 실상무상(實相無相)의 묘법(妙法)은 전해받지 못했다.

한편 두타제일(頭陀第一)의 가섭 존자는 세 곳의 사건 즉, 영산회상거염화(靈山會上擧拈花), 다자탑전분반좌(多子塔前分半座), 사라쌍수곽시쌍부(沙羅雙樹槨示雙趺)에서 법기(法器)를 인정받고 상수(上首) 제자가 되었다. 부처님 열반 후, 가섭 존자는 경율(經律)을 편찬하는 결집(結集) 회의에서 주석(主席)을 맡았고 여기서 아난 존자와 부딪치는 상황이 있게 된다.

가섭 존자는 깨치지 못한 아난 존자를 문밖으로 내보낼 수밖에 없었다.

위의 본칙(本則)에서 소개된 이야기는 둘의 관계 사이에서 극단적인 일이 벌어지기 직전의 상황으로 보인다. 섭섭한 마음을 가진 아난 존자의 요청에 의한 법거량이 이루어진 것이다.

"금란가사 외에 따로이 전해 받은 것이 있습니까?"

오기의 강한 발동이라고 밖에 볼 수 없다.

그때 가섭 존자는 "아난아." 하고 부른다. 아난이 "예." 하고 대답하자 다짜고짜 "문 앞의 찰간을 넘어뜨려라." 하고 질책한다. 아난 존자는 이 말의 뜻을 알아차리지 못하고 자기의 살림밑천이 부족함을 한탄하면서 문밖에서 7일간 용맹정진에 들어간다. 다행히 일대사(一大事)를 해결하고 결집장소의 칠엽굴 문을 두드리며 말한다.

아금초제루득진(我今初諸漏得盡) 즉, 이제 깨쳤으니 문을 열어 달라는 것이다. 가섭 존자는 크게 반색하며 시험한다.

"때가 이미 깊은 밤중이라 문을 열 수 없으니 깨친 도력(道力)으로 자물쇠 구멍을 통하여 들어오라."라고 하였다.

아난 존자는 그리하여 1차 결집에서 큰 역할을 하게 된다. 여기서 문제의 핵심은 왜 아난 존자가 이렇게 더디게 참여 하였는가 이다.

"아난아!" 하고 가섭 존자가 불렀을 때 "예."하고 대답할 줄 아는 그 놈을 잘 쓰지 못했기 때문이었다. 아난 존자는 체인(體認), 체득(體得)이 없었으므로 말귀를 알아듣지 못하였다. 찰간을 넘어뜨리라고 한 이유가 여기에 있었다.

그런데 아집(我執) 법집(法執)을 파(破)했을 때 그에게 인가(印可)가 떨어졌다. 드디어 두 형제가 가문의 추태를 보여주었다고 할만하다.

무문 스님의 억하탁상(抑下托上)의 역설이 돋보인다. 청정본원심의 자리는 음양이 부리는 차별세계가 아닌 절대 영원한 봄 계절이다.

Case 22
Mahakasyapa's Flagpole

A. Original Case

Ananda asked Mahakasyapa, "Aside from the golden robe, what else did the World-honored One transmit to you?"

Mahakasyapa called out, "Ananda!"

Ananda answered, "Yes."

"Knock over the flagpole in front of the gate!"

B. Commentary and Verse

If you can give a suitable answer here, then you'll soon realize that the Dharma assembly at Vulture Peak has not finished and still continues today. If not, then as the ancient Vipasyin Buddha once said, though he came long ago and devoted himself to practice, until this day he still has not attained the mystical realm of enlightenment.

Ven. Mu Mun said it again with a verse:

Which was kinder, the question or the answer?

How many people will glare fiercely at this point?

Older brother asks, younger brother answers-the family shame is revealed.

This is the independent news of spring, without regard for Yin and Yang.

C. Explanation

While attending the Buddha for twenty-five years, Ananda attained renown among Buddha's disciples as being foremost in seeking knowledge of the Dharma by asking the greatest number of questions. However, he did not receive Buddha's treasury of the true eye of the Dharma, the mystical Dharma of reality devoid of phenomenal characteristics. Mahakasyapa, foremost in ascetic practices, received confirmation of his Dharma attainment in three situations: when Buddha held up a flower on Vulture Peak and Mahakasyapa smiled; at the Stupa of Many Children, when Buddha shared his seat with him; and when Buddha put his feet through the coffin after entering Nirvana.

After Buddha entered Nirvana, Mahakasyapa was head of the

special council to compile the Vinaya(monastic precepts) and scriptures; this is where Ananda was confronted by Mahakashyapa. Mahakasyapa could not but kick the unenlightened Ananda out the door, so the story related above seems to be a situation that occurred just before something extreme arose between the two of them. The Dharma combat took place at the prompting of Ananda, who was disappointed at not being accepted.

"Aside from the golden robe, what else did you receive?" this is nothing if not a strong provocation!

At that moment, Mahakasyapa called out, "Ananda!" When Ananda answered, "Yes," Mahakasyapa abruptly scolded him and told him to "Knock down the flagpole in front of the gate." Ananda couldn't perceive the meaning of this phrase, so while lamenting the inadequacies of his practice, he began a seven day intensive retreat outside the gate. Fortunately, he resolved the great matter, returned to the Cave of Seven Leaves where the council was being held, and knocked on the door. Ananda shouted, "I've awakened, so open the door!" Mahaksyapa greatly rejoiced, then tested him and said, "It's already late at night-I can't open the door. Use your Dharma power and come on in through the keyhole."

Ananda had an important function at the first Buddhist council, but this story explains why he joined so belatedly - when Mahakasyapa called out "Ananda!" he couldn't very well have used someone who simply answered, "Yes." Since Ananda had no attainment, no realization, he couldn't perceive the meaning of what he had said; this is the reason that Mahakasyapa told him to "knock down the flagpole." However, when he smashed through his attachments to self and the teachings, he obtained his approval. In the end, we can say that the two brothers "revealed their family secret."

Ven. Mu Mun's paradox of pushing down while simultaneously pulling up really stands out. The pure, original state of the mind is not the relative world arising out of the utilization of Yin and Yang, but the absolute and eternal spring.

제 23 칙
不思善惡(불사선악)

❦

선도 악도 생각마라
Case23: Don't Think of Good and Bad

가. 본칙(本則)

六祖因明上座趁至大庾嶺, 祖見明至, 卽擲衣鉢於石上云, 此衣表信, 可力爭耶. 任君將去. 明遂擧之, 如山不動, 踟躕悚慄. 明曰, 我來求法, 非爲衣也. 願行者開示. 祖云, 不思善, 不思惡, 正與麼時, 那箇是明上座本來面目. 明當下大悟, 遍體汗流. 泣淚作禮問曰, 上來密語密意外, 還更有意旨否. 祖曰, 我今爲汝說者, 卽非密也. 汝若返照自己面目, 密却在汝邊. 明云, 某甲雖在黃梅隨衆, 實未省自己面目. 今蒙指授入處, 如人飮水, 冷暖自知. 今行者卽是某甲師也. 祖云, 汝若如是, 則吾與汝同師黃梅. 善自護持.

육조 대사가 행자로서 혜명 스님에게 쫓겨 대유령에 이르렀을 때의 일이다. 대사가 혜명이 뒤따라 온 것을 보고 가사와 발우를 바위 위에 올려놓고 말했다.

"이 가사는 법의 믿음을 표시하는 것이니 힘으로 다툴 일이 아니다. 그대에게 맡기니 알아서 하라."

그래서 혜명이 그것을 들어 올리려 했으나 산처럼 움직이지 않았다. 혜명은 주저앉아 무서움에 떨며 말하였다.

"저는 진리를 구하러 온 것이지 가사 때문이 아닙니다. 원컨대 가르침을 열어 보여주십시오."

이에 대사가 말하였다.

"선도 생각지 않고 악도 생각지 않는 바로 그때, 어떤 것이 그대의 본래면목(本來面目)인가?"

혜명은 이 말을 들은 즉시 크게 깨달았다. 그는 온 몸이 땀에 흠뻑 젖은 채 눈물을 흘리며 예배하고 물었다.

"조금 전 비밀의 말씀과 비밀의 뜻 외에 또 다른 어떤 가르침이 있습니까?"

대사가 말했다.

"내가 지금 그대에게 한 말은 비밀이 아니라네. 그대 스스로 자신의 본래면목을 돌이켜 비추어 본다면 비밀은 바로 그대 쪽에 있느니라."

혜명이 아뢰었다.

"제가 비록 황매산에서 대중과 함께 수행해왔습니다만, 실은 아직 자신의 본래면목을 깨닫지 못했습니다. 그런데 지금 깨달음에 드는 바른 가르침을 주시니, 마치 물을 마셔 차고 따뜻함을 스스로 아는 것과 같은 체험을 하였습니다. 이제부터 행자께서는 저의 스승이십니다."

그러자 대사가 다시 말했다.

"그대가 만약 그렇게 생각한다면 나는 그대와 함께 황매의 오조(五祖) 선사를 스승으로 모신 셈이 된다. 스스로 그 경지를 잘 지켜가도록 하거라."

나. 평창(評唱) 및 송(頌)

無門曰. 六祖可謂. 是事出急家. 老婆心切. 譬如新荔支. 剝了殼去了核. 送在爾口裏. 只要爾嚥一嚥.

육조 대사는 다음과 같이 평해도 좋으리라. 즉, 이 일은 급박한 궁지에 몰려서 한 일이었지만, 노파의 친절함과도 같은 마음이 진실로 절실하다. 이를테면, 신선한 여지(荔支) 과일의 껍질을 벗기고 씨도 발라내서 그대의 입 속에 넣어주는 격이니, 그대는 그저 그것을 한입에 삼키기만 하면 된다.

頌曰. 描不成兮畫不就. 贊不及兮休生受. 本來面目沒處藏. 世界壞時渠不朽.

무문 스님이 게송으로 다시 말하였다.

"본떠 묘사할 수도 없고, 그림으로 그릴수도 없네.

찬탄도 미칠 수 없으니 괜한 마음 쓰지 마시게.

본래면목은 아무데도 감출 곳 없으니,

세계가 무너져 내려도 그것은 썩는 것이 아니라네."

다. 강론(講論)

선(善), 악(惡)은 없다. 그러려면 무분별지(無分別智)라야 한다. 그 거룩한 자리에서 본래면목이 드러나 참 생명활동의 지혜 작용이 실력을 발휘한다.

차별심, 사량분별심을 떨쳐버리고 스스로의 불성을 자각하는 일은 근원적인 본래심으로 돌아가는 대작불사(大作佛事)이다. 그것은 곧 중도(中道)의 실천이다.

육조 대사는 단경(檀經)에서도 제자들에게 진여본성(眞如本性)을 확인시키기 위해 양변(兩邊)을 떠날 것을 말한 바 있다.

대법(對法)을 취해서 오고 감이 서로 인(因)이 되게 하다가, 마지막에는 두 법을 모두 없애 달리 갈 곳이 없게 해야 한다고 하였다. 즉 36가지의 대법이 있는데 이 상대법을 잘 쓰면 양변을 떠나

중도에 들게 된다는 것이다.

  이는 바로 일체의 삼라만상이 비롯되는 무한한 절대적 근원에 이르게 하는 원리이다. 중도의 실천을 통해 본래면목, 진여본성, 본래심(本來心) 등의 체험적 언어를 진정 자신의 것으로 받아 들일 수 있어야 한다.

Case 23
Don't Think of Good and Bad

A. Original Case

When the Sixth Patriarch was still a young monk in training, he was pursued by the Ven. Hye Myong as far as the Dayuling mountain range. The Seon Master saw Hye Myong pursuing him, so he put his robe and bowl atop a rock and said, "This robe represents faith in the Dharma, it is not something to be violently fought over. As it's yours, take it!"

Hye Myong tried to pick them up, but they were immovable, like a mountain. He collapsed, trembling with fear and said, "I have come seeking the truth, not for the robe. I beg of you, please give me your teaching!"

The Sixth Patriarch replied, "Don't think of good and bad. At that time, what is your original face?" As soon as Hye Myong heard this, he was greatly enlightened. His whole body was soaked in sweat, and as tears poured down his face he bowed and asked, "Is there any other teaching aside from these secret words and meaning?"

The Sixth Patriarch replied, "What I have just told to you is not a secret at all. If you reflect within and illuminate your original face, the secret is inside of you." Hye Myong told him, "Though I practiced with the community on Hwang Mae Mountain, I couldn't realize my original face yet. The teaching you have given me, it's as if drinking water and knowing for myself whether it is hot or cold. From now on, reverend postulant, you are my teacher."

The Sixth Patriarch then said, "If you think that way, then let's both call Seon Master Oh Jo on Hwang Mae mountain our teacher. Be careful to maintain this stage."

B. Commentary and Verse

Though in the above case the Sixth Patriarch reacted as he did as he was pushed into an urgent situation; we can safely say that he had grandmotherly and sincere kindness. In other words, it is as if he peeled a fresh lychee, took out the seeds, and put it in your mouth. All you have to do is swallow it at once.

Ven. Mu Mun said it again with a verse:

> You cannot imitate or describe it; it cannot be pictured.
>
> You cannot praise it; therefore, don't strive in vain.
>
> Your original face cannot hide anywhere;
>
> Though the world is destroyed, it does not decay.

C. Explanation

There is no good or bad? that requires awareness without relative distinctions. One's original face is revealed in that sacred place; the functioning of wisdom in a truly vibrant life demonstrates one's capacity. Completely discarding this mind of discrimination and relative thought, returning to the fundamental, original mind and realizing one's very own Buddha-nature-this is none other than the practice of the Middle Way.

In the Platform Sutra, the Sixth Patriarch instructs his disciples to leave all opposites behind in order to reaffirm the original-nature of suchness, things just as they are. He chose the opposites-method Dharma, wherein coming and going become causes for each other, and finally the two opposites must be completely discarded, so that one is left with no place to go.

There are thirty-six opposites-method Dharmas, but if you use these opposite teachings wisely, you can leave all opposites behind and attain the Middle Way.

This principle leads to the infinite, absolute root, which is the origin of all creation. Through the practice of the Middle Way, one should be able to accept that resonant phrases such as original-face, original-nature of suchness, and original-mind as one's very own.

제 24 칙
離却語言(이각어언)

❦

말을 끊고서
Case 24: Severing Speech

가. 본칙(本則)

風穴和尙, 因僧問, 語默涉離微, 如何通不犯. 穴云, 長憶江南三月裏, 鷓鴣啼處百花香.

  풍혈(風穴) 큰스님에게 한 스님이 물었다.
  "말하거나 침묵을 지키거나 이미(離微)에 걸리는데, 어떻게 하면 두루 통해서 그것을 범하지 않겠습니까?"
  풍혈 큰스님이 말했다.
  "강남의 춘삼월을 오래도록 기억하고 있는 것은 자고새 우는 곳에 온갖 꽃이 향기롭기 때문이지."

나. 평창(評唱) 및 송(頌)

無門曰. 風穴機如掣電, 得路便行. 爭奈坐前人舌頭不斷. 若向者裏見得親切, 自有出身之路. 且離却語言三昧, 道將一句來.

  풍혈 큰스님의 근기는 번갯불 같아서 길을 알자 금세 간다. 그런데 옛사람의 혀를 잘라버리지 않은 것이 유감이다. 만일 여기서 꼭 알맞게 그 소식을 보고 취할 수 있다면 저절로 모든 속박으로부터 벗어나는 길이 있으리라.

자, 말장난 삼매는 걷어치우고 한마디 일러보라.

頌曰. 不露風骨句, 未語先分付. 進步口喃喃, 知君大罔措.

무문 스님이 다시 게송으로 말하였다.
 "격조 높은 한마디를 드러내지 않고도,
 아직 말하기도 전에 벌써 나누어 주었네.
 더 나아가서 풍혈이 좔좔 설명했다면
 그대들은 그야말로 어떻게 해볼 수가 없었겠지."

다. 강론(講論)

여기서 이(離)는 어구(語句)를 떠난 묘처(妙處)이고 미(微)는 묘용(妙用)을 가리킨다.

묘처는 존재의 본체요, 묘용은 그 활용을 말한 것이다. 묘처는 공(空), 무(無), 평등(平等), 진여(眞如) 등으로 표현되고 묘용은 색(色), 유(有), 차별(差別), 묘유(妙有) 등으로 표현된다. 다시 말해서 이(離)란 일체의 분별을 벗어난 무분별한 그 자리로서 색(色)과 상(相)을 끊은 평등지(平等智)를 가리키는 말로서 진여(眞如)의 본체(本體)이다.

미(微)란 무분별한 그 자리를 벗어난 현상의 구체적인 차별로 나타난 작용을 가리키는 말로 진여(眞如)의 작용(作用)이다. 즉 이(離)는 묵(默)이요, 미(微)는 어(語)이다.

여기서 문제의 핵심은 말을 해도 불법(佛法)에 어긋나고 말을 안 해도 불법에 어긋나니 어떻게 해야 하느냐는 것이다. 말을 하면 미(微)에 떨어지고 입을 다물고 있자니 이(離)에 떨어지게 되어 진여(眞如)의 한쪽 밖에 통하지 못하니 낭패가 아닐 수 없다. 이 이(離)와 미(微)의 양변을 범하지 않고 두루 통하려면 어떻게 해야 하느냐의 질문에 풍혈 큰스님은 두보(杜甫)의 시를 빌려와 응수한다. '강남의 춘삼월', '자고새 울음', '온갖 꽃과 그 향기'.

유언무언(有言無言)에 떨어지지 않는 절대의 경지는 그대 본인 스스로 그 곳에 나아가서 관찰하고 체득해 보라는 일침이다. 복잡하고 이론적인 질문 따위는 접어두고 대자연에 펼쳐진 제법(諸法)의 실상(實相)을 직접 느껴 볼 것을 주문하고 있다. 즉 대자연의 참된 모습을 자각할 때 언어 문자에 집착하지 않고 침묵에도 떨어지지 않는다.

본래 청정한 진리의 본체(本體)는 이(離)와 미(微)가 하나인데, 그 본체에 대하여 이러쿵 저러쿵 말하면 미(微)에 떨어지고 침묵하면 이(離)에 떨어진다.

평등의 세계만을 나타내도 그르치고 차별의 세계만을 나타내도 그르치니 진퇴양난의 딜레마에서 자기 자신을 구제할 방법은 중도(中道)의 실천을 통하여 근원적인 본래의 불성(佛性) 자리로 되돌아가버리는 일이다.

본래면목(本來面目)의 주인공은 오롯이 여여(如如)해서 대상경계와는 한 묶음, 한자리에서 숨쉰다. 그래서 도인(道人)의 눈에는 삼라만상이 그대로 진리의 모습으로 비추어진다. 이(離), 체(體)를 따질 이유도, 필요도 없다.

청산을 보면 산은 푸르고 강물을 보면 물은 흘러갈 뿐이다. 여기에 무슨 이설이 있겠는가.

Case 24
Severing Speech

A. Original Case

A monk asked Seon Master Pung Hyeol, "Whether speaking or keeping silence, one is either caught by the fault of transcendence or subtle functionality; what can we do so as to never commit these transgressions?"

Seon Master Pung Hyeol answered, "I'll long remember March in Gang Nam, as there are so many fragrant flowers where the partridges sing."

B. Commentary and Verse

Seon Master Pung Hyeol's Seon spirit is like a bolt of lightning? he realizes the Way, then goes at once-though it's a pity he couldn't sever the ancients' words. If you can properly grasp the situation here, the way to be free from all hindrances appears by itself. Hey! Clearing away all this Samadhi word-play, give me one word!

Ven. Mu Mun said it again with a verse:

> Without using a dignified phrase,
> Even before speaking, he had already shared it.
> If Pung Hyeol had continued to freely explain,
> There is nothing you could have even tried.

C. Explanation

This story refers to both the mystical, transcendental point which has discarded all speech and the subtle functioning of this transcendence. This point of mystical transcendence is the substance of all existence; its mystical function is the practical application of it. This mystical, transcendental point can also be expressed as emptiness, nothingness, absolute equality, and true-suchness; its function can be expressed as form, existence, distinction, and mystical existence. In other words, the substance of true suchness refers to, with speech, this non-discriminating awareness which severs both form and phenomenal characteristics? the point free from opposites, without any relative distinctions at all. The function of true suchness points to, also with speech, the function that appears with the concrete discrimination of phenomena, separate from that point of non-discrimination. That is to say, transcendence is silence, whereas its function is speech.

Here is the crux of the problem: though one speaks, it's separate from the Buddha-Dharma, yet when one doesn't speak, it's also separate from the Buddha-Dharma. What should you do? If you speak, you fall into functioning(form), but if you close your mouth you fall into transcendence(emptiness). Since you always penetrate only one aspect of true-suchness, there will always be this predicament. When asked how not to commit the fault of making opposites but to utilize them both thoroughly, Seon Master Pung Hyeol replied by borrowing a poem from Du Bo. "March in Gang Nam," "partridges sing," "many flowers and their fragrance,"? this absolute realm doesn't lapse into either speech or silence; this single point encourages you to go there, penetrate and attain it yourself. It is asking you to put aside such a complicated, theoretical question, and directly experience for yourself the true aspects of all Dharmas unfolding in the natural world. In other words, when you are aware of the true aspects of the natural world, you do not attach to speech and words, nor do you attach to silence.

In the originally pure, clear essence of truth, transcendence and function are one; when we speak this way and that about this original essence, we fall into function(form), when we keep silence we fall into transcendence(emptiness). Since, though only the realm of absolute equality appears, it is a transgression, but also if the realm of discrimination appears, it is also a mistake, the way to help oneself out of this dilemma is through realization of the Middle Way? returning to this fundamental, original Buddha-nature.

The master of one's original face is perfectly just-like-this, both one bundle with the relative realms, and resting in the same spot. Therefore, to the eyes of an enlightened man, all of creation reflects an aspect of truth, just as it is; there is no reason or necessity to distinguish between form and emptiness. If you look at the mountain, it is just blue; if you look at the river, the water is simply flowing. What's the use of any conflict here?

제 25 칙

三座說法(삼좌설법)

❦

삼좌가 설법함
Case25: Third Seat Dharma Speech

가. 본칙(本則)

仰山和尙, 夢見往彌勒所, 安第三座. 有一尊者, 白槌云, 今日當第三座說法. 山乃起白槌云, 摩訶衍法, 離四句, 絶百非, 諦聽諦聽.

앙산(仰山) 큰스님은 꿈에 미륵 보살의 처소에 가서 세 번째 자리에 앉았다.

그때 한 존자(尊者)가 추(槌)를 울리고 말하였다.

"오늘은 세 번째에 앉은 사람이 설법을 해야 할 차례입니다."

그러자 앙산 큰스님이 일어나 추를 울리고 말했다.

"대승의 법은 4구(四句)를 떠나고 100비(百非)를 끊는 것이니 똑똑히 들으시오. 똑똑히 들으시오."

나. 평창(評唱) 및 송(頌)

無門曰, 且道, 是說法不說法, 開口卽失, 閉口又喪. 不開不閉, 十萬八千.

말해보라. 이것은 설법을 한 것인가, 하지 않은 것인가? 입을 열면 바로 잃고, 입을 다물어도 또한 목숨을 잃는다. 입을 열지 않아도, 입을 다물지 않아도 십만 팔천리 멀어진다.

頌曰. 白日靑天, 夢中說夢. 捏怪捏怪, 誑諄一衆.

무문 스님이 다시 게송으로 말하였다.
"맑은 날 푸른 하늘,
꿈 속에서 꿈을 말하네.
괴이하고 또 괴이하여라.
한 산의 대중을 속이는구나."

다. 강론(講論)

참으로 꿈 속에서 꿈 이야기를 하고 있다. 하지 않아도 될 이야기를 4구니, 100비니 하는 유식한 언어로 둘러친다.

장수라는 사람이 꿈에 나비가 되어 공중을 훨훨 날아다녔다. 그러면 장수가 나비인가, 나비가 장수인가? 나비와 본인 스스로를 분간 못하였다고 장수가 꿈 얘기를 한 적이 있다. 나비와 자기가 한 몸이 될 때 꿈이니 생시니 하는 구분은 없어진다. 나비와 한 몸이 되어버려야 한다. 나비라는 것도 없어질 때 온 천지는 나비가 된다.

진리와 하나 되고 주객이 하나 되는 자리에 들어가는 교학적 가르침이 4구 100비이다. 위대한 선사들이 4구 100비를 들먹거리는 것은 선(禪)과 교(敎)의 근본자리가 한바탕임을 증명하는 일이 된다. 즉, 4구를 여의고 100비를 끊으면 공(空)의 자리에 들어서고 마침내 자성불(自性佛)이 스스로의 모습을 드러낸다. 그렇다면 4구 100비가 구체적으로 무엇인가?

4구는 일(一), 이(異), 유(有), 무(無)의 네 가지 범주를 말한다.

100비는 일(一), 이(異), 유(有), 무(無)에 대해서 부정하는 것인데 백 가지가 되는 것은 이러하다. 우선, 같다(一)는 것에 대해 '실제 같다는 것이 아니고, 같지 않다는 것도 아니며, 같지도 않고 같지 않은 것도 아니고, 같지 않고 같지 않은 것도 아니다는 것도 아니다.' 하고 부정한다.

즉, 네 번의 부정하는 방법을 쓰는데 이와 같이 나머지 이(異), 유(有), 무(無)를 적용하면 도합 열여섯 번이 된다. 이 열여섯 번 부정을 과거, 현재, 미래로 곱하면 마흔 여덟 가지의 경우가 된다. 이를 다시 이미 부정한 것과 아직 부정하지 않은 것으로 계산하면 아흔여섯 번이 된다. 여기에 맨 처음 부정을 제공한 4구를 합하면 100비가 된다. 앙산 큰스님이 '똑똑히 들으시오.' 하고 말한 것은 교학적 언어를 빌려 선의 요체를 바로 드러낸 모습이다. 즉, 언어를 초월하여 단박에 깨쳐 보라는 주문이다.

꿈속에서조차 이런 가르침을 내렸다는 것은 참으로 대단한 일이다.

4구를 떠나고 100비를 끊는다는 말은 일체의 인식론적인 분별을 떠나 참된 공에 들어간다는 의미이다. 공의 자리는 언어도단(言語道斷)하고 심행처멸(心行處滅)하므로 일찍이 나지도 않았고 죽지도 않았다. 더 이상 할 말이 없다. 계합하는 일만 남았다. 대승법의 요지이며 반야, 공사상의 핵심인 4구 100비는 어떤 수단, 방법을 동원하여도 그것은 피상적인 설명일 뿐이다. 스스로 터득하지 않으면 다 남의 살림살이이다.

Case 25
Third Seat Dharma Speech

A. Original Case

While in a dream, Seon Master Ang Sahn went to the Bodhisattva Maitreya's place and sat in the third seat. A disciple then struck the gavel and said, "Today the one sitting in the third seat should give the Dharma speech."

Whereupon Seon Master Ang Sahn stood up, struck the gavel, and said, "The teaching of Mahayana transcends the four propositions and severs the hundred negations. Listen carefully, listen carefully!"

B. Commentary and Verse

Tell me! Did he give a Dharma speech or not? If he opens his mouth he is lost, but even if he closes his mouth, he loses his life. Even if he neither opens nor closes his mouth, he is still one hundred and eight thousand miles away(from the truth).

Ven. Mu Mun said it again with a verse:

> On a clear day, with a blue sky,
>
> He speaks of a dream in the midst of a dream.
>
> How bizarre and strange -
>
> He deceives the whole mountain community.

C. Explanation

This is truly speaking of a dream in the midst of a dream. But even were it not, the story is surrounded by clever speech about the four propositions and hundred negations. A man named Jang Su had a dream in which he became a butterfly and flew away flapping into the sky. So was Jang Su the butterfly, or was the butterfly Jang Su? Jang Su once spoke about his dream, and said that he couldn't distinguish the butterfly from himself. The distinction between dream and reality disappeared when his body became one with the butterfly. Your body must become one with the butterfly; when even the butterfly disappears, the whole universe becomes the butterfly.

The four propositions and hundred negations are academic teachings about entering the realm of becoming one with truth, where both subject and object are one. The great Seon masters mentioned the four propositions and the hundred negations because they confirmed this fundamental point-the unified essence of both Seon and doctrine. In other words, transcending the four propositions and severing the hundred negations, one enters the realm of emptiness, and eventually the attainment of Buddhahood reveals its own aspect.

But concretely, what are the four propositions and the hundred negations? The four propositions refer to the four categories of sameness, difference, existence and nonexistence. The hundred negations are denials of sameness, difference, existence and nonexistence, but there are one hundred of them for a reason. First, concerning "sameness," it is not "the same as the truth," but it is also not "not the same," also not "not the same and not not the same," also not "not not the same and not not the same."

In other words, using this method of negating each case four times, when this is applied to the rest? difference, existence, and nonexistence? then the total becomes sixteen negations. If these sixteen negations are multiplied by the past, present, and future, then we have forty-eight cases. If this is again added to that which we have already negated, and to that which has not been negated, then we have a total of ninety-six. If we include here the original four negations, we arrive at a total of one-hundred negations. Seon Master Ang Sahn's exhortation to "Listen clearly!" directly reveals the main point of this academic phrase, borrowed from the Seon tradition. That is to say, it's urging us not to attach to the words, but to wake up right away. It's really incredible that this sort of teaching has been handed down, even from the midst of a dream.

"Transcending the four propositions and severing the hundred negations," means that one should not attach to any intellectual distinctions at all, and enter true emptiness. As emptiness is the realm where all speech and words have been cut off, the place where all cleverness and mental activity have ceased, it is never even once born or dies. There is nothing more to say-all that's left is to tie it together. While the four propositions and hundred negations are the main teaching of Mahayana Buddhism and the core principle of Prajna(wisdom) and the theory of emptiness, no matter what method or technique you rely on, these are only superficial explanations. If you don't attain it yourself, it's only someone else's life experience.

제 26 칙
二僧卷簾(이승권렴)

두 스님이 발을 걷어 올리다
Case26: Two Monks Roll Up the Blinds

가. 본칙(本則)

淸涼大法眼, 因僧齋前上參, 眼以手指簾. 時有二僧, 同去卷簾. 眼曰, 一得一失.

   청량원의 법안 큰스님에게 점심공양 전에 스님들이 찾아왔다. 법안 큰스님이 손가락으로 발을 가리켰다.
   그때 두 스님이 함께 일어나 발을 걷어 올렸다. 그러자 법안 큰스님이 말했다.
   "하나는 됐지만 하나는 틀렸다."

나. 평창(評唱) 및 송(頌)

無門曰. 且道, 是誰得誰失. 若向者裏著得一隻眼, 便知淸涼國師敗闕處. 然雖如是, 切忌向得失裏商量.

   자, 말해보라. 누가 옳고 누가 그른 것인지를.
   만일 여기에서 바른 안목을 가지고 볼 수 있다면, 곧 청량 국사가 어디서 잘못했는가를 알 수 있을 것이다.

비록 그와 같다 할지라도, '누가 됐고, 누가 틀렸다.'라고 분별하여 헤아려서는 안 된다.

頌曰. 卷起明明徹太空, 太空猶未合吾宗. 爭似從空都放下, 綿綿密密不通風.

무문 스님이 다시 게송으로 말하였다.
"발을 걷어 올리니 탁 트인 밝은 하늘,
그 하늘도 나의 종지에는 맞지 않네.
어찌 그 하늘마저 내던져 버리지 않았을까?
전혀 빈틈없게 바람도 통하지 않아야 하리."

다. 강론(講論)

무문 스님은 득(得)과 실(失)을 초월한 경지에서 이 상황을 보라고 말한다. 득과 실이라는 차별 세계에서의 사량분별함을 경계하고 있다. 법안 큰스님이 두 스님의 행동을 보고 득과 실을 논한 것에 대해서 무문 스님 또한 득, 실을 따지고 있으니 자못 큰일이 아닐 수 없다.

득과 실이라는 상대적인 차별심을 초월한 정법에 대한 안목 즉, 일척안(一隻眼)의 입장에서는 법안 큰스님의 두 스님에 대한 평가가 문제가 될 성싶다.

무문 스님의 게송에서 보여지는 것처럼 방의 안과 밖을 구분하는 발을 걷어 올리면 바로 밝은 하늘 즉, 허공과 하나가 되어버리는 마당에 무슨 시비(是非)와 선악(善惡)과 득실(得失)의 분별이 있겠는가. 허공 가운데는 텅 비어 한 물건도 없다. 그래서 반야경에서도 일체개공(一切皆空)이라 하였던 것이다. 사실, 절대평등의 세계에서는 그러한 말들조차 용납치 않는다.

즉, 일체 언어적인 흔적과 자취를 용납치 않는다. 아공(我空), 법공(法空)의 그윽한 곳에 들어가면 세상과 하나가 되어 버린다. 전혀 빈틈이 없어서 바람도 통하지 않는다.

여기에서, 만법일여(萬法一如)적인 깨달음의 생활이 펼쳐진다. 이쯤되면 오히려 득실과 시비 등 일체의 차별이 소용된다. 그래서 사사무애(事事無碍)라는 대자유(大自由)의 삶이 펼쳐진다. 이런 각도로 법안 큰스님의 "한 사람은 됐으나 한 사람은 틀렸다."라고 한 말을 이해해야 한다.

이 말씀 자체가 분별 이전의 소식으로 이미 살핀 주감암주(州勘庵主)의 공안과 맥이 같다.

어떠한 간택(揀擇)도 용납치 않아서 상대적 분별을 떠났고, 떠났다는 그 생각마저도 떠난 자리이다. 사구(死句)가 아닌 활구(活句)의 대답을 요구하는 것이 선(禪)의 도리일진댄 얻었다는 생각이 남아 있는 한 자기 성취에 대한 분별이 있으므로 공부가 덜 되었다. 밝고 깨끗한 경지를 얻었다는 그 마음, 그러한 의식은 자기 스스로를 집착하고 있다는 반증이다. 다시 부언하면, 우리는 공(空)에 이르러야 한다.

그런데 진짜 불법(佛法)은 공이란 것도 없다. 만약 공에 걸리면 완전한 자유인이 못된다. 차별과 평등을 종횡무진 할 수 있어야 한다. 평등에 이르러야 차별을 쓸 수 있고, 차별에 제대로 철저한 사람은 이미 평등을 섭렵하였다.

어느 한쪽만을 고집해서 될 일이 아니다. 차별 속에서 평등을 잊어버리지 않아야 하고, 평등 속에서 차별을 쓸 줄 알아야 무애도인(無碍道人)이라 할 수 있다.

법안 무애도인의 득실에 대한 법문을 무문 스님이 비판하고 있는 듯한 말들은 후학들의 사량분별심을 없애기 위한 방편이지 큰 스님의 법기(法器)에 흠을 내자는 것이 아니다.

두 어른 모두 살활자재한 모습을 보여주고 있다.

Case 26
Two Monks Roll Up the Blinds

A. Original Case

Before the midday meal, some monks came to pay respect to Seon Master Beop An of the temple Cheong Ryang Won. The Seon Master pointed to the blinds. At that moment, two monks stood up together and rolled up the blinds. Seon Master Beop An then said, "One has succeeded, the other one failed."

B. Commentary and Verse

Hey, tell me! Who succeeded and who failed? If you have the correct Dharma eye at this point and can penetrate it, you can soon realize where National Teacher Cheong Ryang was mistaken. But though you wish to do that, you should not make distinctions and think of "who succeeded and who failed."

Ven. Mu Mun said it again with a verse:
Rolling up the blinds, the sky is bright and vast;

But even that sky does not match up to my school's doctrine.

Why don't you even throw away the sky?

Then not even the slightest wind can pass through.

C. Explanation

Ven. Mu Mun asks us to look at this situation from the view of not attaching to gain or loss, since both gain and loss are limited by conceptual thinking in the realm of relative distinctions. Seon Master Beop An saw the actions of the two monks, and talked about gain or loss; also Ven. Mu Mun made the similar distinction of gain and loss? this was nothing but a big issue. From the point of view of the true, singular eye of Dharma, which transcends the relative, distinguishing mind of gain and loss, it seems that Seon Master Beop An's judgment of the two monks was a problem. Like Ven. Mu Mun's verse shows, if you roll up the blinds, which divide the room into inside and outside, there is only the bright sky; in this place which has completely become one with empty space, what kind of distinctions could there possibly be of right and wrong, good and bad or gain and loss? In the midst of space, there is not even anything that is empty.

Therefore, in the Heart Sutra it says that "Everything is empty." Actually, in this realm of absolute equality, even that speech is not allowed - that is to say, no verbal traces or vestiges are permitted at all. If you enter that profound place, where both self and Dharma are empty, the whole world completely becomes one; since there is no gap left at all, not even the wind can pass through. From this point, an enlightened life unfolds, wherein the absolute is part of everything. When this happens, all distinctions such as gain and loss, right and wrong can be utilized; therefore, a life of great liberation, where nothing at all is any hindrance unfolds. Seon Master Beop An's sentence that "one succeeded, the other failed," should be understood from this perspective.

The point of this speech, a teaching before relative distinctions appear, was already examined in the case of "Joju Sees Through the Hermits," which is of the same tradition. Since no choice or separation is allowed at all, this point transcends relative distinctions and even thinking itself. The Seon tradition itself requires an answer that is either live or dead speech; if there is any thought at all remaining concerning one's attainment, since this is a relative distinction, one's practice has failed. If one attaches to the mind which has attained this level of purity and brightness, then this disproves it.

In addition, we must reach the level of emptiness. However, the true Buddha-Dharma has no such thing as emptiness at all. If you are attached to emptiness, you can't become a completely free person; one must be able to move freely between relative distinctions and absolute equality. If one reaches absolute equality, distinctions can be used; one who is thoroughly aware of relative distinctions has already mastered absolute equality.

This is not about stubbornly holding fast to one side or another. If one does not forget absolute equality amidst relative distinctions, and knows how to use relative distinctions in the midst of absolute equality, one can be called an enlightened man of no hindrance.

Ven. Mu Mun appears to be criticizing Beop An's enlightened, unhindered Dharma speech - but this is a technique to take away the conceptual thinking of future disciples, not to make a crack in Seon Master Beop An's Dharma-vessel. Both monks are showing everyone an unrestricted, liberated life.

제 27 칙
不是心佛(불시심불)

❦

마음도 아니요, 부처도 아니다
Case27: Not Mind, Not Buddha

가. 본칙(本則)

南泉和尙, 因僧問云, 還有不與人說底法麼. 泉云, 有. 僧云, 如何是不與人說底法. 泉云, 不是心, 不是佛, 不是物.

    남전(南泉) 큰스님에게 한 스님이 물었다.
    "지금까지 사람들에게 설하지 않은 법이 있습니까?"
    남전 큰스님이 대답했다.
    "있지."
    그 스님이 여쭈었다.
    "사람들에게 설하지 않았던 법이 무엇입니까?"
    남전 큰스님이 대답했다.
    "마음(心)도 아니요, 부처(佛)도 아니요, 물건(物)도 아니다."

나. 평창(評唱) 및 송(頌)

無門曰. 南泉被者一問, 直得揣盡家私, 郞當不少.

    남전이 이 한 질문을 받고 자기 재산을 모두 다 써버렸다. 아주

형편없는 꼴이 된 것이지.

頌曰. 叮嚀損君德, 無言眞有功. 任從滄海變, 終不爲君通.

무문 스님이 다시 게송으로 말하였다.
"정중한 것이 도리어 덕을 손상시키니
말 없음이야말로 참 공덕이로다.
설령 푸른 바다가 뽕밭으로 변하여도
끝내 그대 위해 말하지 않으리."

다. 강론(講論)

선리(禪理)는 교외별전(敎外別傳)이요 불립문자(不立文字)이기 때문에 상대에게 설하지 못하는 법이 있음은 당연하다.
진리 당체는 글로 표현할 수 없고, 그림으로도 나타낼 수 없다. 그리고 말로 전달할 수 있는 것도 아니다.
남전 큰스님은 마음도 아니요, 부처도 아니요, 물건도 아니라고 분명하게 말씀하셨다. 여기에 대해서 무문 스님은 너무 자상하게 말씀하셨다고 불평한다. 하지 않아도 될 말까지 해서 스스로의 체면을 구겼다고 비판한다. 진리는 말할 필요도 없거니와 다 표현할 수도 없다는 점에서는 남전 큰스님의 말씀이 큰 하자가 있는 것처럼 보이나 그 또한 가르침의 방편이라는 것을 감안한다면 큰스님의 자비가 한량없으시다는 것을 느끼게 된다. 어쩜, 남전 큰스님으로서는 그저 불시심(不是心), 불시불(不是佛), 불시물(不是物)이라 했을 뿐인데 무문 스님 같은 후학들이 괜한 시비를 하고 있는지도 모른다. 물론 이 또한 자비의 방편이라 한다면 할 말이 없다.

『금강경(金剛經)』 여법수지분(如法受持分)에 다음과 같은 말씀이 있다.

불설반야바라밀 즉비반야바라밀 시명반야바라밀(佛說般若波羅蜜, 卽非般若波羅蜜 是名般若波羅蜜), 즉 부처님이 설하는 반야바라밀이 곧 반야바라밀이 아니라 그 이름이 반야바라밀이라는 뜻이다. 『금강경』의 그 아래 문장에서는 미진(微塵), 세계(世界), 32상(三十二相)을 예를 들면서 똑같은 논리 전개로 즉비(卽非) 사상을 유감없이 드러내고 있다. 즉 중도정견(中道正見)으로 보면 그 당체는 말할 필요도, 말로 표현할 길도 없다는 의미이다.

그렇고 보면, 선(禪)과 교(敎)는 정확히 일치한다는 것을 알 수 있다.

한 대상을 어떤 개념으로 덧씌우면 거기에서 오류가 발생한다.

차차 그 이름을 실재화(實在化)의 대상으로 삼게 된다. 그런데 나중에 돌아보면 본체와는 터무니없이 동떨어져 있음을 자탄한다. 이름이라는 것은 그 순간 만들어진 고정관념이요 찰라적인 상황 설명일 뿐이다.

마음(心), 부처(佛), 물건(物) 등도 마찬가지이다. 이미 망상과 분별심으로 고착화 될 지경에 이르렀다. 거기에 대해서 "아니다."라고 하는 단 한마디가 각성을 추구한다. 모든 것을 뒤집어엎고 새로이 출발한다. 그 자리에 본래심이 드러나고 자기 생명력이 살아 숨 쉰다.

개념으로부터 해방되면 그 어떤 경계에도 끄달리지 않는다. 여여(如如)할뿐이다.

즉비(卽非)의 위대한 힘이다.

Case 27
Not Mind, Not Buddha

A. Original Case

A monk asked Seon Master Nam Jeon, "Is there any Dharma that has not yet been taught to people?"

Nam Jeon answered, "There is."

The monk asked again, "What is the Dharma which has not yet been taught to people?"

Nam Jeon answered, "It's not mind. It's not Buddha. It's not a thing."

B. Commentary and Verse

When Nam Jeon got this one question, he used up all his possessions? what a dreadful sight it was!

Ven. Mu Mun said it again with a verse:
    Being polite spoils one's merit;
    Silence is indeed the true virtue.

Though the blue sea changes into a mulberry patch,

I'll never give you any comment.

C. Explanation

The Way of Seon is known as a "special transmission, outside of scriptural teachings." As it is also "not depending on words and speech," naturally certain Dharma cannot be taught to another person. The essence of truth cannot be expressed in writing; it also cannot be represented pictorially.

Seon Master Nam Jeon clearly said that, "It is not mind. It is not Buddha. It is not a thing." Regarding this Ven. Mu Mun spoke too attentively? he didn't have to go that far. We can criticize Nam Jeon for losing face by saying too much unnecessarily. If you consider whether Seon Master Nam Jeon's speech was a big mistake, as it is not necessary to speak of truth and also since it cannot be completely expressed, or whether it was an expedient means of teaching, the Seon Master's limitless compassion can be felt. Yes, Seon Master Nam Jeon just said that "It is not mind. It is not Buddha. It is not a thing," not realizing that future disciples such as Mu Mun would be checking right and wrong. Of course, we must stop this debate over whether it was meant to be a compassionate technique.

In Chapter XIII of the Diamond Sutra, "How the Dharma Should Be Received and Retained," there is the following passage: "The Prajna(wisdom) Paramita that Buddha taught is not the true Prajna Paramita; only its name is the Prajna Paramita." A later passage in the Diamond Sutra says that, by the same principle, using particles of dust, the entire world, and the thirty-two distinguishing marks as examples, this theory of "not-suchness" appears fully everywhere. In other words, it means that when seen by the correct view of the Middle Way, the essence need not be spoken of, that there is no way to express it with speech. If you see that, then you can realize that Seon and doctrine are of exactly the same principle.

If you impose a certain fixed concept on an object, mistakes arise from that point of view, and then gradually you begin to regard this concept as something that exists. However, later when you look back on it, you'll feel regret because it's so far removed from the original essence. A name is a fixed idea produced in a particular moment? only the explanation of momentary state of being.

The same is true with the words mind, Buddha, or a thing? they have already reached the boundaries set by delusion and relative distinctions. This requires a one-word awakening?

"No!"

Everything is turned over, a fresh departure. The original-mind is uncovered at that point, and one's life force breathes fresh vitality.

If you are free from conceptual thinking, then you are not caught by any limitations? it is just so. This is the great power of "not-suchness."

제 28 칙
久響龍潭(구향용담)

오랫동안 용담의 소문을 듣다
Case28: Well-known Yong Dam

가. 본칙(本則)

龍潭, 因德山請益抵夜. 潭云, 夜深, 子何不下去. 山遂珍重, 揭簾而出. 見外面黑, 却回云, 外面黑. 潭乃點紙燭度與. 山擬接. 潭便吹滅. 山於此忽然有省. 便作禮. 潭云, 子見箇甚麽道理. 山云, 某甲 從今日去, 不疑天下老和尙舌頭也. 至明日龍潭陞堂云, 可中有箇漢, 牙如劍樹, 口似血盆, 一棒打不回頭, 他時異日, 向孤峰頂上, 立吾道在. 山遂取疏抄, 於法堂前, 將一炬火提起云, 窮諸玄辨, 若一毫致於太虛, 竭世樞機, 似一滴投於巨壑. 將疏抄便燒, 於是禮辭.

    용담(龍潭) 큰스님의 처소를 찾아간 덕산(德山) 스님이 큰스님의 법문을 청하여 듣고 참문하는 사이에 밤은 깊어갔다.
    용담 큰스님이 말했다.
    "밤이 깊었으니 이제 그대는 물러가는 것이 좋겠네."
    덕산 스님이 드디어 인사를 올리고 발(簾)을 걷으며 문밖으로 나갔다. 바깥은 온통 칠흑처럼 깜깜했다. 덕산 스님이 이에 돌아와서 말하기를,
    "밖이 매우 캄캄합니다."라고 했다.

그러자 용담 큰스님이 지촉(紙燭)에 불을 붙여서 덕산 스님에게 건네주었다. 덕산 스님이 그것을 받으려고 할 때 용담 큰스님이 확 불어서 꺼버렸다. 이에 덕산 스님은 홀연히 깨달은 바가 있어서 큰 절로 감사의 인사를 올렸다. 용담 큰스님이 물었다.

"그대는 무슨 도리를 보았는가?"

덕산 스님이 대답하였다.

"저는 오늘 이후로는 천하 노스님들의 말씀을 의심하지 않겠습니다."

그 다음 날 용담 큰스님은 법상에 올라 말했다.

"여기 한 사내가 있어서 이빨은 칼을 세워 놓은 나무와 같고, 그의 입은 피를 담아 놓은 그릇과 같다. 그런 그가 방망이로 한 대 얻어맞고도 뒤도 돌아보지 않는다. 그는 후일 저 우뚝 솟은 정상에서 나의 도(道)를 크게 확립하게 될 것이다."

이에 덕산 스님은 『금강경소초(金剛經疏抄)』를 꺼내 법당 앞에 놓고 불이 붙은 장작개비를 치켜들며 말했다.

"여러 가지 심오한 진리를 파헤쳤다 하더라도 그것은 허공의 한 개 티끌에 불과하다. 또 세상의 모든 진리를 모두 설파했다 하더라도 그것은 깊은 골짜기에 던져진 물방울 하나에 불과하다."

그는 금강경주석서를 모두 불사른 뒤 작별인사를 올렸다.

나. 평창(評唱) 및 송(訟)

無門曰. 德山未出關時, 心憤憤口悱悱, 得得來南方, 要滅却教外別傳之旨. 及到澧州路上, 問婆子買點心. 婆云, 大德, 車子內是甚麼文字. 山云, 金剛經抄疏. 婆云, 只如經中道, 過去心不可得, 見在心不可得, 未來心不可得, 大德要點那箇心. 德山被者一問, 直得口似匾擔. 然雖如是, 未肯向婆子句下死却. 遂問婆子, 近處有甚麼宗師. 婆云, 五里外有龍潭和尙. 及到龍潭, 納盡敗闕. 可謂是前言不應後語. 龍潭大似憐兒不覺醜, 見他有些子火種, 郞忙將惡水 驀頭一澆澆殺. 冷地看來, 一場好笑.

덕산이 아직 깨치지 못했을 때는 분한 마음 때문에 말이 잘 나오지 않았다.

그는 의기양양하게 남방으로 오며 '교외별전을 주장하는 무리들을 없애 버리고 말 것'이라고 했다. 그가 예주 땅에 이르러 한 노파에게 점심을 주문할 때였다. 노파가 물었다.

"스님의 걸망 속에는 무슨 책이 들어 있습니까?"

덕산이 대답했다.

"금강경 주석서라오."

그러자 노파가 말했다.

"그 경에는 이런 말씀이 있다고 들었습니다. '과거의 마음도 얻을 수 없고 현재의 마음도 얻을 수 없고 미래의 마음도 얻을 수 없다.' 그렇다면 스님께서는 어느 마음에 점을 찍으려 하시는지요?"

덕산은 이 한마디 질문을 받고 말문이 막히고 말았다. 비록 그렇기는 하였지만, 덕산은 이 노파의 한마디 말에 기가 꺾여 버리지는 않았다. 그래서 노파에게 한 마디 더 물어보았다.

"이 근처에 어떤 큰스님이 계십니까?"

노파가 대답했다.

"오 리쯤 밖에 용담 큰스님이 계십니다."

그렇게 하여 덕산은 용담에까지 오게 되어 완전히 패배감을 맛보게 되었다.

덕산이 고향을 떠나올 때는 호언장담했었는데, 용담에서 일어난 일과는 완전히 앞뒤가 맞지 않게 되었다고 할 수 있다. 용담은 아이가 너무 귀여워 자신의 추태도 의식하지 못한 부모처럼, 덕산에게 불씨가 남아있음을 보고 느닷없이 머리에 구정물을 끼얹어 버렸다.

이러한 모습을 냉정히 관찰해보면 이는 한바탕 웃음거리가 아니겠는가?

頌曰. 聞名不如見面, 見面不如聞名. 雖然救得鼻孔, 爭奈瞎却眼睛.

무문 스님이 다시 게송으로 말하였다.
"이름 듣기보다는 얼굴을 보는 것이 낫고
때론 얼굴보다 이름만 듣는 것이 낫네.
설령 콧구멍은 얻었을지는 모르겠지만
어찌하랴, 눈알이 멀고 말았으니."

다. 강론(講論)

본칙의 제목인 구향용담은 덕산(德山) 스님이 떡 파는 한 노파의 안내로 용담숭신(龍潭崇信) 큰스님을 찾아가서 첫 대면 때 한 말에서 유래된다.
"오랫동안(久) 용담의 소문(響)을 들어왔는데, 용담에 와보니 못도 없고 용도 없구나."
즉 덕산 스님이 천하의 용담 큰스님이라는 이름을 듣고 큰스님을 찾아가게 되었고, 그 자리에서 자기 기세를 보여주는 장면이다. 큰스님은 덕산의 법기(法器)가 범상치 않음을 직감적으로 파악하고 덕담 아닌 덕담을 하였다.

"아- 그대가 이미 용담에 들었네."

용담숭신 스님은 당대의 선승인 천황도오(天皇道吾)의 법을 이었다. 용담 큰스님은 원래 속가에서 떡장수를 하다가 절 집안에 들어왔다. 기연은 이러하다.

천황도오 스님은 당대의 선지식으로서 이름이 있었으나 사람을 통 만나지 않았다. 공양 때면 유독 떡장수의 호떡공양은 받았다. 그런데, 무슨 일로 스님은 매번 10개씩의 호떡을 받으면서 꼭 하나는 도로 떡장수에게 돌려주었다. 떡장수는 그것이 궁금하여 그렇게 하는 까닭을 물었다. 스님의 대답이다.

"내가 그대에게 이렇게 주어서 자손의 공덕을 삼노라."

며칠 후 떡장수는 속 깊은 고민을 털어놓았다.

"스님, 제가 사는 꼴이 분주하기만 합니다. 어찌하면 좋겠습니까?"

스님의 대답이다.

"집에 있으면 감옥이라 옹색하고, 출가하면 자유롭고 넓으리라."

떡장수는 말씀 끝에 바로 출가하여 머리를 깎으니 숭신이라는 법명을 받았다. 용담숭신 큰스님은 훗날 덕산 스님을 제자로 맞게 되는데 여기 '구향용담'의 화두를 낳는 사건이 발생한다.

덕산 스님은 성이 주(周)씨로서 『금강경』에 능통하였으므로 주금강이라 불렸다. 당시 남쪽지방에서는 육조혜능 스님의 영향으로 선풍(禪風)이 크게 일어나 선종(禪宗)이 발달하였다. 교상학(教相學)이 주류를 이루는 북쪽지방의 대표주자인 덕산 스님은 남쪽 선가(禪家)에서 부르짖고 있는 불립문자, 교외별전이 맘에 들지 않았다. 그래서 손수 쓴 『금강경』의 소초(疏抄)를 걸망에 짊어지고 남쪽 행을 결행하였던 것이다.

'마음이 곧 부처다.'라는 언사 따위에 분한 마음이 일어나 말이 잘 나오지 않았다고 할 정도니 덕산 스님의 정의감도 대단하다. 아무튼 그러한 그의 패기가 위대한 스승, 용담 큰스님을 친견케 한 것이다. 대각(大覺)을 이루는 데는 어떤 식으로든 발심이 있어야 함을 보여주는 좋은 예이다.

아무튼 용담 큰스님으로부터 촛불을 꺼버리는 친절과 은혜를 입고 덕산 스님은 깨달음을 얻었다. 무문 스님의 게송에 보이는 것처럼 덕산 스님은 처음에는 콧등만 높아 으쓱하였다. 그렇지만 용도 못도 보지 못하는 눈뜬 장님이었다.

그 눈을 뜨게 한 사건, 계기가 구향용담의 본론이다.

사방천지가 칠흑같은 어둠에 덮여 있었는데 온전한 의지처인

촛불이 갑자기 꺼지자 덕산 스님은 한발자국도 움직일 수 없었다.

생사(生死)라는 칠흑같은 어둠 속에서 덕산 스님의 알량한 지식들은 무용지물이었던 것이다. 그런데 의외였다. 꼼짝도 할 수 없는 크나큰 충격을 받자 오히려 마음이 확 열려 버렸다. 아주 극한 상황에서 전혀 새로운 빛을 본 것이다.

그래선지 덕산 스님은 후일 제자들의 교화방법으로, 생각할 틈도 주지 않고 무지막지하게 몽둥이를 휘두르는 수법을 썼다. 그 유명한 덕산방(德山棒)이다.

실참(實參)만이 살 길이지, 이것저것 헤아려서는 될 일이 아님을 스승으로부터 뼈저리게 느꼈기 때문이다. 불을 확 불어서 꺼버렸는데 어째서 도를 통했는가? 불이 꺼져야 밝아짐을 용담숭신 큰스님은 이미 알고 계셨다.

Case 28
Well-known Yong Dam

A. Original Case

The Ven. Deok Sahn visited Seon Master Yong Dam and asked him about the Dharma until late at night.

Seon Master Yong Dam then said, "As the night is late, why don't you retire?" Deok Sahn finally bowed to him, rolled up the blinds, and went out the door. Outside it was pitch-black, so Deok Sahn came back in and said, "Outside it's very dark."

Seon Master Yong Dam lit a paper candle and handed it to Deok Sahn, but as he was about to take the candle the Seon Master blew it out. Deok Sahn had a sudden experience of enlightenment through this, so he offered a deep bow of gratitude to Yong Dam.

The Seon Master then asked him, "What did you realize?"

Deok Sahn answered, "From today onwards I will never doubt the words of the ancient masters anywhere in heaven or on earth."

The next day, Seon Master Yong Dam ascended the rostrum

and said, "There is a man here whose teeth are like a forest of knives, and whose mouth is like a blood bowl. Though you strike him with this staff, he doesn't turn and look around. At a later date, he will establish his Dharma on that lofty peak over there."

After this, Deok Sahn took all his Diamond Sutra commentaries and put them in front of the Buddha Hall. He raised a burning log and said, "Though I have revealed all the various profound truths, they are nothing more than a dust particle in empty space. Though I have completely expounded all the truths of the world, they are nothing more than a drop of water in a vast ravine."

He then burned all his notes and commentaries, bowed to his teacher, and bade farewell.

B. Commentary and Verse

Before Ven. Deok Sahn awakened, he was speechless with anger. He proudly came to the South in order to eradicate the teachings of those who advocated a "special transmission outside of the scriptures." When he reached the land of Yae Ju, he ordered lunch from an old woman, who asked him, "Venerable, what kind of books are inside your sack?"

Deok Sahn answered, "They are commentaries and notes on the Diamond Sutra."

Whereupon the woman said, "I've heard it is said in that sutra, 'Past mind cannot attain it, present mind cannot attain it, and future mind cannot attain it.' Therefore, venerable monk, with which mind would you have your lunch?"

When Deok Sahn heard this question, he became stuck? he couldn't say anything. But though this was the case, his spirits were not dampened, so he asked the old woman, "Is there a Seon Master in this area?"

The old woman answered, "Seon Master Yong Dam lives about five miles from here."

When Deok Sahn called on Seon Master Yong Dam, however, he felt completely defeated. Deok Sahn had been very proud when he was leaving his village, but with Yong Dam, it might be said that the daily activities were not consistent at all. Yong Dam was like a parent who has lost all sense of shame because their child is so cute; seeing a burning ember remaining in Deok Sahn, he would suddenly pour filthy water over his head. If we look at this objectively, wasn't he just making a fool of him?

Ven. Mu Mun said it again with a verse:

> Seeing the face is better than hearing the name;
>
> Occasionally only hearing the name is better than the face.
>
> Even though you have two nostrils?
>
> Alas, you are blind!

C. Explanation

The name of this case, "Well-known Yong Dam," comes from the time when Ven. Deok Sahn, at the direction of the old woman selling rice-cakes, first went to visit Seon Master Yong-Dam Sung-Shin. During this initial meeting he said, "I've long heard of Yong Dam('Dragon pond'), but now that I've come here there isn't a dragon or a pond." That is to say, Deok Sahn had heard the name Yong Dam everywhere, so having coming there to visit him he showed him his spirit. The Seon Master intuitively realized that Deok Sahn's level of Dharma attainment was not ordinary, so he complimented him in an off-handed way:

"Oh, so you're already in the Dragon Pond(Yong Dam)."

Ven. Yong-Dam Sung-Shin was a Dharma heir of the Tang Dynasty Seon teacher Cheon-Hwang Do-Oh. Seon Master Yong

Dam had originally been a rice-cake peddler in lay life and had then entered the temple. There was a strange coincidence, as Ven. Cheon-Hwang Do-Oh already had established a name for himself as a Seon teacher in the Tang Dynasty. Though he never met anybody at all, he alone would receive stuffed pancakes during the midday meal from only this rice-cake peddler. For some reason, every time he received ten pancakes, he would always give one back to the peddler for the road. The rice-cake peddler wondered about this and asked him the reason.

The monk answered, "When I give this to you, I'm making merit for your descendants."

A few days later, the rice-cake peddler revealed his deep anguish, "I'm living my life so busily. What should I do?"

The monk answered, "If you're in a house, it's being stuck in prison; leaving home(being ordained) is vast and liberating." The rice-cake peddler became a monk right away, and when he had his head shaved he received the Dharma name Sung Shin. At a later time, when Seon Master Yong-Dam Sung-Shin took Deok Sahn as his disciple, the Zen question "Well-known Yong Dam" was created.

Ven. Deok Sahn's family name was Ju, and as he had mastered the Diamond Sutra, he was called "Diamond Ju." At that time, due to the influence of the Sixth Patriarch Hui-neng, the spirit of Seon had predominantly arisen in the South, and the Seon sect was beginning to develop there. Deok Sahn, who was representative of the northern region's scriptural school, was not fond of the southern sect's declaration "Not depending on speech and words; a special transmission outside the scriptures."

He therefore loaded the Diamond Sutra commentaries he had personally written into his monk's bag and vowed to head towards the South. Ven. Deok Sahn's sense of injustice was so great that he became enraged at irresponsible teachings such as "Mind is Buddha." At any rate, his ambitious spirit soon brought him face to face with a great teacher, Seon Master Yong Dam. This is a good example showing us that if one has this initial "beginner's mind" that it's possible to have a great awakening by any sort of means. At any rate, Deok Sahn attained enlightenment after receiving the kindness and favor of Seon Master Yong Dam, who blew out the candle. As is shown in Ven. Mu Mun's verse, at first Deok Sahn held his head high with pride; however, the blind man who couldn't see the dragon or the pond was eventually able to open his eyes. This is the main point of the story "Well-known Yong Dam"? providing a situation or a moment for awakening. The whole universe is completely submersed in pitch-black darkness, but when the candle, the perfect prop, was suddenly blown out, Deok Sahn couldn't even move an inch.

In the midst of the pitch-black darkness(ignorance) of life and death, Deok Sahn's petty knowledge was completely useless; unexpectedly, when he received an unavoidable jolt, his mind was completely opened. He saw a totally new light through this extreme situation.

From then on Deok San used the technique of wildly swinging his staff, not giving any space for thought, as a method for teaching his disciples. This is the renowned "Deok Sahn's Hit." He keenly attained from his teacher that the way to live one's life is only through investigation of truth, not by thinking about this thing and that. How could he have penetrated the Way when the candle was suddenly blown out? Seon Master Yong Dam already understood this original radiance when he blew out the candle.

제 29 칙
非風非幡(비풍비번)

❦

바람도 아니요, 깃발도 아니다
Case29: Not the Wind, Not the Flag

가. 본칙(本則)

六祖, 因風颺刹幡, 有二僧對論, 一云, 幡動, 一云, 風動, 往復曾未契理. 祖云, 不是風動, 不是幡動, 仁者心動. 二僧悚然.

   육조 스님 앞에서 두 스님이 바람에 나부끼는 깃발을 보고 서로 다른 주장을 하였다. 한 스님은 깃발이 움직인다고 했고, 또 한 스님은 바람이 움직인다고 했다. 이치에 맞지 않는 말을 주고받는 것을 보고 육조 스님은 이렇게 말하였다.
   "바람이 움직이는 것도 아니고 깃발이 움직이는 것도 아니다. 그대들의 마음이 움직이는 것이다."
   이에 두 스님은 놀라워했다.

나. 평창(評唱) 및 송(頌)

無門曰. 不是風動, 不是幡動, 不是心動. 甚處見祖師. 若向者裏見得親切, 方知二僧買鐵得金. 祖師忍俊不禁, 一場漏逗.

   바람이 움직이는 것도 아니요, 깃발이 움직이는 것도 아니다.

또한 마음이 움직이는 것도 아니다. 그렇다면 조사를 어디서 볼 수 있겠는가?

만약 이 속내를 절실하게 알게 된다면 바야흐로 이 두 스님은 철을 샀는데 금을 얻게 되었음을 알게 된 것이다. 그런데 조사는 참지 못하여 한바탕 창피스러운 꼴을 연출한 셈이다.

頌曰. 風幡心動, 一狀領過. 只知開口, 不覺話墮.

무문 스님이 다시 게송으로 말하였다.
"바람과 깃발과 마음이 움직인다고 한 자들
한 장의 영장으로 같은 죄로 끌려 가리.
다만 입을 열 줄만 알았지,
말실수하는 줄은 생각도 못했네."

다. 강론(講論)

마음이 움직인다는 것은 유심론(唯心論)적 입장이다. 일체유심조(一切唯心造)니 삼계유심(三界唯心)이니, 유식(唯識)이니 하는 말들은 불교 교상(敎相)의 근간을 이룬다. 혜능 역시 문제의 초점을 자신에게 돌린다. 즉, 바람과 깃발 사이의 물리적 관계를 논하지 않고 사물을 인식하는 우리의 의식 즉, 마음에 책임을 던진다. 과연, 일체만물의 움직임이 마음으로부터 비롯된다면 도대체 그 마음은 어떻게 생겼단 말인가.

마음은 분명히 관념이다. 그 누구도 마음을 직접보고 마음을 논하지는 않는다. 이조혜가가 달마대사를 찾아갔을 때 멱심불가득(覓心不可得)이라고 하였다.

저 『금강경』에서도 과거심불가득, 현재심불가득, 미래심불가득이라고 하였다. 그런데 육조 스님이 그대들의 마음이 움직인다고 한 것은 외경(外境)에 사로잡혀 내심(內心)의 주인공을 놓친 것을 탓하는 말이다.

우리가 사물을 인식할 수 있는 것은 인식기관이 존재하고 그 기관이 활동을 하기 때문임은 틀림없다. 인식은 곧 마음이다. 마음 때문에 희로애락이 일어난다. 그런데 그러한 경험 내용이 같은 사건을 두고도 사람마다 서로 다르다. 이는 곧 일체의 삼라만상은 독립성이 없으며 실재하지도 않음을 반증한다. 모든 현상은 우리의 인식주관이 대상을 표상하여 만들어 낸 심연상으로서 존재한다. 객관의 대상은 인식주관과 상관관계를 가진다는 뜻이다. 마음이라고 불리는 인식주관은 스스로의 독자성이 없고 반드시 객관의 대상에 따라 좌우된다. 즉, 마음은 무자성(無自性)이다. 상의상관하는 연기의 작용만 있을 뿐 그 아무것도 없다. 따라서 움직이는 것은 바람도, 깃발도, 마음도 아니다. 여기에 이르러야 모든 분별이 그친다.

바람, 깃발, 마음이 없어진 자리는 이론이 필요치 않다. 그저 하나가 되어버리면 그만이다. 한 덩어리가 되면 객관도, 주관도 없어진다. 대상과 자기 자신의 구별이 없어져야 진리에 완전히 계합한 것이 된다. 개구즉착(開口卽錯)이다.

그래서 혜능 스님 조차도 핀잔을 받고 있는 것이다. 그렇지만 혜능 스님 이상의 인물 또한 없다.

Case 29
Not the Wind, Not the Flag

A. Original Case

Two monks saw a flag fluttering in the wind and began to argue with each other in front of the Sixth Patriarch. One monk said that the flag was moving, while the other one said that it was the wind that was moving. After the Sixth Patriarch saw them irrationally arguing back and forth he said, "It is not the wind that is moving, nor is it the flag that is moving? both of your minds are moving!" The two monks were awe-struck by this.

B. Commentary and Verse

It is not the wind that is moving, nor is it the flag that is moving; also it is not mind that is moving. But how can you see the patriarch? If you sincerely understand his intention, you will realize that the two monks bought iron but ended up getting gold. However, the patriarch's impatience produced this rather shameful scene.

Ven. Mu Mun said it again with a verse:

> Those who say the wind, flag and mind are moving
>
> Are all dragged off by the same crime, with one warrant.
>
> They only knew how to open their mouths -
>
> But they couldn't conceive of their faults while speaking.

C. Explanation

The phrase "mind is moving" is the view of the principle of 'mind-only.' The teaching phrases, "everything is created by mind alone," "the three realms are only mind," and "consciousness-only" form the basis of Buddhist doctrine. The Sixth Patriarch Hui Neng also turns the focus of the matter to oneself? in other words, not discussing the physical relationship between the wind and the flag, but putting the responsibility on mind, our consciousness which perceives everything. Indeed, if the movement of all creation originates in the mind, where did that mind itself arise from? Mind is clearly conceptual thought? no one who discusses mind has directly perceived it. When the Second Patriarch Hye Ga went to visit Bodhidharma, he said, "Though I've searched for my mind, I could not find it anywhere." In the Diamond Sutra it also says "Past mind cannot attain it, present mind cannot attain it, and future mind cannot attain it." However, the Sixth Patriarch told them "your minds are moving" blaming them for being caught by outside appearances and losing the true inner master.

Our ability to perceive things in the world is without doubt due to the existence and function of bodily organs of perception? this cognizance is none other than mind. Human feelings and emotions also arise because of this mind. However, even in the same situation, each person will have a different perception in their own mind. This is because, in all of creation, there is no independent, autonomous nature, which proves that in reality, things don't actually exist. All appearances, subjectively represented by our "overseer" consciousness, are created and exist due to our inner mental perceptions. This means that there is some correlation between one's subjective perceptions and this "overseer" consciousness.

This "overseer" consciousness, that which is called mind, has no independent nature itself, and is most definitely influenced by this subjective perception. In other words, mind itself has no self-nature, there is only the functioning of dependent origination (cause and effect) corresponding to objects of perception-but actually nothing exists at all. Therefore, that which is moving is not the wind, not the flag and also not the mind. If one continues to this point, all relative distinctions cease.

At the point where the wind, flag and mind do not exist, there is no need for dissent? when they completely become one, that's it. When they become one mass, both subject and object disappear. If the separation between oneself and the object of one's perception completely disappears, one completely unites with the truth. "Opening your mouth, there is separation."

Therefore, even the Sixth Patriarch gets a scolding, but there is nobody greater than him.

제 30 칙
卽心卽佛(즉심즉불)

이 마음이 곧 부처이다
Case30: This Mind Itself is Buddha

가. 본칙(本則)

馬祖, 因大梅問, 如何是佛. 祖云, 卽心卽佛.

마조(馬祖) 큰스님에게 대매(大梅) 스님이 찾아와 여쭈었다.
"무엇이 부처입니까?"
마조 큰스님은 대답했다.
"이 마음이 곧 부처이다."

나. 평창(評唱) 및 송(頌)

無門曰. 若能直下領略得去, 著佛衣, 喫佛飯, 說佛話, 行佛行, 卽是佛也. 然雖如是, 大梅引多少人, 錯認定盤星. 爭知道說箇佛字三日漱口. 若是箇漢, 見說卽心是佛, 掩耳便走.

만일 이 말을 곧바로 이해할 수 있다면, 부처의 옷을 입고 부처의 밥을 먹으며, 부처의 말을 하고, 부처의 행동을 하리니, 그대로 부처이다. 비록 그렇기는 하지만, 대개는 많은 사람들로 하여금 저울의 눈금을 잘못 읽게 했다.

어찌 알리오. 부처라는 말을 하고서 3일간 양치질을 한 사연을. 만약 이 사람이 '이 마음이 곧 부처이다.'라는 말을 듣는다면 귀를 막고 도망갈 것이다.

頌曰. 青天白日, 切忌尋覓. 更問如何, 抱臟叫屈.

무문 스님이 다시 게송으로 말하였다.
　"푸른 하늘에 빛나는 태양
　절대 찾아 나서지 말라.
　더욱이 무엇이냐고 묻는 것은
　훔친 물건을 껴안고 죄 없다 우기는 일."

다. 강론(講論)

마조 큰스님에게 어떤 스님이 찾아와 "무엇이 부처입니까?" 하고 여쭈었더니 "이 마음이 곧 부처이다." 라고 대답했다.

그 스님이 다시 "어떻게 해서 이 마음이 곧 부처입니까?" 하고 여쭈었더니 마조 큰스님은 "아기의 울음을 막기 위함이니라." 라고 일침을 놓았다.

그 스님이 또 다시, "아기의 울음이 그칠 때 어떠합니까?"
하고 여쭈니 마조 큰스님은 "마음도 아니고 부처도 아니다."라고 쐐기를 박았다.

그 스님이 또 다시 "이 두 가지 즉, 즉심즉불(卽心卽佛)과 비심비불(非心非佛)을 부정하는 사람이 온다면 어떻게 하시겠습니까?" 하고 여쭈니 마조 큰스님은,

"만약 그러한 사람이 온다면 이 물(物)이 아니라고 대답하리라." 라고 언성을 높였다.

그 스님이 또 다시 "그러면 이 세 가지 다 불문(不問)에 붙이는 사람이 온다면 어떻게 말씀하시겠습니까?" 하고 여쭈니 마조 큰스님은, "위의 세 가지를 자유로이 처리할 수 있는 사람이라면 비로소 대도를 체회(體會)한 이라 하겠다." 라고 속 시원히 대답하셨다.

본 칙에 등장하는 대매 스님은 '이 마음이 곧 부처이다.' 라는 스승 마조 큰스님의 평소 가르침에서 확철대오하였다. 대매 스님은 그 후 스승을 떠나 명주(明州)의 대매산(大梅山)에서 은거하며 30년간을 지냈다.

스승 마조 큰스님은 한 스님을 보내어 그를 시험하였다.

"마조 큰스님의 교법(敎法)이 요즘 와서 달라졌습니다. 비심비불(非心非佛)이라고 가르칩니다."

이에 대매 스님은 "큰스님이 그러셔도 나는 여전히 즉심즉불(卽心卽佛)을 굳게 믿습니다."라고 하였다.

이런 사실을 알리자 큰스님은 매실이 잘 익었다며 기뻐하셨다. 원래의 법명인 법상(法常)에 대매(大梅)라는 법호가 붙은 것은 이 때 부터였다.

현대인들에게 '즉심즉불' 같은 말씀이 진실하게 와 닿지 않은 것은 이미 이런 말씀에 익숙해져서 색 바랜 언어가 되어 버렸기 때문이다. 그래서 이런 화두를 접하더라도 깨치기는커녕 별 느낌이 없는 것이다. 문제의 한계는 여기서 끝나지 않는다.

"무엇이 부처입니까?"하고 물으면 "마음이 부처이다."라고 말들은 잘한다.

부처, 부처라고 하지만 대부분의 사람들은 자기의 고정관념으로, 자기식의 부처를 끌어안고 있다. 주인공이 부처를 상대적으로 알고 있기 때문에 부처의 생명력이 이 마음 쓰는 순간에 살아 숨쉰다는 것을 놓친다. 이 마음이 곧 부처라는 사실만 존재할 뿐 객관화된 이상적이고 권위적인 부처는 없다. 즉, 사람마다 자기 개념으로 덧씌워진 부처를 들먹거리고 있을 뿐이지 진정 참 부처는 알지 못한다는 말이다.

그래서 무문 스님은 도둑놈이 죄의식이 없다고 한 것이다.

Case 30
This Mind Itself is Buddha

A. Original Case

Ven. Dae Mae asked Seon Master Ma Jo, "What is Buddha?"

Seon Master Ma Jo answered, "This mind itself is Buddha."

B. Commentary and Verse

If you can directly grasp this phrase, then you wear the Buddha's clothes, eat the Buddha's food, speak the Buddha's words, and do the Buddha's deeds? just as a Buddha. Though that is true, usually most people are led into misreading the scale on the balance. How can you know? Even mentioning Buddha is a reason to wash out your mouth for three days. If such a person hears the phrase "Mind is Buddha," he will stop up his ears and run away.

Ven. Mu Mun said it again with a verse:
    The sun shines in the blue sky?

Never search around!

The more you ask "What?"

Holding the stolen goods and yet proclaiming one's innocence.

C. Explanation

A monk came to Seon Master Ma Jo and asked him, "What is Buddha?"

Ma Jo answered, "This mind itself is Buddha."

The monk asked again, "How can this mind itself be Buddha?"

Ma Jo hit the mark and answered, "To stop the baby from crying."

The monk then asked, "What if you stop the baby from crying?"

Seon Master Ma Jo struck the nail right on the head? "It is not mind, not Buddha."

The monk asked once again, "What would you do if someone came here who denies both that 'Mind itself is Buddha' and 'Not mind, Not Buddha.'"

Ma Jo raised his voice? "If that kind of person came here, I would answer, 'It's not anything!'"

The monk persisted, "But what if someone came here refuting all three of these statements?"

Relieved, Seon Master Ma Jo answered, "If there is someone who can freely manage these three statements, I would say that he has personally attained the Great Way."

Ven. Dae Mae, who appears in the original case, attained final enlightenment with his teacher, Seon Master Ma Jo's usual teaching 'This mind itself is Buddha.' Dae Mae later left his teacher and went into seclusion at the mountain Dae Mae San in Myong Ju for 30 years.

His teacher Seon Master Ma Jo sent a monk there to test him. The monk said, "Seon Master Ma Jo's Dharma teaching has changed these days. Now, it is not mind, not Buddha." Dae Mae answered, "The Master may teach that, but I still strongly have faith that this mind itself is Buddha."

When the Seon Master was told of this, he was very happy, because the plum had become ripe; the transmission name Dae Mae("Great Plum") was then added to his disciple's original Dharma name, Beop Sang. The reason people these days don't truly connect with teachings like 'This mind itself is Buddha' is that they've become accustomed to this kind of speech, so it's become very commonplace; therefore, though one may encounter this kind of Great Question, one has no sense of awakening at all. The problem doesn't stop there; if you ask someone, "What is Buddha?" they readily answer, "This mind itself is Buddha." Though they say "Buddha, Buddha," but most people are holding their own fixed, personal idea of what Buddha is. As one's inner-master knows the Buddha relatively, the Buddha's life force loses its vitality in this very moment; since only this idea that 'Mind is Buddha' exists, the objective, ideal, all-powerful Buddha is not there. In other words, since everybody only talks about the Buddha they have created with their thinking, they can't truly realize the actual Buddha.

Everyone who has their own idea of Buddha can't realize the true Buddha. Therefore, Ven. Mu Mun said that the thief is unaware of his crime.

제 31 칙
趙州勘婆(조주감파)

조주 큰스님, 노파를 점검하다

Case31:
Seon Master Joju Investigates the Old Woman

가. 본칙(本則)

趙州, 因僧問婆子, 臺山路向甚處去. 婆云, 驀直去. 僧纔行三五步. 婆云, 好箇師僧. 又恁麼去. 後有僧擧似州. 州云, 待我去與爾勘過這婆子. 明日便去, 亦如是問. 婆亦如是答. 州歸謂衆曰, 臺山婆子, 我與爾勘破了也.

조주 큰스님을 찾아오던 한 스님이 노파에게 물었다.
"오대산으로 가는 길이 어느 쪽입니까?"
노파가 말했다.
"곧장 가시오."
그 스님이 서너 발자국을 옮기자 노파가 말했다.
"참 멀쩡한 스님이 또 저렇게 가시다니!"
뒤에 누가 이 사실을 조주 큰스님에게 아뢰었다. 큰스님이 말씀하셨다.
"어디, 기다려 보게. 내가 가서 너희들을 위해 그 노파를 살펴보고 오겠다."
다음 날 당장 노파를 찾아간 큰스님은 그 스님과 똑같이 질문을 했다. 노파 역시 똑같이 대답을 했다. 조주 큰스님은 돌아와 대중들에게 말했다.

"오대산 가는 길의 그 노파를, 내가 그대들을 위해 점검했노라."

나. 평창(評唱) 및 송(頌)

無門曰. 婆子只解坐籌帷幄, 要且著賊不知. 趙州老人, 善用偸營劫塞之機, 又且無大人相. 檢點將來, 二俱有過. 且道, 那裏是趙州勘破婆子處.

노파는 다만 막사에 앉아서 계략을 세울 줄만 알았지 안타깝게도 도둑이 와서 붙어 있는 줄 알지 못했다. 조주 늙은이는 적진에 몰래 들어가 요새를 빼앗는 솜씨는 훌륭했지만, 역시 대인의 모습은 아니었다. 잘 살펴보면, 두 사람 모두에게 다 잘못이 있다.
자, 말해보라. 어디가 조주가 노파를 점검한 자리인가?

頌曰. 問旣一般, 答亦相似. 飯裏有砂, 泥中有刺.

무문 스님이 게송으로 다시 말하였다.

"물음이 그토록 같으니
대답 또한 비슷하구나.
밥 속에는 모래가 있고
진흙 속에 가시가 있도다."

다. 강론(講論)

이 공안의 핵심은 세 군데에 있다.
'곧장 가시오(驀直去)', '또 저렇게 가시다니(又恁麽去)', '점검했노라(勘破了也)'이다. 모든 공안이 그렇지만 여기 조주감파(趙州勘婆)도 중의적(重義的) 내용을 담고 있다. 후학들의 입장에서는 그 깊은 속뜻을 가늠한다는 것이 예사로운 일이 아니다. 근기(根機)와 법기(法器)에 따라 얻는 답이 다를 수가 있다. 선에서의 대답은 천편일률적이지 않아서 자유분방한데, 그것이 곧 선사상(禪思想)의 또다른 매력이다.

이 공안에서 '곧장 가시오'는 직지인심(直指人心)을 염두에 둔 법문이다. 오대산을 향한 스님들의 행각은 분명, 진리의 추구였다. 그런 스님들을 상대로 곧장 가는 길 즉, 직지인심의 선적인 길을 노파는 제시했던 것이다. 그렇지만 대부분의 스님들은 알아듣지 못하고, 아무 생각 없이 발걸음만 그쪽을 향했다. 노파의 입장에서는 참으로 답답할 노릇이었다. 그래서 '또 저렇게 가시다니!' 하고 비아냥댄 것이다.

그런데, 이 노파는 다 좋았지만 조주의 정체를 알아보지 못한 것은 큰 실수였다. 조주는 오대산 가는 길을 물으러 간 것이 아니었기 때문이다. 노파는 꼼짝없이 조주의 시험에 걸려들었다. 밥 속에 있는 돌을 씹고 진흙 속에 있는 가시를 밟는 꼴이 되었다.

이 공안의 깊은 속뜻을 다음과 같이 볼 수도 있다. 길을 묻는 사람에게 있어서 '곧장 가다' 라는 말은 하나의 명령체계이다. 그것을 종교에서는 교리라고 한다.

그런데 그러한 교리는 자칫 잘못하면 독선이 되기 쉽다. 그래서 자비를 실천해야 할 종교인들이 전쟁까지 일으킨다. 교리가 오히려 아집과 편견을 조장, 유도한 결과가 된 것이다. 교리라는 길을 밟아 곧이곧대로 가려는 수행자들에게 노파는 '또 저렇게 가시다니!' 하고 걱정한다. '그것마저 놓아버리지 못하고 한사코 한쪽 길만을 고집해서 어쩌자는 것인가!' 하고 한탄한다.

무문 스님은 그의 평에서 조주 큰스님이나 노파 모두에게 다 잘못이 있다고 지적한다. 조주 선사를 몰라본 노파나 노파의 입을 막지 못한 조주 선사나 다 어설픈 데가 있었던 것이다. 때문에 이 화두는 활구(活句)의 체면을 차렸다.

깊이 생각해 볼 일이다.

Case 31

Seon Master Joju Investigates the Old Woman

A. Original Case

A monk who had come to see Seon Master Joju asked an old woman on the road, "Which way to Oh Dae Mountain?"

The old woman said, "Only go straight."

After the monk had gone three or four steps the old woman said, "Such a clear, capable monk also goes that way!"

Later someone told this story to Seon Master Joju, who said, "Wait a while? I'll go and investigate this old woman for you."

The next day, the Seon Master went right away, found the old woman, and asked her the same question the monk had asked her. The old woman also gave the same answer.

Joju returned and told the community,

"I have investigated the old woman of Oh Dae Mountain for you."

B. Commentary and Verse

The old woman only knew how to sit in the barracks and plot her strategy; unfortunately, she didn't realize that a thief had come and was sticking close to her.

Joju entered the old woman's camp without her knowing, and had the excellent skill to occupy the fortress, though he did not seem like a great man. If we look at it carefully, both of them have faults. So, tell me! At what point did Joju investigate the old woman?

Ven. Mu Mun said it again with a verse:
 The question was exactly the same,
 The answer was also similar.
 There is sand in the rice,
 Thorns in the mud.

C. Explanation

The main point of this story can be found in three phrases: "Only go straight," "Another one also goes that way," and "I have investigated the old woman." All Koan cases are like this, but this story of "Joju Investigates the Old Woman" also has a dual meaning. From the point of view of disciples, evaluating the deep hidden meaning is not something they do every day. The answer one receives may differ according to one's capacity for practice and level of attainment. Seon answers are not lacking in variety? they are wild and free, which is yet another appeal of Seon teaching.

In this episode, the phrase "only go straight" is a Dharma speech that should be remembered? it points directly to mind. The monks were making a pilgrimage to Oh Dae Mountain in search of truth and clarity.

The old woman showed them the way to "go straight," in other words, the Seon method of pointing directly to people's minds. Most of the monks couldn't understand it, however, and thoughtlessly only their feet went in that direction. The old woman who had the role to truly answer them must have been troubled by their lack of understanding; she therefore made the sarcastic remark, "Another one also goes that way!"

Though this old woman did everything well, she made a big mistake when she didn't recognize Joju's true face, since Joju had not gone there to ask about the way to Oh Dae Mountain. The old woman got hopelessly caught by Joju's test? chewing on stones in the rice, walking on thorns in the mud.

This episode's deep meaning can be seen this way. For those asking for the direction, the phrase "only go straight" is one method of instruction? in religion it is called doctrine. However, with even the slightest deviance from the truth, this doctrine can become self-righteousness.

Therefore, religious people who should be practicing compassion have even caused wars? when a religious doctrine promotes obstinacy and biases, the result is that it induces people to do such a thing. For those practitioners who would tread the path of doctrine in a straightforward manner, the old woman admonishes them, saying "Another one also goes that way!" She laments, "How is it that they can't put it down, and adamantly attach to only one way?"

Ven Mu Mun, in his judgment, points out that both Seon Master Joju and the old woman made mistakes. Both the old woman, who failed to recognize Seon Master Joju, and Joju himself, who couldn't silence the old woman, were rather careless, which keeps up the appearance of this story's 'live speech.'

This is something that needs to be considered deeply.

제 32 칙
外道問佛(외도문불)

✧

외도가 부처님께 여쭙다

Case32:
An Outer-path Practitioner Asks the Buddha

가. 본칙(本則)

世尊, 因外道問, 不問有言, 不問無言. 世尊據座. 外道贊歎云, 世尊大慈大悲, 開我迷雲, 令我得入. 乃具禮而去. 阿難尋問佛, 外道有何所證, 贊歎而去. 世尊云, 如世良馬, 見鞭影而行.

세존께 한 외도가 찾아와 물었다.
"말 있음으로도 묻지 않고 말 없음으로도 묻지 않겠습니다."
이에 세존께서는 묵묵히 앉아 계셨다. 이를 본 외도가 찬탄하며 말했다.
"세존께서는 대자대비하셔서 나의 미혹한 마음의 구름을 다 걷어 내시고, 저로 하여금 깨달음에 이르게 해주셨습니다!"
그리고는 예의를 갖춰 인사한 뒤 돌아갔다. 곧이어 아난 존자가 세존께 여쭈었다.
"저 외도가 무엇을 증득했기에 저렇게 찬탄하고 갔습니까?"
세존께서 말씀하셨다.
"세간의 준마가 채찍의 그림자만 보아도 내달리는 것과 같은 것이니라."

나. 평창(評唱) 및 송(頌)

無門曰. 阿難乃佛弟子, 宛不如外道見解. 且道, 外道與佛弟子, 相去多少.

아난은 부처님의 제자이면서도, 외도의 견해에도 미치지 못한 것 같구나. 자, 일러보라. 외도와 부처님의 제자와의 거리가 어느 정도인지를.

頌曰. 劍刃上行, 氷稜上走. 不涉階梯, 懸崖撒手.

무문 스님이 게송으로 다시 말하였다.
　　"칼날 위를 걷고
　　얼음 모서리를 달린다.
　　계단이나 사다리를 쓰지 않고
　　절벽에서 손을 놓도다."

다. 강론(講論)

진리의 참된 본성은 이언설상(離言說相)이며 이명자상(離名字相)이며 이심연상(離心緣相)이다. 말과 표현들은 실체 그 자체가 아니다. 단지, 그것을 보여주기 위한 수단에 불과하다.

그래서 세존께서도 팔만 사천 법문을 하셨음에도 불구하고 마지막에는 일자불설(一字不說)이라고 선언하셨던 것이다. 개념화된 말로써는 천변만설(千辯萬說)이라도 진실 그 자체를 나타내기 어렵다는 뜻이다.

외도(外道)의 질문은 그런 점에서 예리했다. 언어문자로 대답하면 유언(有言)이 되고 벙어리처럼 입 다물고 있으면 무언(無言)이 되어 비난 받을 수밖에 없는 상황이다. 유언이 되었던 무언이 되었던 진실의 반쪽밖에 나타내지 못한다. 여기서 세존께서 그대로 앉아 계신 것은 본래의 자리에서 여여불(如如佛)의 경지를 보여주고 있는 입장이다.

이러한 세존의 모습에 외도는 일초직입여래지(一超直入如來地)하였다. 그렇지만 부처님 제자, 아난은 깜깜하기만 했다. 그럴 수밖에 없었던 것이 저 외도는 백척간두진일보(百尺竿頭進一步)하는 구도심이 있었고, 아난은 그렇지 못하였기 때문이다. 대사일번(大死一番)하지 못하면 확철대오는 요원하다. 외도는 아난 존자의 정신영역을 훨씬 넘어서 있었다. 채찍의 그림자만 보아도 내달릴

줄 아는 양마(良馬)였던 것이다.

 진여본성을 알아차리는 데는 그 어떤 차별도 없음을 보여준다. 진리의 체성(體性)이 그렇게 되어있기 때문이다. 어떤 종교를 믿는가 하는 것이 문제가 아니라 얼마나 더 정신적으로 성숙되어 있는가가 관건이다.

 묵묵히 앉아 답을 대신하는 선가(禪家)의 양구(良久)는 웬만한 경지로써는 수용하기 힘들다. 그 자리는 이미 인식론적 분별을 떠나 절대와 궁극이라는 본래면목(本來面目)과 맞닿아 있다.

 양구의 전형적인 형태는 『유마경(維摩經)』에도 나타나 있는데, 비사리성의 유마장자가 묵연(默然)함으로써 불이법문(不二法門)을 드러내 보였다는 유마일묵(維摩一默)의 이야기는 너무나도 유명하다.

 양구(良久)는 유언(有言)과 무언(無言)을 초월한 모습의 표현이다. 초월하였다 함은 유언(有言) 가운데 무언(無言)이고 무언(無言) 가운데 유언(有言)이라는 뜻이다. 철저한 무아(無我)가 되지 않고서는 할 말이 없는 신성한 자리이다.

Case 32

An Outer-path Practitioner Asks the Buddha

A. Original Case

An outer-path(non-Buddhist) practitioner came and asked the Buddha, "I do not ask with speech, nor do I ask with silence."

The World-honored One just sat there silently.

The practitioner praised him and said, "The World-honored One, with his great love and compassion, has removed all the clouds from my deluded mind, allowing me to reach enlightenment." After bowing properly, he then left.

Ananda soon asked the Buddha, "What did that outer-path practitioner attain that he praised you so much?"

The World-honored One responded, "It is as if a fine, worldly horse runs after having just seen the shadow of the whip."

B. Commentary and Verse

Even though Ananda was the Buddha's disciple, it seems that he couldn't measure up to the insight of an outer-path practitioner. Ven. Mu Mun wrote a verse about the difference between Buddha's disciple and the outer-path practitioner:

> Walking on the blade of a sword,
> Running on the edge of the ice;
> Without using steps or a ladder?
> Let your hands go from the cliff wall.

C. Explanation

The original-essence of truth is that which transcends speech and words, name and form, and any kind of dry cognition? speech and expressions(of truth) are not the truth itself. It's not too much to say that these are just methods for showing us the truth. Therefore, even though the World-honored One gave eighty-four thousand kinds of Dharma speeches, in the end he declared that he had never spoken a single word? though one says innumerable things, as this is only conceptual speech, it's difficult for the truth itself to be revealed.

The outer-path(non-Buddhist) practitioner keenly questioned the Buddha on this point. The situation was such that, if Buddha had answered by speaking, he would have been criticized for using speech, but if he had closed his mouth like a mute, he would have been criticized for keeping silence. Whether he used speech or kept silence, either way, only half of the truth would have been revealed. In this case, the World-honored One sat quietly, just as he was, demonstrating the realm of "suchness", the original point. When the outer-path practitioner saw the Buddha doing this, he "directly entered the realm of the Tathagata." However, Buddha's disciple Ananda was still in the dark. This was unavoidable, since the outer-path practitioner had the sincerity needed to "take one more step off the top of the hundred-foot pole," whereas Ananda did not.

If one cannot "die the great death" (i.e. completely extinguish the ego) then one's path to enlightenment is too far to be reached. The outer-path practitioner's mental capacity was far beyond Ananda's, i.e. he was like a fine horse who runs, having only seen the shadow of the whip. When one perceives the original nature of true-suchness, there is no distinction or discrimination whatsoever, as this is the essential nature of the truth. The key point is not a matter of believing in a particular religion, but of how spiritually mature one becomes. It is difficult to use the Seon-style answer, in other words, replacing an answer with sitting in silence appropriately. This point, which has already transcended theoretical distinctions, touches one's absolute, ultimate original face.

The typical form of this 'silent answer' also appears in the Vimilakirti Sutra, when Vimilakirti of Vaisali demonstrated a 'not-two Dharma speech' by keeping silence; this story of "Vimilakirti's Silent Unity" is very well-known, and shows that this 'Seon-style silence' transcends both speech and silence. This transcendence means that there is silence in speech, and speech in silence. The ego must be thoroughly emptied? this is a sacred spot where nothing can be said unless no-self has been thoroughly attained.

제 33 칙
非心非佛(비심비불)

마음도 아니고 부처도 아니다
Case33: No Mind, No Buddha

가. 본칙(本則)

馬祖, 因僧問, 如何是佛. 祖曰, 非心非佛.

마조(馬祖) 큰스님께 한 스님이 여쭈었다.
"어떤 것이 부처입니까?"
큰스님이 대답하셨다.
"마음도 아니고 부처도 아니다."

나. 평창(評唱) 및 송(頌)

無門曰. 若向者裏見得, 參學事畢.

만약 여기서 알 수 있다면 참선 공부는 다 끝났다.

頌曰. 路逢劍客須呈, 不遇詩人莫獻. 逢人且說三分, 未可全施一片.

무문 스님이 다시 게송으로 말하였다.

"길에서 검객을 만나면 칼을 바쳐야 하리라.
그러나 시인이 아니거든 시를 바치지 말라.
사람을 만나면 삼 할 만 말해야 한다.
마음 속의 것을 완전히 내놓아서는 안 된다."

다. 강론(講論)

 마조 큰스님의 제자, 복우산자재(伏牛山自在) 선사는 즉심즉불(卽心卽佛)은 무병구약(無病救藥)의 구(句)이고 비심비불(非心非佛)은 약병대치(藥病對治)의 구(句)로 보았다.
 즉, 비심비불(非心非佛)은 즉심즉불(卽心卽佛)의 무기(無記)에 빠진 대중들을 전혀 다른 방법으로 제도하는 말씀이다. 여기서 무기(無記)는 아이러니하게도 집착(執着)과 상통하는 말임을 이해할 필요가 있다. 선(禪)에서 늘 경계하는 차별심, 집착심, 고정관념 등은 중생의 병인데 즉심즉불의 화두가 오히려 병의 원인이 되었다면 그때는 정반대의 처방을 내리는 수밖에 없는데 그것이 바로 비심비불인 것이다.
 『전등록』 마조전에는 다음과 같은 이야기가 있다.
 어떤 스님이 마조 큰스님에게 질문을 했다.

"화상(和尙)은 어째서 즉심시불(卽心是佛)이라고 합니까?"
큰스님이 말했다.
"우는 아기의 울음을 그치게 하기 위한 것이다."
"울음을 그친 뒤에는 어떻게 합니까?"
"비심비불(非心非佛)이지."
"이 두 가지 이외의 사람이 오면 어떻게 합니까?"
"그에게는 '중생이 아니다(不是物).'라고 말하리라."
"갑자기 그러한 사람이 오면 어떻게 합니까?"
"그로 하여금 대도를 체득하라고 지시하리라."

잘 살펴보면 결국, 즉심시불과 비심비불은 어느 것이나 집착을 끊도록 하는 법문임을 알 수 있다.
『조당집』에는 다음과 같은 말씀도 있다.

복우 선사가 마조 대사의 심부름으로 편지를 들고 남양혜충 국사를 찾아가니 국사가 물었다.
"마조 대사는 어떤 가르침을 설하는가?"
복우가 대답했다.
"즉심시불이라고 말씀하십니다."

국사가 말했다.

"다시 다른 말은 없었는가?"

복우가 답했다.

"비심비불이라고 하고, 또는 불시심(不是心) 불시불(不是佛) 불시물(不是物)이라고 합니다."

마조 큰스님의 이런 살활자재하는 말씀의 근본취지는 자가보장(自家寶藏)의 보살핌에 있다. 돈오입도요문론(頓悟入道要門論)으로 유명한 대주혜해(大株慧海)가 처음 마조 큰스님을 친견할 때 이야기이다.

"어디서 왔는가?"

"월주 대운사(大雲寺)에서 왔습니다."

"무엇하러 왔는가?"

"불법을 구하러 왔습니다."

"나는 아무것도 없다. 불법이 어찌 나에게 있겠는가! 그대는 왜 자기 집에 있는 보물을 돌보지 않고 밖에서 찾고 있는가?"

"저에게 보배가 있다니 무슨 뜻인지요?"

"지금 나에게 묻고 있는 그대가 보배일세. 왜 밖으로 찾아다니는가?"

 이렇게 마조 큰스님은 부처가 따로 있는 것이 아니라 '마음이 곧 부처'라는 사실을 가르치려고 부단히 노력하였다.
 그런데 이러한 큰 희망의 뉴스가 학인들에게는 차츰차츰 고정관념이 되어갔다. 즉심즉불이 당연한 것으로 수용되면서, 무기의 늪에 빠져 또렷한 자기 의식이 사라지고 말았다.
 마음이란 곳에 강한 집착심이 생긴 결과였다. 그래서 집착과 무기가 양면성의 서로 다른 표현이라고 본다면 이 '비심비불'이야말로 이 둘을 단숨에 날려버리는 화두이다.

Case 33
No Mind, No Buddha

A. Original Case

A monk asked Seon Master Ma Jo, "What is Buddha?"

Ma Jo answered, "No mind, no Buddha."

B. Commentary and Verse

If you can understand this, your Seon practice is completely finished.

Ven. Mu Mun said it again with a verse:
> If you meet a swordsman on the road, present your sword;
> However, don't offer a poem to a non-poet.
> If you meet someone, say only one-third of it;
> You should not completely disclose everything in your mind.

C. Explanation

Seon Master Ma Jo's disciple, the Seon Master known as the "liberated man of Mt. Bok Woo," said the phrase 'Mind is Buddha' was "looking for medicine without a disease," whereas the phrase 'No mind, No Buddha' was "prescribing medicine fit for the disease." In other words, 'No mind, No Buddha' was a phrase to help those practitioners who had become lost in dullness with a completely different method. Ironically, at this point one should understand that 'dullness' has the same meaning as attachment. In Seon, the limitations of the mind of distinctions and attachment, as well as fixed concepts, are the sicknesses of sentient beings, so when the teaching 'Mind itself is Buddha' now becomes the cause of the disease, it's necessary to prescribe the complete opposite medicine? 'No mind, No Buddha.'

The following story about Ma Jo is related in the Record of the Transmission of the Lamp:

A monk asked Seon Master Ma Jo, "Venerable, how can this mind itself be Buddha?"

Ma Jo answered, "To stop the baby from crying."

"After you stop the baby from crying, then what?"

"No mind, no Buddha."

"What if someone came here who took exception to both of these?"

"I would tell him, 'It's not any being.'"

"If that person suddenly came here, what would you do?"

"I would instruct him to attain the Great Way."

If you examine it carefully, you can realize that both 'Mind itself is Buddha' and 'No mind, No Buddha' are Dharma speeches that sever any attachment whatsoever.

In the Record of the Patriarchs, the following story is related:

Seon Master Bok Wu was asked by Seon Master Ma Jo to carry a letter to National Teacher Nam-Yang Hye-Chung, who asked him, "What does Seon Master Ma Jo teach?"

Bok Wu answered, "He teaches 'Mind itself is Buddha.'"

The National Teacher said, "Doesn't he say anything else?"

Bok Wu answered, "He also teaches, 'No mind, no Buddha,' as well as 'Not mind,' 'Not Buddha,' and 'Not anything.'"

The basic reason Seon Master Ma Jo used this kind of living, independent speech was to help people take care of the treasure in their own house.

This is the story of how the well-known Ven. Dae-Ju Hye-Hae, known for his Treatise on the Attainment of Sudden Enlightenment, first encountered Seon Master Ma Jo.

"Where have you come from?"

"I've come from Dae Wun Sa temple in Wol Ju."

"Why have you come here?"

"I've come in search of the Buddha-Dharma."

"I don't have anything. How could I have any Buddha-Dharma?! Why aren't you taking care of the treasure in your own house instead of searching outside?"

"What do you mean that I have a treasure?"

"Now, that which is asking me is your treasure! Why are you going around looking outside?"

In this way, Seon Master Ma Jo ceaselessly tried to teach that Buddha is not something separate, that 'This mind itself is

Buddha.' However, this kind of encouraging teaching gradually became a fixed concept for his disciples; since they used 'Mind is Buddha' as a natural, obvious thing, they became immersed in the swamp of dullness, and their clear self-awareness disappeared. The result was that a strong attachment to this "mind" arose. Therefore, if we look at both attachment and dullness as two sides of the same coin, then the question 'No mind, no Buddha' blows both of them completely away with one breath.

제 34 칙
智不是道(지불시도)

지혜는 도가 아니다
Case34: Wisdom is Not the Way

가. 본칙(本則)

南泉云, 心不是佛, 智不是道.

   남전 큰스님이 말씀하셨다.
   "마음은 부처가 아니요, 지혜는 도가 아니니라."

나. 평창(評唱) 및 송(頌)

無門曰. 南泉可謂, 老不識羞. 纔開臭口, 家醜外揚. 然雖如是, 知恩者少.

   말하자면, 남전은 이제 늙어서 부끄러움을 모르는구나. 잠깐 입을 열었는데 집안의 더러운 모습이 밖으로 다 드러났다. 그러나 비록 이와 같다 할지라도 그 은혜를 아는 놈이 적구나.

頌曰. 天晴日頭出, 雨下地上濕. 盡情都說了, 只恐信不及.

   무문 스님이 다시 게송으로 말하였다.

"하늘이 맑으니 해가 솟고,
비가 오니 대지가 젖는구나.
마음을 다해 설명해 주어도,
믿어주지 않을까 걱정이로다."

다. 강론(講論)

『무문관』에 등장하는 남전보원(南泉普願) 관련 화두는 총 4개이다. 제 4칙의 남전참묘(南泉斬猫), 제 19칙의 평상시도(平常是道), 제 27칙의 불시심불(不是心佛), 제 34칙의 지불시도(智不是道)가 그것인데, 이 모두가 분별심과 집착을 떨쳐버리라는 공통된 주문을 하고 있다.

『조당집』 제 15권에 마조(馬祖)의 제자 동사여회(東寺如會)는 마조 대사가 즉심시불(卽心是佛)을 설하였다고 주장하는 당시의 사람들을 보고 '부처가 어디에 머무르기에 마음이라고 하는가? 마음이란 환화(幻化)와 같은 것인데, 부처를 비방함이 너무 심하다.'고 말하면서 다음과 같이 외쳤다.

"마음은 부처가 아니요, 지혜는 도가 아니다. 칼을 잃어버린 지 오래인데, 이제야 뱃전에 표시를 하는가."

이는 무문관 본 제 34칙의 화두와 꼭 일치하는 이야기로서 모두가 마조의 즉심시불(卽心是佛) 등에 대한 논쟁을 종식시키고 말에 집착하는 병폐를 지적하기 위함이다.

즉, '이 마음이 부처다.'라고 주장하면 마음에 집착하고 '지혜가 도이다.'라고 주장하면 도에 집착하는 범부들을 위해서, 남전 보원이나 동사여회는 '마음은 부처가 아니고, 지혜는 도가 아니다.'라고 주장하게 된 것이다.

마조 스님이 스스로 뱉은 즉심시불(卽心是佛)에 대해서 후일 정반대 의미의 비심비불(非心非佛)을 주장하고, 나아가 그의 제자 남전 스님이 심불시불(心不是佛), 지불시도(智不是道)를 말하는 것은 엄청난 모순과 어패가 있다. 이는 곧 분별과 망념에 의한 집착을 경계하는 역설적 가르침이다.

살불살조(殺佛殺祖)의 반항기와 예리한 정신을 갖지 않으면 소위 마음 닦는 이는 언제나 스스로 위험해진다. 새롭고 독창적이지 못한 것은 예속이요 우상의 노예라는 것이 선(禪)의 일관된 입장이다.

돌로 만든 계집(石女), 나무로 만든 사람(木人)에게 까지도 생명력을 불어 넣을 수 있어야 진정 깨어있는 수행자이다. 구멍 없는 피리(無孔笛)를 불고, 줄 없는 거문고(沒絃琴)를 탈려면 현재의 사고방식을 죄다 부수지 않으면 안 된다. 그림자 없는 나무(無影樹) 아래에서 한여름 편히 낮잠 잘 수 있으려면 번뇌의 밑천인 일체 알음알이를 내려 놓아야 한다.

'마음이 부처이고 지혜는 도이다.' 라는 선입견을 가지고는 자유로울 수 없다. 그러한 지식의 찌꺼기에 오염되면 자성(自性)의 청정성(淸淨性)이 떨어진다.

화두의 실천력은 탈고정관념(脫固定觀念)에 있으므로 마음이 부처이고 지혜가 도인 사람에게는 당연히 마음은 부처가 될 수 없고 지혜는 도가 될 수 없다.

이쯤 되면 자연 그대로 볼 줄 안다. 산은 높고 강은 길게 흐른다. 꽃은 붉고 버드나무 가지는 푸르다. 하늘 밝으면 해가 솟고 비가 오면 대지가 젖는다. 삼독심의 안개가 걷히었으므로 온 세상이 있는 그대로 환하게 드러난다.

이쯤 되면 믿어주지 않을까 걱정할 것도 전혀 없다.

Case 34
Wisdom is Not the Way

A. Original Case

Seon Master Nam Jeon said, "Mind is not Buddha; wisdom is not the Way."

B. Commentary and Verse

In a word, Nam Jeon has now grown old, and knows no shame. He opened his mouth for a moment and showed the dirty face of his family outside. Though he did this, there were few who knew his kindness.

Ven. Mu Mun said it again with a verse:
    As the sky is clear, the sun shines brightly;
    When rain comes, the earth is moist.
    Though he explains with a most sincere mind,
    He worries he will not be believed.

C. Explanation

A total of four cases appear in the Gateless Gate which are related to Nam-Jeon Bo-Won: Case 4, "Master Nam Jeon Cuts the Cat," Case 19, "Everyday Mind is the Way," Case 27, "Not Mind, Not Buddha" and Case 34 "Wisdom is Not the Way." They all have the common theme of completely ridding oneself of attachments and relative distinctions. In volume 15 of the Records of the Patriarchs, Ma Jo's disciple Dong-Sa Yeo-Hwe asked those people of the era promoting Seon Master Ma Jo's teaching 'This mind itself is Buddha,' "Where does Buddha reside that you call it mind? Mind is like an illusion? you go too far by slandering the Buddha." He then proclaimed, "Mind is not Buddha, wisdom is not the Way. You lost the knife long ago, and now you are marking on the bow of the ship."

This story is in complete accord with the aforementioned case 34 of the Gateless Gate, as it points out the sickness of attaching to speech, and puts an end to all the arguments concerning Ma Jo's 'This mind itself is Buddha.' In other words, for all the common people advocating 'Mind itself is Buddha' and attaching to mind, or promoting 'Wisdom is the Way' and attaching to the Way, Nam-Jeon Bo-Won and Dong-Sa Yeo-Hwe taught "Mind is not Buddha; wisdom is not the Way."

Ven. Ma Jo himself proclaimed the teaching 'Mind itself is Buddha,' but then later advocated the complete opposite teaching 'No mind, No Buddha.' His disciple Nam Jeon went on to proclaim, 'Mind is not Buddha,' and 'Wisdom is not the way,' which were huge contradictions? these were paradoxical teachings to guard against attachments due to relative distinctions and delusions.

If one who does not cultivate the rebellious spirit and keen-eyed mind to "Kill the Buddha and Patriarchs," he can become a danger to himself. The Seon tradition has the consistent opinion that anything which is not original and creative is dependent? enslaved to some false idol(idea). A truly awakened practitioner is one who can instill vitality with even a stone girl or wooden man. If you want to play the flute with no holes or the harp with no strings, you have to completely smash through your current way of thinking. If you want to take a comfortable nap in the middle of summer under the tree with no shadow, you have to put down all intellectual understanding, which is the very root of delusion.

You cannot be free while holding the Seon view that 'Mind is Buddha; wisdom is the Way.' If the residue of that understanding taints you, the pure and clear nature of your true-self is lost. As the practice of keeping a Great Question involves freeing oneself from conceptual thinking, to the person who believes 'Mind is Buddha; wisdom is the Way,' naturally mind cannot become Buddha and wisdom cannot become the Way. When this happens, one can see nature just as it is? the mountain is high and the river flows into the distance; the flower is red and the willow-branch is green. When the sky is clear, the sun shines brightly; when rain comes, the earth is moist. When the fog of the three poisons(desire, anger, ignorance) is removed, the whole world is clearly revealed, just as it is. When this happens, there is no reason to worry if someone believes you or not.

제 35 칙

倩女離魂(천녀이혼)

천녀의 혼이 나가다

Case35: Cheon Nyeo's Soul Has Left

가. 본칙(本則)

五祖問僧云, 倩女離魂, 那箇是眞底.

오조법연(五祖法演) 큰스님이 한 스님에게 물었다.
"천녀(천女)의 혼이 떠났는데, 그렇다면 어느 쪽이 진짜인가?"

나. 평창(評唱) 및 송(頌)

無門曰. 若向者裏悟得眞底, 便知出殼入殼, 如宿旅舍. 其或未然, 切莫亂走. 驀然地水火風一散, 如落湯螃蟹, 七手八脚. 那時莫言不道.

 만약 여기에서 진짜를 깨달아 알 수 있다면, 육체의 껍데기를 들고 나는 것이 마치 여관을 들어갔다 나오는 것과도 같은 것임을 알 것이다. 혹시나 아직도 알지 못한다면 결코 날뛰어서는 안 된다. 돌연히 지(地)·수(水)·화(火)·풍(風)의 사대(四大)가 흩어지는 그날이 오면, 뜨거운 물속에 빠진 게처럼 일곱 개의 팔과 여덟 개의 다리를 버둥거리며 괴로워 할 것이니, 그때에서야 말해주지 않았다고 원망하지 말지어다.

頌曰. 雲月是同, 溪山各異. 萬福萬福, 是一是二.

무문 스님이 다시 게송으로 말하였다.
"구름사이 달은 하나인데
비추는 계곡과 산은 다 다르도다.
좋고 좋도다.
이것은 하나인가, 둘인가?"

다. 강론(講論)

본 화두는 진현우(陳玄祐)가 지은 당대(唐代)의 전기(傳奇) 『리혼기(離魂記)』의 이야기에서 끌어왔다.
줄거리는 다음과 같다.

중국 형양(衡陽)땅에 장감(張鑑)이라는 사람이 살고 있었는데, 그에게는 천낭(倩娘)이라는 예쁜 딸이 하나 있었다.
장감은 평소 외조카인 왕주(王宙)에게 색시감으로 천낭을 데려

가라 하였다. 그런데 그 지방의 고관이 천낭의 미모에 반해 혼인을 요청하자 장감은 이전의 약속을 잊고 그에게 천낭을 시집보내려 하였다.

서로를 연모하던 왕주와 천낭은 상심하였고, 왕주는 천낭을 잊기 위해 그곳을 떠나기로 결심하기에 이르렀다. 그래서 왕주가 막 배를 타고 떠나려 하는데 천낭이 그곳에 나타나서 둘은 함께 머나먼 촉(蜀)나라로 도피하여 5년을 애기도 낳으며 재미나게 살았다.

그런 세월 중 어느 날부터 천낭이 시름시름 앓기 시작했는데, 그들은 부모 마음을 아프게 한 과보로 병이 되었다고 생각하여 부모님께 정식으로 결혼 승낙을 얻으려고 고향으로 향했다.

고향집 근처 나루에 도착한 왕주는 천낭을 배에 남겨두고 장감에게 가서 그동안의 사정을 이야기하였다. 그러자 장감은 놀라며 천낭은 규방에서 오랫동안 앓아누워 있는데 무슨 소리냐는 것이었다.

집안 식구들이 모두 규방으로 달려가 자초지종을 전하는 사이 천낭은 생기를 되찾고 있었다. 장감은 배로 사람을 보내어 또다른 천낭을 집으로 데려오게 하였다.

수레를 타고 온 천낭과 규방에서 걸어 나온 천낭이 마당에서 마주치는 순간, 둘은 하나로 합쳐지는 것이었다.

장감이 천낭에게 이것이 도대체 어떻게 된 것이냐고 물으니, 천낭은 "서방님을 차마 혼자 떠나 보낼 수가 없어서 그때 제 혼이 서방님을 따라서 배에 올랐던 것 같습니다."라고 말하였다.

장감과 그의 식구들은 그제서야 규방의 천낭이 시름시름 앓으며 정신없는 사람처럼 과거 5년을 지낸 것이 천낭의 혼이 왕주를 따라 갔었기 때문에 일어난 일임을 알았다.

이 이야기에서 진(眞), 위(僞)를 가린다는 것은 곧 분별심을 일으킨 결과이다.

차별계를 버리고 평등체에 들어가려면 무상(無常)이고 무아(無俄)인 공(空)의 세계를 터득하지 않으면 안 된다.

진, 위가 따로 존재하는 것이 아니라 그 바탕은 공(空)이다.

신심일여(身心一如)이며 번뇌즉보리(煩惱卽菩提)요, 생사즉열반(生死則涅槃)이다.

무명(無明)의 실성(實性)이 곧 불성(佛性)이고, 환화공신(幻化空身)이 곧 법신(法身)이다.

진망불이(眞妄不二)요, 천지동근(天地同根)이며, 만물일체(萬物一切)이니 생명의 근원인 불성(佛性) 자리는 일체의 차별경계를 떠나있다.

영육이원론(靈肉二元論)이 아니라 심신일여론(心身一如論)의 입장에서 본칙을 해결해야 한다.

Case 35
Cheon Nyeo's Soul Has Left

A. Original Case

Seon Master Oh-Jo Beop-Yeon asked a monk, "Cheon Nyeo's soul has left her, so which one was the real Cheon Nyeo?"

B. Commentary and Verse

If you can realize which one is real here, you will know that the birth and death of this shell of a body is like entering and leaving a hotel. If you still haven't realized that yet, you should not boast of yourself. When the day comes that the four great elements of earth, water, fire and air are scattered, it's like when a crab is immerse in hot water? its seven arms and eight legs flail about in agony. At that time, don't blame me for not having told you!

Ven. Mu Mun said it again with a verse:
    Between the clouds, there is one moon;
    The illuminated valleys and mountains

Are all distinct - beautiful, so beautiful!

Are they one or two?

C. Explanation

The original episode was taken from a story in the Tang Dynasty Records of Soul Departures, written by Hyeon-Wu Jin. A synopsis of the story is as follows:

A man named Jang Gam lived in the Chinese land of Hyeong Yang, and he had one beautiful daughter named Cheon Nang. Jang Gam often used to promise his nephew Wang Ju that he could marry his daughter. However, a government official in the area was captivated by Cheon Nang's beauty and asked for her hand in marriage; Jang Gam forgot about his previous commitment and sent her off to be married to him.

Wang Ju and Cheon Nang were broken-hearted, as they were in love with each other? he eventually told Cheon Nang that he had decided to leave that place in order to put her out of his mind. Wang Ju boarded a ship and was about to depart, when suddenly Cheon Nang appeared, and the two of them escaped together to the faraway land of Chok. They lived happily there for the next five years and had a child.

During this time, one day Cheon Nang began to get sicker and sicker, and believing that this sickness was retribution for the pain they had caused their parents, they headed home in order to formally ask their parents' permission for marriage. After arriving in the port near his hometown, Wang Ju left Cheon Nang in the boat and went to his father Jang Gam to explain what had happened all that while. Jang Gam was astonished? for a long time, Cheon Nang had been lying sick for in the women's quarters? what was he talking about?! All of the family members ran to the women's quarters? while the story was being told, Cheon Nang had suddenly regained her strength. Jang Gam sent someone to the boat to bring home the other Cheon Nang.

At the moment when the other Cheon Nang came home by cart and the Cheon Nang who was walking out of the room met face to face in the yard, the two of them became one. When Jang Gam asked her how in the world this could have happened, Cheon Nang answered, "I couldn't bear to let my husband go alone, so it seems my soul followed him onto the ship." At this point, Jang Gam and his family realized what had happened?

Cheon Nang had been constantly sick in the room, like someone in a daze, because her spirit had followed Wang Ju.

The discrimination between true and false in this story is a direct result of the mind of relative distinctions arising. If one wants to discard this realm of discrimination and enter the level of absolute equality, one must attain the world of emptiness, the realm of no permanent self. "True" and "false" do not exist separately? their essence is emptiness. The body and mind are not separate? delusion is none other than Bodhi, and life and death are not different from Nirvana.

The true nature of ignorance is none other than the Buddha-nature; the illusory, empty body is none other than the Dharmakaya(Dharma body). True and false are not separate? heaven and earth have the same origin, all of creation is one body. The realm of Buddha-nature, the root of life, transcends all relative distinctions. This episode should be resolved from the point of view that body and soul are not separate principles? mind and body are one and the same.

제 36 칙
路逢達道(노봉달도)

길에서 도인을 만나면

Case36:
When you Meet a Sage on the Path

가. 본칙(本則)

五祖曰, 路逢達道人, 不將語默對. 且道, 將甚麼對.

 오조법연(五祖法演) 큰스님이 말씀하셨다.
 "길에서 도인(道人)을 만나면, 말로써도 대답하지 말고 침묵으로써도 대답하지 말라. 자아, 일러보아라. 그러면 어떻게 응대해야 하겠는가?"

나. 평창(評唱) 및 송(頌)

無門曰. 若向者裏對得親切, 不妨慶快. 其或未然, 也須一切處著眼.

 만약 여기에 대해 딱맞게 대답할 수 있다면 참으로 즐겁고 기쁘지 않겠는가? 아직 그렇지 못하다면, 모름지기 어느 곳에서나 착안(著眼)코저 노력하여야 한다.

頌曰. 路逢達道人, 不將語默對. 攔腮劈面拳, 直下會便會.

무문 스님이 다시 게송으로 말하였다.

"길에서 도인을 만나거든,

말로도 침묵으로도 대하지 말라.

주먹으로 뺨따귀를 올려 붙여라.

그 순간에 알 사람은 바로 안다."

다. 강론(講論)

『무문관』에 오조법연 관련 화두는 4번이나 등장한다. 제 35칙, 제 36칙, 제 38칙, 제 45칙이 그것이다.

무문 스님이 이 오조법연 선사의 법손이었기 때문에 이처럼 많은 배려를 한 것으로 보인다. 그렇지만 객관적으로 보더라도 오조 스님은 임제종의 중흥조(中興祖)라 불릴만큼 특출한 인물임에는 틀림없다.

홍인 대사가 주석했던 동산(東山)을 일컬어 오조산이라 하였는데, 법연 스님이 그곳에서 오래 머물렀기 때문에 오조라는 대단한 호칭을 얻게 된 것이다.

본 36칙 노봉달도(路逢達道)는 그리 생소한 화두는 아니다. 제 24칙의 이각어언(離却語言)의 화두와 제 32칙의 외도문불(外道問

佛)의 화두와 그 성격이 비슷하다.

'길에서 도인을 만나면 어떻게 응대할 것인가?', 여기서 오조 법연이 요구하는 것은 소위 말후구(末後句)의 대답이다. 말후구는 구경(究竟)으로서 곧 즉여(卽如)를 말한다.

무심(無心)한 인식상태인 여여(如如)와 무심의 작용인 즉여(卽如)의 힘은 부단한 정진 끝에 얻어지는데 이 즉여가 말후구이다.

'최후의 구절' 말후구는 그 어떤 것이라도 관계없다. 무분별후득지(無分別後得智)의 일체작용은 진리(眞理)에 그대로 부합된다.

다음 얘기들은 그 좋은 예이다.

어떤 스님이 설봉 화상에게 질문했다.

"고인(古人)이 노봉달도인(路逢達道人) 막장어묵대(莫將語默對)라고 하였는데, 그러면 어떻게 상대해야 합니까?"

선사는 대답하기를 "차를 마시게."라고 하였다.

『조주어록』 하권(下卷)에는 이런 얘기가 있다.

조주 선사는 임제가 참문하러 왔을 때 마침 발을 씻고 있었다.

임제가 "조사가 서쪽에서 오신 의도가 무엇입니까?"하고 물으니 조주 선사가 대답하였다.

"지금 막 발을 씻고 있는 참이다."

임제는 앞으로 다가가서 귀를 기울였다. 조주가 말했다.

"알았으면 그것으로 좋고, 알지 못했으면 또 다시 입을 벌리지 말라."

유록화홍(柳綠花紅) 청산유수(靑山流水)가 자성(自性)의 드러남인 것처럼 말을 하던, 말을 하지 않던 도인의 경계는 다 구경인 말후구이다. 즉, 행주좌와 어묵동정이 모두 불사(佛事)이다. 그리고 선(禪) 아닌 것이 없다.

말하면서도 말한 바 없이하고 말하지 않으면서도 우뢰와 같은 메시지를 보낸다. 상을 벗어버리고 상대와 모두 하나가 되었기 때문이다.

자타일여(自他一如)라 하였던가!

이 자리에서는 말하는 자체가 침묵이요, 침묵하면서도 장광설을 퍼붓는다.

부처님께서도 『열반경』에서 일자불설(一字不說)을 말씀하신바 있다.

무문 스님이 일체처에 착안(着眼) 하라고 한 그 착안의 자리는 시비, 선악의 분별을 떠난 몰입의 경지이다. 그리하여 상대와

100% 합일하면 마치 사물이 명경(明鏡)의 대(臺)를 의식하지 않고 그대로 빨려드는 것과 같다.

산을 만나면 산이 되고, 강을 만나면 강이 된다. 아이를 만나면 아이가 되고, 거지를 만나면 거지가 된다.

어묵(語默)의 차별 경계에 떨어지지 않고 도인을 상대하는 방법은 아주 간단하다. 그리고 거룩하다.

Case 36

When you Meet a Sage on the Path

A. Original Case

Seon Master Oh-Jo Beop-Yeon said, "If you meet a man of the Way on the path, do not answer him with words, nor with silence. So, tell me! How should you respond to him?"

B. Commentary and Verse

Wouldn't it truly be joyous and gratifying if you could answer correctly in this situation? But if you can't, by all means you should really try to pay attention everywhere.

Ven. Mu Mun said it again with a verse:
 Meeting a man of the Way on the path,
 Don't greet him with either words or silence;
 Punch him in the face with your fist,
 At that moment, those who realize it will know it right away.

C. Explanation

Episodes connected with Oh-Jo Beop-Yeon are introduced four times in the Gateless Gate, in cases 35, 36, 38 and 45? since Ven. Mu Mun was the Dharma-grandson of Oh-Jo Beop-Yeon, it seems he held him in high regard. However, even objectively, Ven. Oh-Jo was a very prominent individual, to the extent that he is known as the one who revitalized the Linchi school during its decline. Seon Master Hong In renamed the mountain Dong Sahn, where he was head of the community, Oh Jo Sahn; Ven. Beop Yeon then received this name as his honorable title, as he resided there for a long time. Case 36, "When You Meet a Sage on the Path," is not such an unusual case. The characteristics of this episode are similar to case no. 24, "Severing Speech," and case no. 32, "An Outer-path Practitioner Asks the Buddha." If you meet a man of the Way on the path, how should you respond to him? Oh-Jo Beop-Yeon is looking for the so-called 'last word' style of answer here.

As the 'last word' is the final, the ultimate, it refers to true suchness(the realm of 'just-like-this'). The state of awareness, of no-mind, is 'like-this,' whereas its function is just-like-this, true suchness? one attains the energy of true suchness at the completion of concentrated practice. This true suchness is none other than the last word. The last word, the 'final phrase,' has nothing to do with this at all. Every function of this awareness that is attained when there are no relative distinctions is in accordance with the truth, just as it is. This next story is a good example of this.

A monk asked Seon Master Seol Bong, "An ancient master said, 'If you meet a man of the Way on the road, you should greet him with neither speech nor silence.' But how should one greet him?" The Seon Master answered, "Drink tea."

The following story is related in the second volume of the Records of Joju. Linchi came to seek instruction from Seon Master Joju, who was just then washing his feet.

Linchi asked him, "What was the purpose of the patriarch (Bodhidharma) coming from the West(India)?"

Seon Master Joju answered, "I am just now washing my feet."

Linchi came closer and cocked his ears.

Joju said, "If you understood from that, great; if you didn't understand, don't open your mouth again."

Just like "The willow is green, the flower is red," and "The mountain is blue, the water is flowing," reveal self-nature, whether an enlightened sage uses speech or not, it is all the last, ultimate word. That is to say, whether walking, resting, sitting or lying down, whether speaking, keeping silence, moving or sitting quietly, everything is Buddhism? there is nothing that is not Seon.

While speaking, do not say anything; while not speaking, send a message like a thunderclap. Completely discard relative objects, as all opposites become one.

Self and others are actually one!

At this point, speech itself is silence, and even while keeping silence, lengthy speeches come pouring out. In the Nirvana Sutra Buddha said "I never spoke a single word." Ven. Mu Mun says "pay attention everywhere," this point of attention is the stage of complete immersion which transcends the relative distinctions of good and bad, or right and wrong. Therefore, if all opposites are completely united, it's as if images are reflected by the mirror, regardless of the mirror's stand.

If you encounter a mountain, you become a mountain; if you encounter a river, you become a river. If you meet a child, you become a child; if you meet a beggar, you become a beggar.

Without falling into the discrimination between speech and silence, the way to encounter a man of the Way is very simple and sacred.

제 37 칙
庭前柏樹(정전백수)

뜰 앞의 측백나무

Case37:
The Cypress Tree in Front of the Courtyard

가. 본칙(本則)

趙州, 因僧問, 如何是祖師西來意. 州云, 庭前柏樹子.

조주 큰스님에게 한 스님이 찾아와 물었다.
"달마대사가 서쪽에서 온 뜻이 무엇입니까?"
큰스님이 대답하셨다.
"뜰 앞의 측백나무니라."

나. 평창(評唱) 및 송(頌)

無門曰. 若向趙州答處見得親切, 前無釋迦, 後無彌勒.

만약 조주가 대답한 그 의미를 딱 들어맞게 알아차릴 수 있다면 앞에 석가모니 부처도 없고 뒤에 미륵 부처도 없을 것이다.

頌曰. 言無展事, 語不投機. 承言者喪, 滯句者迷.

무문 스님이 다시 게송으로 말하였다.

"말은 사실을 다 나타낼 수 없고,
말은 적확(的確)하게 드러내 주지도 않는다.
말을 쫓아가는 자는 잃게 될 것이고,
말 구절에 걸리는 자는 헤매게 되리라."

다. 강론(講論)

조주 큰스님이 만년에 주석하셨던 관음원의 지금 이름은 백림 선사(柏林禪寺)이다.

필자가 중국 선종 사찰을 순례하면서 가장 먼저 들른 곳이 백림 선사였는데 경내에서 한참 동안이나 잣나무를 찾았다. 본칙에서 보여지는 것처럼 '여하시조사서래의(如何是祖師西來意)'에 대한 답이 '정전백수자(庭前柏樹子)'인데 이 정전백수자가 한국의 스님들에게는 '뜰 앞의 잣나무'로 통용되어 왔다. 그런데 백림 선사에서 잣나무는 그림자도 보이지 않았다. 큰 고목나무가 절 마당 여기저기 서 있어서 다가가 살펴보니 '柏' 자(子)의 패찰이 달려 있었다. 1800년 수령의 나무도 있었는데 그 나무들은 다름 아닌 측백나무였다.

백림 선사의 사명(寺名)에 나타나는 의미는 '측백나무 숲 참선

도량'이다. 그런데 우리 한국에서는 아직도 대부분 사람들이 측백나무를 잣나무로 오인하고 있다. 그러니까 '柏(백)'자(子)의 실체를 전혀 몰랐던 것이다.

혹자는 그것이 측백나무가 되었든 잣나무가 되었든 다 마찬가지 아니냐고 한다. 그렇게 말하는 것이 더 웃긴다. 화두참선의 소재는 현재적이고 사실적이어야 하는데 앞에 측백나무를 두고 잣나무라고 말한다면 아주 우스꽝스러운 일이 아닌가!

그러한 측면에서 보면, 특수한 상황에서 만들어진 화두를 그 현장에도 없었던 전혀 다른 제 삼자가 그저 빌려 쓴다는 것이 얼마나 무리한 일인지 짐작 할 수 있다.

사실 1700 화두 가운데 극히 몇 개의 화두를 제하고는 화두로서 큰 가치가 없다. 비현재적, 비사실적이기 때문이다. 그렇다면 기존의 화두를 어떻게 활용할 것인가?

기존의 화두가 정신수준, 깨달음의 근기를 가늠하는 잣대로는 가능하다. 즉, 실제참구의 소재로서의 생명력은 떨어지지만 공부점검의 소재로는 별 문제가 없다.

각설하고, 본칙의 원 주제로 돌아가서 살펴본다.

상식적으로 말한다면, 달마가 서쪽에서 온 뜻은 '심법(心法)을 전하여 중생을 구제하기 위함' 이었다. 조금 더 차원을 높여서 '마음이 곧 부처이다.', '평상심이 도다.', '너의 본 마음이다.' 라는 등으로 답할 수도 있다.

그런데 여기서는 이러한 상식을 넘어서서 '뜰 앞의 측백나무'라고 하니 기가 막힌다. 그러자 앞에 앉은 제자가 또 묻는다.

본칙에서는 생략되어 있지만 오등회원(五燈會元)에서는 다음과 같은 뒷 얘기가 소개되고 있다.

스님이 다시 말했다.
"스님, 대상(對象)으로서 보이지 마십시오."
조주 스님이 응대했다.
"나는 대상을 들어 설명한 바가 없네."
다시 그 스님이 여쭈었다.
"무엇이 조사가 서쪽에서 온 뜻입니까?"
조주 큰스님이 대답했다.
"뜰 앞의 측백나무니라."

조주 큰스님은 인식주관도 인식대상도 모두 사라져 버린, 오로지 측백나무의 또렷한 자각만이 있을 뿐임을 말씀하셨는데 공부가 덜 된 사람은 쓸데없는 분별심을 내고 앉았다.

'정전백수자'의 화두가 만들어진 현재 백림선사는 스님들이 간화선은 하지 않고 수식관을 하고 있다.

깊이 생각해 볼 문제다.

Case 37

The Cypress Tree in Front of the Courtyard

A. Original Case

A monk came and asked Seon Master Joju, "What is the meaning of Bodhidharma coming from the West(India)?"

The Seon Master answered, "The cypress tree in front of the courtyard."

B. Commentary and Verse

If you can precisely grasp the meaning of Joju's answer, there is no Sakyamuni Buddha before you and no Maitreya Buddha later.

Ven. Mu Mun said it again with a verse:
  Words cannot show the whole truth,
  Speech does not reveal it with certainty;
  One who follows words will be lost,

One who is caught by phrases will be confused.

C. Explanation

The Gwanum temple, of which Joju was the head during the latter part of his life, is now called Baekrim Seon Temple. When this author was making a pilgrimage to Chinese Seon temples, the very first place I visited was Baekrim Seon temple; after a long search, I found the cypress tree. Like is shown in the original case, to the question, "Why did the patriarch come from the West?" Joju answered, "The cypress tree in front of the courtyard." This has been commonly passed down to Korean monks as the "pine tree in front of the courtyard." However, at Baekrim Seon Temple, even the shadow of a pine tree could not be seen. Giant, ancient trees stood here and there in the temple courtyard, and when I looked closely, there was a tablet with the character "cypress" hanging there. There were also some trees that were eighteen-hundred years old that were none other than cypress trees. The name of the temple Baekrim Seon-sa also has the meaning, "Cypress Forest Seon Temple." However, most people in Korea still mistake the cypress tree for a pine tree, so they don't know at all about the existence of this character reading "cypress." Perhaps somebody might wonder, whether it's a cypress tree or a pine tree? they're all similar, aren't they? Speaking like that is even more ridiculous!

The subject matter of a Great Question in Seon Meditation must be based on the current situation and truth in this moment? so isn't it completely ridiculous if you disregard the cypress tree and instead call it a pine tree. Seen from that point of view, one can get a sense of how illogical it is for a completely different third party to use a question that was created in a specific situation, especially when the situation itself no longer exists. Actually, out of the 1,700 cases, except for a very few, most episodes do not have significant value as Great Questions, since they are not based on the current situation and reality. Therefore, how to make use of these preexisting cases?

It is possible to utilize the standard cases as criteria for evaluating one's level of spiritual development or capacity for enlightenment. That is to say, their efficacy may have decreased as far as being subject matters for the investigation of truth, but there is no problem with using them to check one's practice.

Moving on, let's turn to the main subject of the case and take a look at it. According to common sense, Bodhidharma came from the West(India) in order to transmit the Dharma of the Mind and save sentient beings. Taking it to a higher level, one might answer, "Mind itself is Buddha," "Everyday mind is the Way," or "Your original-mind is the Way," and so on.

However, at this point when you transcend common sense, saying "The cypress tree in front of the courtyard" is beyond ones imagination. Therefore, the disciple sitting in front asked once again. It was omitted from the original story, but in the Five Lantern Records, the following story is introduced.

The monk asked again, "Venerable, don't make it seem like a relative object."

Joju answered, "I didn't use any object when I explained it to you."

The monk asked again, "What is the reason Bodhidharma came from the West?"

Seon Master Joju answered, "The cypress tree in front of the courtyard."

As all of Seon Master Joju's subjective and objective

understanding has disappeared, he spoke of only a clear awakening to the cypress tree; however, the inferior practitioner was absorbed in making useless distinctions.

The monks who currently reside at Baekrim Seon Temple, where the question of "The cypress tree in the garden," was created, do not engage in Seon practice and investigation, but instead ruminate using dry cognition. This is a problem that should be deeply considered.

제 38 칙
牛過窓櫺(우과창령)

소가 창틀을 빠져 나가다

Case38:
A Buffalo Passes Through a Window

가. 본칙(本則)

五祖曰, 譬如水牯牛過窓欞, 頭角四蹄都過了, 因甚麼尾巴過不得.

　오조법연(五祖法演) 스님이 말씀하셨다.
　"비유컨대 물소가 창틀을 빠져 나간다고 하자. 머리와 뿔, 네 발굽은 다 나갔는데 어찌하여 꼬리는 빠져 나가지 못하는가?"

나. 평창(評唱) 및 송(頌)

無門曰. 若向者裏顚倒著得一隻眼, 下得一轉語, 可以上報四恩, 下資三有. 其或未然, 更須照顧尾巴始得.

　만약 이 말씀의 깊은 뜻을 뒤집어서 지혜의 눈을 갖다 대고 한 마디를 할 수 있다면 위로는 네 가지 은혜에 보답하게 되고, 아래로는 삼계의 중생을 교화하게 되리라.
　혹시 아직 그렇지 못하다면 다시 꼬리를 비추어 되돌아보아야 한다.

頌曰. 過去墮坑塹, 回來却劫被壞. 者些尾巴子, 直是甚奇怪.

무문 스님이 다시 게송으로 말하였다.
"지나가면 구렁텅이에 빠지고,
되돌아오면 도리어 부서져 버릴 터
이 꼬리란 놈이여,
정말 괴상망측한 놈이로구나."

다. 강론(講論)

이 공안의 내용은 경전에 그 근거를 둔 듯하다. 『불설급고장자여득도인연경(佛說給孤長者如得道因緣經)』에 보면 흘율지왕(訖栗枳王)이 하룻밤에 열 가지의 꿈을 꾸었는데 그 중에서 코끼리가 창문을 빠져나오는 이야기가 등장한다.

"왕의 꿈에 한 마리의 큰 코끼리가 창살 사이로 빠져 나오는 것이 보였다. 그런데 몸통은 빠져 나왔는데 꼬리가 그만 창문에 걸려버렸다.

그것은 마치, 부처님께서 열반에 드신 후에도 많은 바라문과 장자, 거사, 혹은 남자 혹은 여자가 권속을 모두 버리고 출가하여 불도(佛道)를 닦았지만, 그들은 아직도 마음이 명예와 이익 등 세속에 대한 욕심과 탐착에서 벗어나지 못하고 있는 것과 같다."

이처럼 경전에서는 큰 코끼리 즉, 대상(大象)을 말했는데 본칙에서는 대신 물소 즉, 수고우(水牯牛)를 등장시키고 있다. 몸은 창틀을 빠져 나갔는데 꼬리가 빠져나가지 못했다는 것은 출가자가 마음 속에 명예와 이익 등 세속적인 가치관을 완전히 떨쳐버리지 못함을 비유했다고 볼 수 있다.

출가에는 세 가지 또는 세 단계의 출가가 있다.

가장 먼저는 육친출가(六親出家)이다. 부모, 형제 등 가까운 친인척을 떠나는 것이다. 실타래처럼 얽힌 육친의 인연을 벗어나는 일은 대단히 어렵다. 꼭 그리해야 하는 이유는 혈육에 대한 집착을 끊고서야 전문 수행을 할 수 있기 때문이다.

둘째는 오온출가(五蘊出家)이다. 자아 즉, 자신에 대한 집착을 떠나는 것이다. 범부중생이 삼독심(三毒心)을 일으키는 것은 자기애(自己愛)로부터 비롯된다. 출가자는 삼의일발(三衣一鉢)을 기본으로 일종식(一種食)공양, 무문관(無門關) 정진 등 고도의 수행도

기꺼이 받아들이면서 살 수 있어야 한다.

세 번째는 법계출가(法界出家)이다. 자기가 진리라고 생각하는 영역을 벗어나야 완전한 자유인이라 할 수 있다. 우리 주위에는 자기 종교사상의 틀에 갇혀 꼼짝달싹 못하는 사람이 많다. 출가자는 자기 도그마(dogma)로부터 벗어났을 때 거룩해진다.

출가는 근본적으로 중생의 차별심과 전도된 착각을 뒤집어 엎는다. 그러한 내면적 성숙이 있은 후의 일전어(一轉語)는 중생심에서 불심으로, 미혹에서 깨달음으로 전향할 수 있는 전미개오(轉迷開悟)의 일구(一句)로서 강한 힘을 갖는다.

물소의 꼬리는 욕망을 나타낸다. 부귀영화를 꿈꾸는 세속적인 욕망은 물론, 부처가 되고져 하는 욕망조차도 사실은 물소의 꼬리인 것이다.

일체의 욕망과 차별심을 초월해야 진퇴양난의 딜레마를 극복할 수 있다. 창문 앞에 있는 공무(空無)의 함정에 빠져서도 안 되고 되돌아와서 번뇌망상의 법집에 빠져 상신실명(喪身失命)하는 경우도 없어야 한다.

유(有)와 무(無), 미(迷)와 오(悟), 선(善)과 악(惡)의 상대적인 차별경계를 벗어날 때 고해(苦海)를 건너 피안(彼岸)에 이르는 불사(佛事)가 될 것이다.

Case 38
A Buffalo Passes Through a Window

A. Original Case

Ven. Oh-Jo Beop-Yeon said, "It's like a water buffalo passing through a window frame; the head, horns, and four legs have all made it through? why can't the tail make it out?"

B. Commentary and Verse

If you can say something with a discerning eye, turning over the deep meaning of these words, then you can repay the four kinds of kindness above, and instruct sentient beings in the three realms below. If you still can't do that, then you should return to and reflect on this tail once again.

Ven. Mu Mun said it again with a verse:
 If you pass through, you fall into an abyss,
 If you turn back, you're completely destroyed;
 This little tail,

What a really peculiar thing it is.

C. Explanation

The subject-matter of this story seems to be based in the sutras. In the sutra of Buddha's Discourses to Elder Sudatta (Anathapindika), King Prasenajit had ten different dreams one night; one of them was of an elephant passing through a window.

"An elephant passing between the bars of a window was seen in the king's dream. Though the entire body passed completely through, the tail got caught in the window. This is as if, after the Buddha entered Nirvana, though many Brahmans, elders, laypeople, both men and women, left their families behind to ordain as monks and nuns and cultivate the Buddha-Dharma, they could not completely free their minds from desire and attachment to worldly fame and profit."

Similarly, while the sutra talks about a "great elephant," the original episode mentions a water buffalo. The body has passed completely through the frame of the window, while the tail couldn't get through? this can be seen as a metaphor for ordained monastics who do not completely discard the desire for fame, profit, and worldly values in the their minds.

There are three types or levels of 'home-leaving(ordination).' The very first kind is termed 'leaving the six types of blood relations,' in other words leaving one's parents, brothers and sisters, and other close relatives behind. It is truly a difficult thing to leave behind the karmic connections with one's close relatives, which are like a tangled knot. The reason this absolutely must be done is because only by cutting the attachment to one's flesh and blood we can truly devote ourselves to practice.

The second level of ordination is 'leaving the five Skandhas,' which means transcending attachments to ego, to oneself. For most sentient beings, 'self-love' or narcissism incites the three poisons of desire, anger and ignorance to become inflamed. Monastics should be able to live possessing only three robes and one bowl, eating one meal a day, doing intensive periods of solo practice, and willfully engaging in other austere trainings.

The third type of ordination is 'leaving the Dharma-realm(i.e. the realm of human experience.)' Only if we leave the realm wherein our idea of self is thought to be the truth can we become completely liberated beings. Many of those around us are completely entrenched in their religious ideas, and can't even budge an inch. A monastic becomes great when he frees himself from his own dogma. Fundamentally, leaving home(ordination) should turn over the discriminating thoughts and backwards illusions of sentient beings. A 'single turning-word' after one achieves that kind of inner maturity has the incredible power to transform the mind of sentient beings into Buddha-mind, and delusion into enlightenment, with 'a single phrase that transforms delusion into awakening.'

The tail of the water buffalo represents desire; of course the worldly desire, which dreams of wealth and prosperity, but the tail of the buffalo is also the desire to become a Buddha. Only by transcending all desires and discriminating thoughts can one overcome this awkward dilemma. One must not fall into the pit of emptiness in front of the window, but also not backslide and get caught by attachment to delusions and defilements, losing your body and life. When we transcend all relative distinctions of being or non-being, love or hate, and good or bad, we truly practice Buddhism in which we cross the sea of suffering and enter the realm of Nirvana.

제 39 칙
雲門話墮(운문화타)

운문의 '말에 떨어지다'
Case39:
Un Mun's "Caught by Words"

가. 본칙(本則)

雲門, 因僧問, 光明寂照遍河沙. 一句未絶, 門遽曰, 豈不是張拙秀才語. 僧云, 是. 門云, 話墮也. 後來死心拈云, 且道, 那裏是者僧話墮處.

운문 큰스님에게 한 스님이 찾아와 게송 한 구절을 읊었다.
"지혜광명이 온 세계를 고요히 비추니…."
첫 구절이 끝나기도 전에 운문 큰스님이 가로막으며 말했다.
"그것은 장졸수재의 말이지 않는가?"
그는 '그렇다.'고 했다. 그러자 큰스님은 이렇게 말했다.
"너는 말에 떨어졌다."
뒷날 사심(死心) 선사가 이 이야기를 집어서 말했다.
"자, 말해보라. 그 스님이 말에 떨어진 곳이 어디인가?"

나. 평창(評唱) 및 송(頌)

無門曰. 若向者裏見得雲門用處孤危, 者僧因甚話墮, 堪與人天爲師. 若也未明, 自救不了.

만약 여기에서 운문의 용처(用處)가 고위(孤危)한 것과 무슨 말로 인하여 말에 떨어진 줄을 더불어 깨달아 알면 감히 인천(人天)의 스승이 될만 하거니와 만약 밝히지 못한다면 자기 자신도 구제하기 어려우니라.

頌曰. 急流垂釣, 貪餌者著. 口縫纔開, 性命喪却.

　　무문 스님이 다시 게송으로 말하였다.
　　　"급류에 낚시를 드리웠더니
　　　먹이를 탐하는 놈이 물었구나.
　　　입을 조금만 달싹거려도
　　　목숨을 잃고 말 것이다."

다. 강론(講論)

　　운문 큰스님에게 한 스님이 읊은 시의 전문은 이러하다.

　　　"지혜광명이 온 세계를 고요히 비추니
　　　범부와 성인 등 모든 생명이 다 나의 가족,

한 생각도 일지 않으면 전체가 드러나고
육근(六根)이 조금만 움직여도 구름에 가리네.
번뇌를 끊으려 하면 되레 병만 많아지고
진여(眞如)를 구하는 것 또한 삿된 짓이로다.
세상 인연에 따르되 걸리는 것이 없으면
열반과 생사라는 것도 허공꽃과 같으리."

이 시의 본 저자는 장졸수재(張拙秀才)로 유학자였다.
선월(禪月)의 소개로 석상경제(石霜慶諸) 선사에게 참(參)했다. 그때 석상 스님은 수재에게 '그대의 성은 무엇인고?'라고 물었는데 수재는 '성은 장이고 이름은 졸(拙)입니다.'라고 답하였다. 그러자 석상 스님은 '교(巧)를 구함도 가히 얻을 수 없는데, 졸(拙)이 어떻게 나왔는고?'라고 다시 말하였다. 이에 장졸수재가 깨달은 바 있어 말 그대로 수재(秀才)답게 위의 게송을 즉석에서 지어 스님에게 바쳤다.

이 시는 다분히 자연주의적이다. 수행자들이 목적하는 전미개오(轉迷開悟), 혁범성성(革凡成聖)의 말들도 구차하다. 생긴 그대로 살아가면 된다. 이미 한 경계를 넘어선 정신세계를 그려내고 있기 때문에 소박하고 담백한 맛이 배어 있다.

아무튼, 이 게송은 당시 많은 사람들에게 회자 되었을 것이 분명하다. 그러니 운문 큰스님은 시를 듣자마자 '그것은 장졸수재의 말이지 않는가?' 하고 꼭 집었던 것이다.

운문 큰스님 앞에 나타난 그 스님은 실력이 있었던 게 분명하다. 그래서 상(相)도 좀 낼 겸 큰스님 앞에서 깝죽거리다가 첫 구절에서 쥐어 박히고 말았다. 남의 시를 가지고 와서 들먹거렸으니 '무간 아비지옥에서 벗어날 지혜가 그 시에 들어 있는 들 무슨 소용 있겠는가.' 하는 메시지이다.

스스로 깨달아서 스스로의 시를 지을 일이지 다른 이의 깨달음을 끌고 와 말장난을 하자고 하니 말이 될 법한 소리인가!

선(禪)에 있어서 모방은 아무짝에도 가치 없다. 전혀 새로운 말 즉, 자기 고함 소리를 지를 줄 알아야 한다. 설령 제불조사(諸佛祖師)의 말이라도 거기에 매달리면 그 순간 말에 떨어지고 만다. 말을 희롱하며 살아가는 자유인이 되지 못하고 말의 노예가 되어서는 주인공적 삶이라고 할 수 없다. 시비와 분별이 모두 남이 한 말 때문에 생기는 것이니 극히 경계하지 않으면 안 된다.

Case 39
Un Mun's "Caught by Words"

A. Original Case

A monk came to Seon Master Un Mun and began to recite a verse: "The light of wisdom silently illuminates the whole world⋯."

Before he had even finished the first line, Seon Master Un Mun cut him off and said, "Aren't those the words of Jol Jang the Genius?"

The monk replied, "Yes, they are."

The Seon Master then said, "You are caught by the words."

At a later time, Seon Master Sa Shim brought up this story and asked the assembly, "Tell me! At what point did that monk get caught by the words?"

B. Commentary and Verse

If you realize Un Mun's deep meaning here and understand at what point the monk got caught by words, then without hesitation you become teacher of gods and men; if you are not clear about that, then it's difficult to even save yourself.

> Ven. Mu Mun said it again with a verse:
> Casting the line into the flowing stream,
> The greedy one is caught;
> Even opening your mouth a little,
> Your life is already lost.

C. Explanation

The entire poem that the monk was reciting to Seon Master Un Mun looks like this:

> The light of wisdom silently illuminates the entire world;
> Ordinary men and saints? all beings are my family.
> If not even a single thought arises, everything is clear;
> When the six senses move even a little, it becomes cloudy.
> The more you try to cut off delusions,
> The worse your sickness becomes;
> Seeking true-suchness is also a mistake.

Even though you follow the ways of the world,

If you don't get caught by them,

Then nirvana, life and death are as if dream-like appearances.

The original author of this poem was the Confucian scholar known as 'Genius Jol Jang.' He studied with Seon Master Seok-Sang Gyeong-Jae, having been introduced by Seon Matser Seon Wol. At that time, Ven. Seok Sang asked the genius, "What's your family name?" The genius replied, "My family name is Jang, and my first name is Jol(dim-witted)." Whereupon Ven Seok Sang responded, "You really can't get any character you seek, so where did this Jol("dim-wit") come from?" Jol Jang the Genius realized something at this, and so as his name would imply, he skillfully composed the aforementioned poem right on the spot and offered it to the monk.

This poem is quite natural. Even phrases that express the aims of practice are quite clumsy? 'changing delusion into enlightenment,' or 'turning an ordinary man into a sage.' Just leave things as they are! As he is depicting the spiritual realm which is already one level beyond, a pure and simple sense is embodied in the poem.

Anyway, it's obvious that this verse was popular with many people during those days. That's why Seon Master Un Mun, as soon as he heard the poem, pointed out "Aren't those the words of Jol Jang the Genius?" It's also clear that the monk who appeared in front of Seon Master Un Mun had some ability; that's why he was hit in the first verse, when he flippantly boasted in front of the master. The implication was, when you bring someone else's poem here and spout it off, "What's the use, even if the wisdom in that poem can save you from eternal hell?"

You should realize it yourself and write your own poem? borrowing another person's attainment and playing around with the words is really ridiculous! In Seon, imitation is utterly useless; you must know how to utter your own "roar" with completely vibrant speech. Though you may use the words of all the Buddhas and patriarchs, if you get caught by them, at that moment you are just trapped in speech. You can't become a truly free individual playing around with words? you become a slave to the speech, and cannot become the master of your own life. You must be very careful, as all thoughts of right and wrong and relative distinctions arise from others' speech.

제 40 칙
趯倒淨瓶(적도정병)

❦

정병을 넘어 뜨리다
Case40: Kicking Over the Water Bottle

가. 본칙(本則)

潙山和尚, 始在百丈會中充典座. 百丈 將選大潙主人. 乃請同首座對衆下語, 出格者可往. 百丈遂拈淨瓶, 置地上設問云, 不得喚作淨瓶, 汝喚作甚麼. 首座乃云, 不可喚作木𣿪也. 百丈却問於山. 山乃趯倒淨瓶而去. 百丈笑云, 第一座輸却山子也. 因命之爲開山.

   위산 스님이 백장 큰스님 회상(會上)에서 공양을 맡아보는 전좌(典座)라는 소임을 살 때였다. 백장 큰스님은 대위산의 주인이 될 만한 인재를 뽑기 위해 수좌(首座)를 포함한 모든 대중들이 나서서 한마디씩 하도록 했다. 뛰어난 사람이 있으면 그리로 가게 할 작정이었다.
   백장 큰스님은 정병(淨瓶)을 집어 땅 위에 놓고 물었다.
   "이것을 정병이라고 불러서는 안 된다. 너희들은 이 정병을 무엇이라고 부르겠는가?"
   그러자 수좌 스님이 말했다.
   "그렇다고 나무토막이라고는 못할 것입니다."
   백장 큰스님은 위산 스님에게도 답할 기회를 주었다. 그러자 위산 스님은 정병을 발로 걷어차 버리고 나갔다. 이에 백장 큰스님이 웃으며 말했다.

"제일좌(第一座)가 촌놈한테 졌구만!"

그래서 위산에게 대위산(大潙山)으로 가 개산(開山)하라고 명하였다.

나. 평창(評唱) 및 송(頌)

無門曰. 潙山一期之勇, 爭奈跳百丈圈圓不出. 檢點將來, 便重不便輕. 何故. 聻. 脫得盤頭. 擔起鐵枷.

위산의 한 시대를 풍미한 용기가 어찌 백장의 울타리 하나를 뛰어넘지 못하겠는가? 자세히 점검해 보면, 무거운 것을 맡고 가벼운 것을 맡지 않았다. 무슨 까닭일까?

니(聻)! 쟁반을 버리고 쇠로 만든 멍에를 짊어지려고 했기 때문이다.

頌曰. 颺下笊籬幷木杓, 當陽一突絶周遮. 百丈重關攔不住, 脚尖趯出佛如麻.

무문 스님이 다시 게송으로 말하였다.
"조리와 국자를 내던져 버리고
정면에서 정병을 걷어차서 논의를 끊어 버렸다.
백장의 여러 관문도 막지 못했으니,
발끝으로 걷어차 버리자 수많은 부처가 흩어졌다."

다. 강론(講論)

백장회해 선사 아래 위산영우는 전좌의 소임을 맡아보고 있었다. 어느 날 풍수와 관상에 밝은 사마(司馬)라는 스님이 행각 중에 들러 백장 큰스님에게 말했다.
"소승이 이번에 호남을 둘러보는데 그곳 대위산의 지세가 주인을 만난다면 천오백 명의 학인을 품을 명산입니다."
"이 노장이 가서 살면 어떻겠는가?"
"큰스님은 골인(骨人)의 상(相)이신데 그 산은 육산(肉山)입니다. 큰스님께서 가셔서 사신다 하더라도 모이는 제자들이 천 명에도 미치지 못할 것입니다."
백장 큰스님은 빈궁한 상이어서 그 산의 주인이 되기에는 부족하다는 것이었다.

그러자 백장 큰스님이 제자들 중에 적합한 사람이 있다면 점검해 달라고 부탁하면서 제일좌인 화림보각(華林普覺)을 불러 보였다. 그러나 사마 스님이 "안 되겠다."고 하여 이번에는 전좌의 소임을 보는 영우 스님을 불러 보였다. 곧 사마 스님이 흔쾌히 "좋다."고 추천하였다.

그런데, 여기서 화림 스님은 단지 관상만으로 결정을 내리는 데 대해 이의를 제기하였다. 그래서 백장 큰스님은 두 사람의 안목을 시험하기로 하였는데 그 본론적인 얘기가 본칙의 내용이다.

문제의 핵심은 정병(淨瓶)을 가리켜 정병이라고 불러서는 안 된다고 하면서 그럼 무엇이라고 해야 하겠느냐는 것이다. 정병이라고 대답하면 고정된 이름과 모양 즉, 명상(名相)에 떨어져 사물에 접촉하는 것이 되고, 정병이 아니라고 말하면 진실을 배반하는 결과를 낳는다.

어느 쪽으로 대답하더라도 정병이라는 진실 그 전체를 나타낼 수가 없는 것이다. 어쨌든 제일수좌의 안목은 백장 큰스님의 덫에 반쯤 걸린 꼴이 되었는데 위산영우의 경우는 큰스님의 덫을 갈기갈기 찢어 버렸다.

위산영우는 정병이라는 이름과 모양을 떨쳐 버리고 주관과 객관의 영역마저 허물어 버렸다.

본래무일물(本來無一物)!
그 어떤 것에도 걸림 없는 초월의 행위가 돋보인다.

Case 40
Kicking Over the Water Bottle

A. Original Case

When Ven. Wi San lived in Seon Master Baek Jang's community, he had the position of kitchen master, and was in charge of preparing the meals. Seon Master Baek Jang assembled the entire community, including the head monk, so that he could choose a competent person to become leader of the Dae Wi Mountain Sangha? they each had to show what they had attained. If there was an exceptional person, his plan was to send him there. Seon Master Baek Jang then took a water bottle, put it on the ground, and asked "You may not call it a water bottle. All of you, what do you call it?"

The head monk said, "Then we also can't call it a block of wood."

Seon Master Baek Jang then gave Ven. Wi San a chance to answer, whereupon Wi San kicked over the water bottle with his foot and left.

Seon Master Baek Jang burst out laughing and said, "The head monk has lost to a country bumpkin!" He then asked Wi San to go to Dae Wi Mountain and start teaching the community.

B. Commentary and Verse

Wi San had the greatest Seon spirit of his day, so how could he not have leapt over one of Baek Jang's gates? If we look at it closely, he undertook the heavier task instead of the lighter one. What was the reason? Look! It was because he threw away the serving tray in order to carry an iron yoke.

Ven. Mu Mun's verse:
   He tossed the strainer and ladle away,
   Kicked over the water bottle and cut off all discussion.
   Baek Jang's various barriers could not stop him,
   When he gave it a kick, all the Buddhas were scattered.

C. Explanation

Ven. Wi-San Yeong-Wu, who was studying under Seon Master Baek-Jang Hwe-Hae, had the position of kitchen master. One day, a monk named Sa Ma, who was skilled in geomancy and physiognomy, came to visit Seon Master Baek Jang during his travels. He said, "I was traveling around the southern province this time? according to the terrain of Dae Wi Mountain, if there is a suitable leader there, then it will become a community with 1,500 practitioners."

The Seon Master asked, "How about this old monk going and living there?"

"Master, your appearance is bony, whereas that is a fleshy mountain. Even if you were to go there and live, the number of disciples would not even reach a thousand."

As Seon Master Baek Jang's destitute appearance was insufficient to allow him to become leader of that mountain, he asked the monk to check and see if there was someone suitable among his disciples; he then called for the head monk Hwa-Rim Bo-Gak and showed him. However, Ven. Sa Ma said "No," so this time he called Ven. Yeong Wu, who was the kitchen master and showed him to the monk. Ven. Sa Ma immediately said, "Great!" and gave his recommendation.

However, at this point Hwa Rim raised the objection that the decision had been made only based on physiognomy(i.e. reading facial features.) Seon Master Baek Jang therefore said that the clear wisdom of the two candidates should be tested, which is the subject of the story in the original case.

The point of the story is pointing to a water bottle, and yet saying that it cannot be called a water bottle? so what should it be called? If you answer that it is water bottle, then you are caught by the fixed name and form whenever you come in contact with objects, but if you say it's not a water bottle, then you go against the truth.

Whichever way you answer, the truth of the water bottle cannot be revealed in its entirety. Anyway, the clear wisdom of the head monk was caught half-way in Seon Master Baek Jang's trap, whereas Wi-San Yeong-Wu tore the master's trap into shreds. Wi-San Yeong-Wu completely cast aside the name and form of the water bottle, and even smashed the realm of subject and object. Originally not even one thing! His superior action, not being hindered by anything at all, really stands out.

제 41 칙
達磨安心(달마안심)

～⁂～

달마가 마음을 편안하게 해주다
Case41: Bodhidharma Pacifies the Mind

가. 본칙(本則)

達磨面壁. 二祖立雪斷臂云, 弟子心未安, 乞師安心. 磨云, 將心來, 與汝安. 祖云, 覓心了不可得. 磨云, 爲汝安心竟.

    달마대사가 면벽(面壁)을 하고 있었다. 이조혜가(二祖慧可)는 서서 스스로 팔을 자르고 말했다.
  "제자의 마음이 편치 못합니다. 스님께서 제 마음을 편안하게 해 주십시오."
  대사가 말했다.
  "그 마음을 가지고 오너라. 내가 너를 편안케 해 주리라."
  혜가가 다시 말했다.
  "마음을 아무리 찾으려 해도 찾지 못하겠습니다."
  이에 대사가 말했다.
  "너를 위하여 이미 마음을 편안하게 해 주었노라."

나. 평창(評唱) 및 송(頌)

無門曰. 缺齒老胡, 十萬里航海, 特特而來. 可謂是無風起浪. 末後接得一箇門人, 又却六根不具. 咦, 謝三郎不識四字.

　이빨 빠진 늙은 오랑캐 늙은이가 십만 리 바다를 항해하여 일부러 여기까지 왔으니 바람도 없는데 풍랑을 일으킨 꼴이다. 뒤늦게 한 제자를 얻었는데 육근을 제대로 갖추지 못한 병신이다.
　우습다! 사삼랑(謝三郎)이 사(四) 자를 알지 못함이로다.

頌曰. 西來直指, 事因囑起. 撓聒叢林, 元來是爾.

　무문 스님이 다시 게송으로 말하였다.
　　"서쪽에서 와서 곧바로 사람의 마음을 가리키니
　　그로 인해 불법을 부촉하는 사건이 일어났네.
　　여기 저기 총림을 요란하게 하는 사람이여,
　　본시 바로 그대 아니냐!"

다. 강론(講論)

　본칙의 단비구법(斷臂求法)의 이야기는 『전등록』, 『조당집』, 『속고승전』 등 여러 문헌에 나타난다. 종합적으로 구성해보면 이러하다.

　달마대사는 양무제와 만났으나 서로 뜻이 계합하지 않아 양쯔강을 건너 숭산의 소림굴에 들어가 벽을 바라보고 앉아 있었다. 사람들은 그를 벽관(壁觀) 바라문이라고 불렀다.

　당시 나이 40이 넘은 신광(神光)이라는 사람이 찾아왔는데, 신광은 오랫동안 낙양에 살면서 여러 서적을 접하였으나 현묘한 깨달음의 경지에는 접근하지 못하였다. 그래서 달마대사의 가르침을 간절하게 원하였던 것이다. 그런데 막상 대면한 달마대사는 그 아무것도 가르쳐 주지 않았다.

　그래서 신광은 하산하였고, 이후 아주 곰곰이 생각하였다.

　'옛사람이 도를 구할 때는 뼈를 부수어 골수를 끄집어내고, 피를 뽑아서 굶주린 이를 구제하고, 머리카락을 진흙땅에 펴서 부처님을 걷게 하고, 벼랑에 몸을 던져 굶주린 호랑이에게 먹이로 육신을 보시하였다고 했다. 옛사람은 이러한 구도정신으로 불도를 구했다고 하는데, 나는 어떠한가!' 하고 반성하였다.

　한참 후 신광은 어느 날 저녁에 다시 달마대사를 찾아가서 꼼짝 않고 서서 구법(求法)의 결의를 보였는데 밤이 깊어지자 마침 눈이 작설하였다. 눈이 무릎까지 쌓인 새벽에서야 달마대사는 입을 열었다.

"어찌 작은 공덕과 경솔한 마음으로 참된 법을 얻기 바라는가?"

신광은 이 말을 듣고 칼을 꺼내 왼팔을 잘라 신표(信標)로써 달마대사에게 바쳤다. 대사는 신광이 법기(法器)임을 알고 그를 인정하면서 이름을 혜가(慧可)라고 하였다.

"스승님, 저에게 부처님의 법인(法印)을 가르쳐 주십시오."

"부처님의 법인은 남에게 얻는 것이 아니니라."

"저의 마음이 편치 못하니 스승께서 편안하게 해 주십시오."

"그 불안한 마음을 가져 오너라. 내가 편안하게 해 주리라."

"마음을 찾아도 찾을 수가 없습니다."

"내가 이미 너의 마음을 편안하게 하였다. 너는 보는가?"

혜가는 드디어 깨닫고 다시 물었다.

"오늘에야 모든 법이 공적(空寂)하고 보리(菩提)가 멀리 있는 것이 아님을 알았습니다. 이 법을 어떻게 전해야 하는지요?"

"나의 법은 이심전심(以心傳心)이라, 불립문자(不立文字)니라."

여기 안심법문(安心法門)의 요점은 '불안한 마음은 실체가 없다.'는 사실이다.

Case 41
Bodhidharma Pacifies the Mind

A. Original Case

Bodhidharma sat facing the wall; the second patriarch Hye Ga stood there, cut off his own arm, and said "Your disciple's mind is not at ease. Venerable, please pacify my mind."

Bodhidharma responded, "Bring me your mind, and I'll pacify it for you."

Hye Ga spoke again, "No matter how much I look for it, I can't find it anywhere."

Bodhidharma then said, "I have already pacified this mind for you."

B. Commentary and Verse

The toothless old barbarian came here deliberately, sailing one-hundred thousand miles over the sea; this was raising waves when there was no wind. Later he got one disciple, a cripple who was not clear in his six senses. How ridiculous! It's like the famous scholar Samrang Sa not even knowing how to write the alphabet.

Ven. Mu Mun said it again with a verse:
Coming from the West, pointing directly to mind;
Because of this, the Buddha-Dharma was entrusted.
The guy making the monasteries everywhere noisy?
Isn't it originally you?

C. Explanation

The original story of "Cutting One's Arm Seeking the Dharma" appeared in various records, including Transmission of the Lamp, Records of the Patriarchs, and Biographies of Eminent Monks. If we were to combine them all in an organized fashion, it would look like this: After Bodhidharma met emperor Wu of the Liang dynasty and the two of them couldn't connect with each other, he crossed over the Yangtze river, entered Sorim cave on Seung Sahn mountain and sat staring at the wall. People referred to him as the "wall-watching Brahmin."

At that time, a man named Shin Gwang, who was more than forty years of age, came to visit him; he had lived in Nak Yang for a long time, had studied many texts, but couldn't reach the level of mystic enlightenment; he therefore earnestly desired Bodhidharma's teaching. However, when he actually met him, Bodhidharma didn't give him any teaching at all, so Shin Gwang came down from the mountain and seriously thought about the situation.

He reflected to himself that, "People in olden times, they used to break their bones and take out their marrow when seeking the Dharma; they would draw their blood to save someone who was hungry, lay their hair out on the mud so that Buddha could walk over it, hurl themselves from a cliff, offering their body as food for a hungry tiger. People in those days sought the Buddha-Dharma with that kind of sincere devotion, so how about me?"

After some time had passed, one day again went to see Bodhidharma in the evening, and stood there not moving at all. He demonstrated his strong determination to attain the Dharma; as the night grew later, eventually snow began to pile up. By dawn, when the snow had piled up to his knees, Bodhidharma opened his mouth and said, "How do you expect to attain the true Dharma with so little merit and such an insincere mind?"

When Shin Gwang heard these words he took out a knife and cut off his left arm, presenting it to Bodhidharma as a token of faith. The master realized Shin Gwang's capacity for the Dharma, so he gave him his consent, and bestowed the Dharma name Hye Ga.

"Master, please teach me Buddha's Dharma seal."

"Buddha's Dharma seal cannot be obtained from someone else."

"As my mind is not at ease, master, please pacify it."

"Bring me your uneasy mind and I'll pacify it for you."

"Even though I've searched for this mind, I could not find it anywhere."

"I have already pacified your mind. Don't you realize it?"

At last Hye Ga had some realization, and then asked, "Today I have realized that all Dharmas are empty and still, and that Bodhi is not far away at all. How should this Dharma be transmitted?"

"My Dharma is a transmission from mind to mind, not dependent on words and speech."

Herein lies the main point of the "Dharma speech that pacifies the mind?" this uneasy mind has no substance at all.

453

제 42 칙
女子出定(여자출정)

여인을 삼매에서 깨우다

Case42:
A Woman Awakens from Samadhi

가. 본칙(本則)

世尊, 昔因文殊至諸佛集處, 値諸佛各還本處. 惟有一女人, 近彼佛坐, 入於三昧. 文殊乃白佛, 云何女人得近佛坐, 而我不得. 佛告文殊, 汝但覺此女, 令從三昧起, 汝自問之. 文殊遶女人三匝, 鳴指一下, 乃托至梵天, 盡其神力而不能出. 世尊云, 假使百千文殊, 亦出此女人定不得. 下方過一十二億河沙國土, 有罔明菩薩, 能出此女人定. 須臾罔明大士從地湧出, 禮拜世尊. 世尊勅罔明. 却至女人前, 鳴指一下, 女人於是從定而出.

    옛날 세존께서 계시는 곳에 문수보살이 찾아왔다. 그곳에는 모든 부처님들이 모여 있다가 각각 본래의 자리로 돌아갔다. 그런데 오직 한 여인이 부처님 근처에 앉아 삼매에 들어 있었다.
    이때 문수보살이 부처님께 사뢰었다.
    "여인도 부처님 곁에 앉아 삼매에 들 수 있는데 저는 어째서 그럴 수 없는지요?"
    부처님께서 문수보살에게 말씀하셨다.
    "그대가 이 여인을 삼매에서 깨어나게 해서 직접 물어보도록 하여라."

문수보살은 여인의 주위를 세 바퀴 돌고 손가락을 '탁' 튕겨보았지만 여인은 일어나지 않았으므로 그 여인을 받쳐 들고 천상(天上)의 범천(梵天)까지 가서 온갖 신통력을 다 하였다. 그러나 여인을 삼매에서 깨울 수가 없었다.

세존께서 말씀하셨다.

"설령 백 천의 문수가 오더라도 저 여인을 선정에서 나오게 하지는 못할 것이다. 여기로부터 아래쪽으로 12억 갠지스 강의 모래알 수만큼 많은 국토를 지난 곳에 망명(罔明)이라는 초지보살(初地菩薩)이 있나니, 그만이 이 여인을 선정에서 나오게 할 수 있을 것이니라."

그러자 순식간에 망명대사(罔明大士)가 땅에서 솟아나와 세존께 예배하였다. 세존께서 그에게 여인을 삼매에서 나오게 하라고 분부하였다. 그는 여인 앞으로 가더니 손가락을 한 번 '탁' 튕겼다. 그러자 여인은 바로 선정에서 깨어났다.

나. 평창(評唱) 및 송(頌)

無門曰. 釋迦老子做者一場雜劇, 不通小小. 且道, 文殊是七佛之師, 因甚出女人定不得. 罔明初地菩薩, 爲甚却出得. 若向者裏見得親切, 業識忙忙, 那伽大定.

　석가 늙은이가 이런 한바탕의 촌극을 벌였으니 시시한 일은 아니었다.
　자, 말해보라. 문수는 과거 칠불의 스승으로 일컫는 보살인데 어찌하여 한 여인을 선정에서 깨우지 못하였는가?
　그런데 망명은 초지보살에 불과한데 어찌하여 선정에서 깨울 수 있었는가?
　만약 여기에서 척하고 알 수 있다면, 망망(忙忙)한 업식(業識)을 여의지 않고 그대로 대룡삼매(大龍三昧)가 될 것이다.

頌曰. 出得出不得, 渠儂得自由. 神頭幷鬼面, 敗闕當風流.

　무문 스님이 다시 게송으로 말하였다.
　　"선정에서 나오게 하든 못하든
　　그는 그대로 나는 나대로 자유,
　　신두(神頭)와 귀면(鬼面)을 쓰고 연극할 때는
　　실패도 그대로 풍류인 것."

다. 강론(講論)

　애시당초 문수의 망념이 문제였다. 오직 한 여인이 부처님 근처에 앉아 삼매에 들어 있었는데 문수는 생각하기로 다섯 가지(범천왕, 제석천왕, 마왕, 전륜성왕, 법왕)가 될 수 없는 오장(五障)의 여인도 저렇게 부처님 옆에서 선정에 들고 있는데 최고 보살인 자신은 어찌 이 모양인가 하는 의식, 망념을 일으켰다. 즉, 차별심을 가졌다는 말이다.
　차별심을 가지고는 어떠한 신통묘용을 발휘하더라도 소용이 없다. 문수의 지혜는 일체의 차별심, 분별심이 없고 불견(佛見), 법견(法見)을 초월한 경지에서라야 그 빛을 발한다.
　초지(初地)인 망명보살은 상대가 여인이라는 일체의 차별심, 분별심이 없는 상태에서 손가락을 튕기는 찰나에 그 여인을 선정에서 깨어나도록 하였다.
　망명보살은 '밝음이 없는 보살'이란 뜻으로 결국 장님을 일컫는데, 장애인인 장님의 법력(法力)이 비장애인보다 더 셀 수도 있음을 촌극으로 보여주는 이야기이기도 하다. 즉, 법신과 법신의 감응은 남녀의 차별, 장애인과 비장애인의 차별을 넘어서서 이루어진다.

선정삼매로 불심의 경지에 있는 여인과 소통하려면 상대도 불심의 경지라야 한다. 문수의 아상(我相)으로는 법성산(法性山)을 오를 수 없다.

시절인연(時節因緣)을 맞음도 결국 자기 소관이 아닌가.

Case 42
A Woman Awakens from Samadhi

A. Original Case

Long ago, Manjushri Bodhisattva came to the place where the World-honored One was staying. All of the Buddhas had assembled there and had each then returned to their original places; only one woman remained, however, seated in Samadhi near the Buddha.

At this time, Manjushri asked the Buddha, "Even a woman is seated in Samadhi next to the Buddha? why can't I do that?"

Buddha spoke to Manjushri, "You should awaken that woman from Samadhi and ask her yourself!"

Manjushri walked around the woman three times and snapped his fingers, but the girl still didn't awaken; so he took her up to the highest Brahma heaven and used all his miraculous powers, to no avail.

The World-honored One said, "Even if a thousand Manjushris were to come here, they still couldn't awaken that woman from

Samadhi. Down below, past millions of lands as innumerable as the sands in the Ganges, is the first level Bodhisattva Mang Myong; he will be able to awaken this woman from Samadhi."

Instantly, Mang Myong Bodhisattva sprung out of the ground and bowed to the Buddha. The World-honored One asked him to awaken the woman from Samadhi, so he went up to the woman and snapped his fingers once; the woman immediately awoke from Samadhi.

B. Commentary and Verse

Old Shakyamuni put on this kind of dramatic scene? it wasn't a trivial thing at all. Tell me! Manjushri was a Bodhisattva who was called 'teacher of the seven past Buddhas' ? why couldn't he awaken one woman from Samadhi?

However, how was it that Mang Myeong, who was only a first level Bodhisattva, was able to awaken her?

If you understand this at once, you will enter the Great Samadhi right away, without concern for the endlessly conceptualizing consciousness.

Ven. Mu Mun said it again with a verse:

> Whether you can wake her up from Samadhi or not,
>
> He does it his way, I do it my way, without hindrance.
>
> One acts with an angel-mask, the other, with a demon-mask?
>
> Even defeat is a pleasure.

C. Explanation

The problem at the beginning is Manjushri's delusion; only one woman seated next to the Buddha has entered Samadhi? but Manjushri believes that she is just a woman with the five hindrances, who can't even become king of Brahma-heaven, Indra-heaven, Mara, the wheel-turning sage or the Dharma, whereas he himself has the delusion the he is the best Bodhisattva.

That is to say, he has this mind of relative discrimination. If you still have this kind of distinguishing mind, then no matter what mystical powers you may possess, they are of no use. Manjushri's wisdom is radiant only when it has no discrimination or distinguishing thoughts at all, and only when it comes from the realm which transcends even the view of Buddha or Dharma.

The first-level Bodhisattva Mang Myong didn't have any discriminating, distinguishing thoughts about this woman, so he was able to instantly awaken her by snapping his fingers. The Bodhisattva Mang Myong was said to be blind, "lacking radiance," and yet this story shows that the Dharma power of a crippled blind man was stronger than the one who was not crippled.

In other words, his Dharma body and its functioning accomplished far more than the discriminating thoughts of man and woman, crippled or not crippled. If you want to connect with this woman who stayed in deep Samadhi, like the Buddha, you must attain this yourself. Manjushri could not reach the mountain of Dharma-nature due to his idea of himself.

Even though the time and place(for enlightenment) may be right, in the end it's up to you.

제 43 칙
首山竹篦(수산죽비)

수산의 죽비

Case43: Su Sahn's Bamboo Clapper

가. 본칙(本則)

首山和尙, 拈竹篦示衆云, 汝等諸人, 若喚作竹篦則觸, 不喚作竹篦則背. 汝諸人, 且道, 喚作甚麽.

   수산성념(首山省念) 큰스님이 대중들에게 죽비를 들어 보이며 말했다.
   "그대들이여, 만약 이것을 죽비라고 부르면 이름에 떨어지는 것이요, 죽비라고 하지 않아도 어긋나는 것이 된다. 그대들이여! 자아, 말해 보라. 이것을 무엇이라고 부를 것인가?"

나. 평창(評唱) 및 송(頌)

無門曰. 喚作竹篦則觸, 不喚作竹篦則背. 不得有語, 不得無語. 速道速道.

   죽비라고 불러도 저촉되는 것이 되고 죽비라고 부르지 않아도 어긋나는 것이 된다.
   말을 할 수도 없고, 말을 하지 않을 수도 없다.

자아, 빨리 말하라! 빨리 말하라!

頌曰. 拈起竹篦, 行殺活令. 背觸交馳, 佛祖乞命.

무문 스님이 다시 게송으로 말하였다.
　　"죽비를 들어 올려,
　　죽고 살리는 영을 내리는구나.
　　자칫하면 어긋나고 저촉되니,
　　여기서는 부처도 조사도 목숨을 구걸할 판."

다. 강론(講論)

　본칙의 주제는 아주 흔하다. 비록 소재는 다르지만 유사한 공안이 많다는 말이다.
　무문관의 40칙인 위산영우 스님의 정병을 차버린 이야기와 제44칙인 파초의 주장자 이야기는 그 맥락이 거의 같다.
　여기서 문제는 촉(觸)과 배(背)이다. 촉은 저촉된다는 뜻으로 특질(特質)에 떨어지는 것을 말하며 배는 위배된다는 뜻으로 본질(本質)에 어긋남을 말한다. 즉, 이름에 떨어지지도 말고 용도에도 어긋나지 않으려면 그놈의 죽비를 어떻게 불러야 할 것인가가 문제의 주안점이다.

특질과 본질의 논리로 예를 들자면 파도는 물이 있음으로 가능하고 물은 파도를 통하여 자기 모양을 나타낸다. 파도와 물은 결국 불일불이(不一不異)의 관계이다.

색즉공(色卽空)으로 설명하여도 그 원리는 비슷하다. 색(色)이란 현상 즉, 특질이고 공(空)이란 내용 즉, 본질인 점에서는 색(色), 공(空)은 표리일체(表裏一體)이다. 여기서 분명한 사실은 색을 떠난 공은 존재가치가 없으며 공을 떠난 색은 허망할 수밖에 없다. 그러한 점에서 색, 공은 언제나 보완의 인연 속에 있어야 한다.

어느 하나로 기울어지면 한쪽만이라도 건질 것 같으나 사실 둘 다 잃어버린다. 그저 피상적으로 보면 색은 색이고 공은 공일뿐이다. 즉, 현상은 현상이고 본질은 본질이다. 그러나 지혜의 안목으로 보면 색, 공은 손등과 손바닥처럼 하나이면서 둘이고, 둘이면서 하나이다. 전체적이고도 균형 잡힌 통찰의 요구는 불교사상의 가장 기본 바탕을 형성하고 있는데, 근본 교리의 8정도(八正道)에서 정견(正見)이 맨 먼저 나오는 것도 이 때문이다. 화두, '수산의 죽비'는 물론 이거니와 모든 화두의 처음과 끝은 정견의 확립이다. 여기에서는 입만 열면 그르친다. 개구즉착(開口卽錯)이다. 언어도단(言語道斷)하고 심행처멸(心行處滅)하지 않으면 답을 얻을 수 없다.

개념화된 언어는 극히 한 부분만을 드러낸다. 죽비라고 해버리면 본질을 잃고 죽비가 아니라고 해버리면 특질을 잃는다. 이런 모순이 어디 있는가! 모순이 합리적으로 조화를 이루는 특단의 길을 찾으려면 끊임없이 궁구하지 않으면 안 된다. 양변(兩邊)을 취하거나 또는 양변을 취하지 않아도 다 문제가 생기니 모순일 수밖에 없다.

숭산에서 찾아온 남악회양을 그의 스승 육조는 '무슨 물건이 이렇게 왔는고?' 하고 다그친다. 제자 회양은 8년의 세월을 보내고서야 '설사, 한 물건이라 해도 맞지 않다.'고 대답하였다.

중도(中道)의 핵심을 낚아챈다는 것이 얼마나 험하고 어려운 일인지를 살펴 볼 수 있는 일화이다. 그렇지만 우리는 반드시 나아가야 한다.

Case 43
Su Sahn's Bamboo Clapper

A. Original Case

Seon Master Su-Sahn Seong-Nyeom held up a Jukpi(bamboo clapper) and showed it to the assembly.

"All of you! If you say it's a Jukpi, you are in conflict with its reality? but it's also wrong not to call it a Jukpi. Tell me! What do you call it?"

B. Commentary and Verse

Calling it a Jukpi conflicts with its reality, but it's also wrong not to call it a Jukpi. Speech and silence both cannot be used. Quickly, tell me! Tell me!

Ven. Mu Mun said it again with a verse:
>   Holding up the Jukpi
>   Both kills and gives life;
>   One mistake, then you are wrong and in conflict;

Here even Buddha and the patriarchs are begging for their lives.

C. Explanation

The subject of this case is quite common; this means that while the topic of this story may be different, there are many Koans that are similar to this one. The point of Gateless Gate case number 40, Ven. Wi-San Yeong-Wu's "Kicking Over the Water Bottle" and case number 44, "Pa Cho's Staff" deal with almost the same subjects.

The story here is about attachment and avoidance; attachment can also imply a contradiction, which means that one is caught by the characteristics of something, whereas this avoidance, implying a violation, means that one goes against the original substance. That is to say, the main point of this story is how one should call the Jukpi so as to not get trapped by the name, but also not contradict the function. An example of this theory of appearances and original substance is that a wave is only possible if there is water, and likewise the form of the water appears through the wave. The water and wave have this relationship of not being the same, and yet also not different.

The principle is similar, even if it is explained in terms of 'form is the same as emptiness.' Seen from the perspective that form, or phenomena, are the specific characteristics, emptiness is the essence or original substance, and form and emptiness are like the inside and outside of the same body. It should be clear at this point that emptiness does not exist without form, and also that form without emptiness must be unreal. From this point of view, form and emptiness must always exist in a karmic relationship, complementing each other.

If you lean to one side, you may think that you can save at least one; however, you in fact completely lose them both. When seen superficially, form is only form, and emptiness is only emptiness? in other words, appearances are just appearances, and original substance is just original substance. However, when seen with the discerning eye of wisdom, form and emptiness are like the palm and the back of the hand? while being two, they are actually one, and while being one, they are actually two. The necessity for a balanced, comprehensive perception forms the basic background of Buddhist philosophy. For that reason, in the fundamental teaching of the Eightfold Path, the very first is "Correct View." This question of "Su Sahn's Jukpi." and not only this one, but the beginning and end of all Great Questions, is based on this Correct View. If you only open your mouth here, it's a mistake. Unless you cut off words and speech and extinguish the place of mental functioning, you cannot get an answer. Conceptual speech only reveals one extreme side; if you call it a Jukpi, you lose the original substance, but if you say it's not a Jukpi, you lose the specific characteristics. What a contradiction! You must ceaselessly investigate if you want to find the best way to rationally harmonize this contradiction. Whether you choose both opposite sides or not, there will always be a contradiction.

Nam-Ak Hwe-Yang, who had come from Mt. Seung Sahn, was prodded by his teacher the Sixth Patriarch, "What kind of thing is it that has come here?" After spending eight years practicing intensively, the disciple Hwe-Yang responded with, "It's not correct even if you call it a 'thing'." This anecdote lets one appreciate what a serious, difficult affair it is to attain the main point of the Middle Way. By all means, however, we must continue.

제 44 칙
芭蕉拄杖(파초주장)

❧

파초의 주장자
Case44: Pa Cho's Staff

가. 본칙(本則)

芭蕉和尙, 示衆云, 爾有拄杖子, 我與爾拄杖子. 爾無拄杖子, 我奪爾拄杖子.

파초혜청(芭蕉慧淸) 큰스님이 대중들에게 말하였다.
"그대들에게 주장자(拄杖子)가 있다면, 내가 그대들에게 주장자를 줄 것이다. 그러나 그대들에게 주장자가 없다면, 내가 그대들에게서 주장자를 빼앗으리라."

나. 평창(評唱) 및 송(頌)

無門曰. 扶過斷橋水, 伴歸無月村. 若喚作拄杖, 入地獄如箭.

주장자에 의지하여 다리가 끊긴 물을 건너고, 주장자를 벗 삼아 달빛 없는 마을로 돌아간다. 그런데, 만약 이것을 주장자라 부른다면 화살같이 빨리 지옥에 떨어지고 말리라.

頌曰. 諸方深與淺, 都在掌握中. 撑天幷拄地, 隨處振宗風.

무문 스님이 다시 게송으로 말하였다.
"제방 선지식의 깊고 얕음이
모두 이 손아귀에 있도다.
하늘을 괴고 땅을 떠받치니,
이르는 곳마다 종풍을 드날린다."

다. 강론(講論)

본칙에서 제시한 것처럼, 무분별한 삼매의 경계에 이르러야 있음(有), 없음(無)의 존재론적 분별을 떠날 수 있다. 그 자리가 비로소 출세간(出世間)의 영역이며 성스러움의 공간이다.

주장자는 스승이 제자들을 지도할 때 공부한 정도의 안목과 역량을 점검하는 법구(法具)로 사용되었다. 그 유명한 덕산의 방(棒)이 대표적인 경우이다.

덕산 스님은 수행자들을 격발하는 도구로써 몽둥이를 사용하였다. 이때의 몽둥이는 바로 주장자이다. 덕산 스님은 학인들이 찾아와서 진리를 묻거나 공부를 점검받으려고 하면 막무가내로 주장자를 휘둘렀다. 성전일구(聲前一句)를 요구하였던 것이다.

한편, 운문종의 개창자 운문문언 스님은 아주 끔찍한 말까지 해 대었다.

"석가모니가 태어나자마자 주행칠보(周行七步)하고 천상천하 유아독존(天上天下 唯我獨尊)을 외쳤다는데, 만약 내가 그 자리에 있었다면 한 방망이로 때려 죽여 개에게 먹이로 던져 주었을 것이다."

또한, 임제 스님에 대한 얘기이다.

스님이 수좌로서 황벽 선사의 문하에서 공부할 때였다. 주위 도반 스님들의 권고에 따라 조실이었던 황벽 선사에게 가서 불법(佛法)의 큰 뜻을 묻다가 세 번씩이나 몽둥이 찜질만을 당하였다. 임제 스님은 스승을 원망하며 다른 절의 조실인 대우 스님을 찾아가 자초지종을 말씀 드렸더니 스님은 "황벽이 그렇게 자상하였구나." 하고 오히려 찬탄하였다. 이에 임제는 크게 깨달은 바가 있었다. 이와 같이 선사들이 사용하는 주장자는 신체활동의 보조기구보다는 교육적인 의미가 더 강하였다.

파초혜청 큰스님도 주장자를 사용하는 데는 일가견이 있었던 것으로 보인다. 파초 스님의 경우, 주장자는 그냥 몽둥이나 지팡이 정도가 아니다. 청정한 마음, 본래면목, 참주인공, 정법안장, 열반묘심, 불심 등을 가리킨다.

"그대들에게 주장자가 있다면, 내가 그대들에게 주장자를 줄 것이다."라고 말한 것은 '있다(有)'고 주장하는 사람에게 하나를 더 주어서 진실로 그것이 맞는지를 확인토록 지시한 법문이다. 또한 "그대들에게 주장자가 없다면 내가 그대들에게 주장자를 빼앗으리라."라고 말한 것은 '없다(無)'고 주장하는 사람에게 그 중생심을 빼앗아서 자신의 본래면목을 드러나게 하려는 법문이다.

주장자가 없다고 한다면 주장자 즉, 본래면목이라는 진실의 위배요, 주장자가 있다고 한다면 주장자 즉, 본래면목이라는 사물에의 집착이다.

아무튼, 본래면목이 있다(有), 없다(無)라고 하는 것은 유, 무(有, 無)의 차별심에 떨어진 결과인데 여기 파초 큰스님은 학인들로 하여금 등짐(背)과 속박(觸), 옳음(是)과 그름(非) 등의 상대적인 경계를 초월하여 대자유적 삶을 구가하도록 주장자까지 동원하는 자비심을 보이고 있다.

후학들은 선지식들의 이러한 배려를 잊지 말아야 할 것이다.

Case 44
Pa Cho's Staff

A. Original Case

Seon Master Pa-Cho Hye-Cheong spoke to the assembly, "All of you, if you have a staff, I will give you a staff. If you have no staff, then I will take it from you."

B. Commentary and Verse

If I rely on it, I can cross the water when the bridge is broken; it is my companion when returning to the village on a moonless night. However, if you call it a staff, you fall into hell quick as an arrow.

Ven. Mu Mun said it again with a verse:
> The depths and shallows of wise teachers everywhere
> Are all in my grasp;
> Holding up heaven and supporting the earth,
> The teachings resound everywhere.

C. Explanation

As alluded to in the original case, if one reaches a state of absolute Samadhi, it transcends all relative, ontological distinctions of "existence" and "nonexistence." That point is the realm which is at last liberated from the dust of the world? a sacred space.

When a teacher instructs his disciples, he uses his staff as a "Dharma tool" to test their attainment and measure their capacity for practice. The quintessential case is the famous story of "Deok Sahn's Hit." Ven. Deok Sahn used his stick as a tool for exploding the minds of practitioners; this stick was none other than the staff mentioned before. Whenever practitioners would come to Ven. Deok Sahn and ask about the truth or request that he check their practice, he would stubbornly swing his staff? a "single phrase before speech." In the same way, Ven. Un-Mun Mun-Eon, who founded the Un Mun School, used quite extreme speech:

"As soon as Shakyamuni Buddha was born, he took seven steps and proclaimed, 'In the heavens above and the earth below, only I am sacred.' If I had been there at that time, I would have hit him with a stick, killed him, and thrown his body to a hungry dog."

There is also a story about Linchi, when he was training under Seon Master Hwang Byeok. Following the advice of his Dharma brothers, he had gone to see the patriarch Hwang Byeok, and had asked him for the deep meaning of the Buddha-Dharma; however, he was only met with as many as three blows from the master's staff. Linchi resented his teacher for doing this, so he went and visited the patriarch of another temple, Ven. Dae Wu, and related the entire story to him. Ven. Dae Wu replied, "Hwang Byeok has been so considerate to you!" and praised him. Linchi greatly attained something when he heard this.

In this way, the staff the Seon Masters used had a more potent educational significance than being a mere crutch to support their bodies. Seon Master Pa-Cho Hye-Cheong's use of his staff shows that he was a real man of attainment. Ven. Pa Cho's staff was not just a club or walking stick? it pointed to the pure and clear mind, the original face, true master, the treasury of the true Dharma eye, the mystic mind of Nirvana, the Buddha-mind and so on.

The phrase "All of you, if you have a staff, I will give you a staff." was a Dharma teaching for those asserting that there "is" something, instructing them to check one more time whether it was really true. Whereas "If you have no staff, then I will take it from you," was a teaching for those asserting that there is "not anything," snatching away their deluded minds and urging them to reveal their original faces.

If you say there is no staff, it denies the truth of the staff, i.e. one's original face; if you say there is a staff, it is an attachment to the physical form of the staff, to one's original face. At any rate, whether one says there "is" or "is not" an original face, you make distinctions between existence and nonexistence as a result. Here, Ven. Pa Cho seems to be using his compassionate mind and even his staff to push his disciples into transcending the relative boundaries of right/wrong and denial/attachment, so that they might realize a life of great liberation. Future disciples should never forget the kindness and consideration of the great Seon teachers.

제 45 칙
他是阿誰(타시아수)

❦

그 사람이 누구인가
Case45: Who is That Person?

가. 본칙(本則)

東山演師祖曰. 釋迦彌勒猶是他奴. 且道, 他是阿誰.

   동산(東山)의 오조법연(五祖法演) 큰스님이 이렇게 말하였다.
  "석가와 미륵이 도리어 그 사람의 노예이다. 한번 말해보라. 그 사람이 누구인가?"

나. 평창(評唱) 및 송(頌)

無門曰. 若也見得他分曉, 譬如十字街頭, 撞見親爺相似. 更不須問別人, 道是與不是.

   만약 그 사람을 분명하게 볼 수 있다면, 마치 환한 네거리에서 아버지와 맞닥뜨린 것과 같아서 다시 다른 이에게 그가 자신의 아버지인지 아닌지 물어볼 필요가 없다.

頌曰. 他弓莫挽, 他馬莫騎. 他非莫辨, 他事莫知.

무문 스님이 다시 게송으로 말하였다.
"남의 활을 당기지 말라.
남의 말을 타지 말라.
남의 잘못을 말하지 말라.
남의 일을 알려고 말라."

다. 강론(講論)

여기 본칙(本則)은 『법연선사어록(法演禪師語錄)』의 상당 법문에도 소개되고 있으며 특히 『종문무고(宗門武庫)』에 상세히 나오는데 전체 이야기는 다음과 같다.

화주의 개성 지각(智覺) 선사는 처음 장로사의 부철각(夫鐵脚), 법수(法秀) 화상(和尙) 아래에서 공부했는데, 깨친 바가 없었다. 뒤에 동산(東山) 오조법연 선사의 법문을 듣고 그의 문하(門下)에 당장 들어갔다.

하루는 방장실에서 오조법연 선사가 지각 선사에게 물었다.
"석가나 미륵도 저 사람의 노복이라고 한다. 자, 말해보라. 저 사람이란 누구인가?"

지각 선사는 대답하였다.

"호장삼(胡張三) 흑이사(黑李四) 즉, 길거리에서 보는 평범한 사람입니다."

오조 화상은 이 말에 고개를 끄덕이며 수긍하였다.

당시, 오조법연 화상 밑에는 원오(圓悟) 선사가 수좌로 있었는데 오조 화상이 이 말을 일러주자 그는 이렇게 말하였다.

"지각의 대답이 괜찮기는 하지만 빈 구석이 있는 것 같습니다. 아직 진실을 체득한 것은 아닙니다. 간과해 버려서는 안 되는 일이니 자세히 살펴주시는 것이 좋겠습니다."

이튿날 지각 스님이 입실하자 오조 화상은 어제와 똑같은 질문을 하였다.

지각 스님은 "어제 화상에게 다 말씀드렸습니다."라고 하였다. 그러자 오조 화상은 "어제 무엇이라고 하였더냐?" 하고 물었다.

지각 스님이 "길거리에서 보는 평범한 사람이라고 말씀드렸습니다."라고 하였다.

그러자 오조 화상은 "아니지, 아니야!" 하고 부정하였다. 지각 스님이 다시 물었다.

"어째서 어제는 옳다고 수긍하셨습니까?"

오조법연 화상이 대답하였다.

"어제는 옳았지만 오늘은 틀렸네!"

지각 스님은 이 말 끝에 크게 깨달았다.

본 화두는 제 11칙인 주감암주(州勘庵主)의 화두와 그 성격이 비슷하다. 똑같은 사안을 두고 전날은 '옳다.' 하였다가 뒷날은 '그르다.' 한다. 다 '그 사람'을 찾도록 안내하고 있다.

그 사람은 누구인가? 그 사람은 주인공이다. 자기의 본래면목(本來面目)이며 무위진인(無位眞人)이다. 사바세계 석가모니불이나 미래 미륵불이 다 그 사람 앞에서는 꼼짝 못한다. 이미 해탈하였으며 열반에 이르렀기 때문에 그 어떤 것에도 걸림없이 자유롭고 행복한 존재이다. 피동적이고 노예적인 인생이 아닌, 능동적이고 주체적인 인생을 살라는 교훈이 담겨져 있다. 즉, 자기 인생의 주인으로 살 일이지 남의 노복으로 살아서는 안 된다. 남의 활이나 당기고 남의 말이나 타고 남의 잘못이나 말하고 남의 일이나 알려고 한다면 그런 인생을 어디다 쓰겠는가!

조고각하(照顧脚下)!
지금, 나는, 여기서, 무엇을 하고 있는가?

이것을 자각하지 않으면 안 된다.

Case 45
Who is That Person?

A. Original Case

Seon Master Oh-Jo Beop-Yeon of Dong-Sahn said, "Shakyamuni Buddha and Maitreya are servants of another. Tell me! Who is that person?"

B. Commentary and Verse

If you can clearly see that person, it's like encountering your own father at a familiar crossroads? there is no need to ask someone else whether it's your father or not.

Ven. Mu Mun said it again with a verse:
    Don't draw another's bow,
    Don't ride another's horse,
    Don't speak of another's faults,
    Don't get to know another's affairs.

C. Explanation

This story is also told in the main Dharma speech of the Records of Seon Master Beop Yeon, and in particular, the entire story is related in detail in the Arsenal for the Seon Lineage as follows:

Seon Master Gae-Seong Ji-Gak of Hwa Ju had initially practiced under Seon Master Bucheol-Gak, Beop-Su of Jang Ro Sa temple, but he had no attainment. He later heard the Dharma speech of Seon Master Oh-Jo Beop-Yeon of Dong Sahn and became his disciple right away.

One day in the patriarch's room, Seon Master Oh-Jo Beop-Yeon asked Seon Master Ji Gak, "Shakyamuni Buddha and Maitreya are both servants of another. Tell me! Who is that person?"

Seon Master Ji Gak answered, "Mr. Chang's third son who has a beard and Mr. Lee's fourth son with a dark face? the common man you see on the road."

Seon Master Oh Jo nodded his head in approval.

At that time, Seon Master Won Oh was head monk of the community, so when Oh Jo told him what had happened he said,

"Ji Gak's answer is not bad, but it's like some part is empty? he has not realized the truth yet. He should closely examine that which must not be overlooked."

The next day, as soon as Ven. Ji Gak entered the room, Seon Master Oh Jo asked him the same question as the day before.

Ji Gak said, "Yesterday I told you everything, master." Whereupon Seon Master Oh Jo asked him, "What did you say yesterday?"

Ji Gak answered, "I said, 'The common man you see on the road.'"

Seon Master Oh Jo then rejected his answer and said, "No, that's not it!"

Ji Gak asked him again, "Then why did you say it was correct yesterday and give your approval?"

Seon Master Oh Jo answered, "Yesterday it was correct, but today it's wrong!" When he had finished speaking, Ji Gak had a great realization.

The character of the original story is similar to case number 11, "Joju Sees Through the Hermits." In exactly the same situation, on the previous day he said, "Correct," whereas on the day after he said, "Incorrect." These are all showing us the way to find 'that person.' Who is that person? It's your master, your original face, the true person of no status. Shakyamuni Buddha of the present world and Maitreya Buddha of the future are all humbled by this person. As one has already become liberated and reached Nirvana, it's a joyful existence, free and unhindered by anything at all.

The lesson inside is not to live a passive and servile kind of life, but an active and independent one. That is to say, live as the master of your own life? you should never be the servant of someone else. What's the use of a life where you draw another's bow, ride another's horse, speak of another's faults, or get to know the affairs of another!

Reflect on yourself first!
What am I doing here and now?

You must be aware of that.

제 46 칙
竿頭進步(간두진보)

장대 끝에서 한걸음 내딛어라

Case46:
Take One More Step from the Top of the Pole

가. 본칙(本則)

石霜和尙云, 百尺竿頭, 如何進步. 又古德云, 百尺竿頭坐底人, 雖然得入未爲眞. 百尺竿頭須進步, 十方世界現全身.

   석상(石霜) 큰스님이 말하였다.
   "백 척의 장대 끝에서 어떻게 한걸음 내디딜 것인가?"
   또 다른 고덕(高德)이 말하였다.
   "백 척의 장대 끝에 앉아 있는 사람은 비록 깨달음의 경지에 들기는 하였으되 아직 진짜는 아니다. 백 척의 장대 끝에서 모름지기 한걸음 내딛어야만 시방세계에 온몸을 나툴 것이다."

나. 평창(評唱) 및 송(頌)

無門曰. 進得步, 飜得身, 更嫌何處不稱尊. 然雖如是, 且道, 百尺竿頭, 如何進步. 嗄.

   한걸음 내딛어 몸을 뒤집으면, 어찌 이르는 곳마다 거룩하다고 칭송받지 않겠는가? 비록 그렇다 하더라도 한 번 일러보라. 백 척의 장대 끝에서 어떻게 내디딜 것인가?

 어허!

頌曰. 瞎却頂門眼, 錯認定盤星. 拌身能捨命, 一盲引衆盲.

 무문 스님이 다시 게송으로 말하였다.
  "정법의 안목을 잃어버리면
  저울의 눈금을 잘못 읽는 법.
  몸을 버리고 목숨을 던지니
  한 소경이 뭇 소경을 인도하네."

다. 강론(講論)

 백척간두(百尺竿頭)는 곧 고봉정상(高峰頂上)이다. 우리의 인식 주관 즉, 분별망상, 사량, 계교, 욕심 등이 완전히 쉬어져 버린 자리이다. 심행처멸(心行處滅)하고 언어도단(言語道斷)하여 한 생각도 일어나지 않는 무분별한 경계이다. 그래서 수행자들은 이곳을 구경이라 지향하여 나아간다.

 오르기 힘든 경지인 것만은 분명하지만 그렇다고 해서 여기가 최종 목적지가 되어서는 안 된다. 만일 그곳에서 안주하고 더 이상 나아가지 않는다면 그런 사람은 완전한 세상을 보지 못한다. 정상(頂上)의 자리마저 내줘버려야 한다. 한걸음 더 내딛어 몸을 뒤집어야 한다. 그리해야 깨달음이 완성된다.

'나'라는 자아의식(自我意識)을 송두리째 없애고 철저한 무아(無我)가 된 뒤에는 허공에 몸을 날려야 한다. 대사일번(大死一番)이라는 과정을 거쳐 마지막 그 안주(安住)의 집착을 놓고 허허로이 텅 빈 세상을 맘껏 날 때 참으로 만법일여(萬法一如)의 재미가 느껴진다.

천길 낭떠러지 아래로 떨어지는 중에 가까스로 나뭇가지를 잡았다면 그것은 그렇게 기이한 일이 못 된다. 그것만으론 다 됐다 할 수 없다. 그것마저 놓아버려야 더 큰 영험을 본다. 만일 깨달음만을 추구하여 정진하는 사람이 있다면 그는 극히 소승적(小乘的)이다. 깨달음이라는 또다른 탐욕의 병에 걸려 전전긍긍할 뿐이다. 깨달음도 과정이 되어야 한다.

체(体)의 튼튼함은 용(用)의 활동에 있는 법인데 백척간두에 올라앉았다 하여 그곳에서 머무르기만 하면 어떡하자는 것인가? 앉은뱅이가 되지 말고 활보해야 한다. 이를 중생제도라고 이름 붙이지만 사실 중생제도라 할 것도 없다. 너무나도 당연하기 때문이다. 시주의 은혜조차 망각하고 아무리 도인(道人) 흉내를 낸들 결국은 염치없는 짓을 하고 앉았을 뿐이다. 자기 한 몸만을 편안히 좋게 하는 것은 깊은 골짜기, 바윗덩어리도 할 수 있다.

견성오도(見性悟道)의 추구도 사실은 욕심이다. 그 업(業)의 한계를 벗어나려면 광도중생(廣度衆生)의 원(願)이 있어야 한다. 그리고 그 원은 언제 어디서고 분출되어야 한다. 원이 함께 있을 때 그 수행은 순수하고 맑아진다. 수행을 통한 철저한 안목의 갖춤, 그 밑자리에 중생제도의 원력(願力)이 전제되지 않으면 깨달음은 완성되지 않는다.

백 척의 장대 위에서 한걸음 내딛는 사람은 시방세계에 온몸을 나투는 사람이다.

저만치 혼자 타고 가던 배를 돌려, 건너는 사람을 맞이할 일이다.

Case 46

Take One More Step from the Top of the Pole

A. Original Case

Seon Master Seok Sang said, "How can you take one more step off of a hundred foot pole?"

Another eminent teacher said, "Someone who is sitting atop a hundred foot pole? though he has entered the realm of enlightenment, it is not yet genuine. By all means, only if he takes one more step off of the pole can his whole body manifest in all the ten directions."

B. Commentary and Verse

If you take one more step and turn your body over, how can you not be divine and receive praise everywhere? But even so, tell me, how can you take one more step from the top of a hundred foot pole? Huh?

Ven. Mu Mun said it again with a verse:

> If you lose the discerning eye of true Dharma,
>
> You misread the mark on the balance.
>
> Though you may cast aside your body and sacrifice your life
>
> You are still a blind man leading the blind.

C. Explanation

'The top of a hundred foot pole' is none other than the highest point of a mountain peak? the point where our subjective intellectual understanding, our delusions, relative distinctions, conjectures, schemes and greed are completely put to rest. It is the realm of no relative distinctions at all, where not a single thought arises? the place where mental functioning is extinguished, where speech and words are cut off. Therefore, practitioners make progress and head towards this ultimate point. It's clear that just reaching that stage is hard enough, but even so, one should not stop here? it is not the final goal. If someone is satisfied with this stage and doesn't progress any more, that person cannot see the entire world. Even having reached the summit, you must give it up, take one more step, and completely turn yourself over? your enlightenment is only complete once you do that.

After all awareness of "self" has been completely extinguished, and one becomes thoroughly selfless, you must blow your body away into space. As one goes through the process of 'dying the great death,' when one puts aside the ultimate attachment to serenity, and the realm of emptiness freely arises at will, then one can truly sense the 'singular suchness of all things.' While falling down the bottomless cliff, if one even just barely grabs onto a branch, then that extraordinary event cannot occur. It can't be said to be complete because of just that? only if that branch is also discarded can one realize an even greater miracle. If one practices only by seeking enlightenment, then it is an extremely narrow path. Enlightenment is yet another desire-sickness that one should be afraid of catching? even enlightenment itself must be a process. The strength of one's body is determined by the way it is used? so how can one just go up on top of the hundred foot pole and stay there? Don't be like a legless cripple, you should take great strides! The name associated with this is 'saving sentient beings,' but actually there is no need to even say that? it's only natural! No matter how much you pretend to be enlightened, if you forget the kindness of your benefactors, ultimately it is shameless of you just to sit. Only caring for the comfort and well-being of one's body is comparable to what a deep valley or a heap of stones can do.

Practicing in order to 'see true nature and realize the Way' is actually also a desire. If you want to free yourself from the limitations of this karma, you must make a vow to save sentient beings everywhere; furthermore, this vow should spring forth at any time, in any place. Practice that is done with this vow becomes pure and clear. Though one may have some thorough discernment through practice, if one does not have the vow to save sentient beings at its base, then enlightenment is not complete. The person who takes one more step off the top of a hundred foot pole is one whose whole body manifests in all parts of the world? it's just like turning the boat around that one has ridden alone and sending it back to ferry someone else across.

제 47 칙
兜率三關(도솔삼관)

❦

도솔의 세 가지 관문
Case47: Do Sol's Three Gates

가. 본칙(本則)

兜率悅和尙, 設三關問學者. 撥草參玄, 只圖見性. 卽今上人性在甚處. 識得自性, 方脫生死. 眼光落時, 作麼生脫. 脫得生死, 便知去處. 四大分離, 向甚處去.

   도솔종열(兜率從悅) 큰스님은 세 개의 관문을 설치하여 수행자들에게 물었다.
   "풀숲을 헤치고 그윽함을 찾는 것은 오로지 자성(自性)을 보고자 함이다.
   바로 지금, 그대의 성품(性品)은 어디에 있는가?
   자성(自性)을 알고 나면 바야흐로 삶과 죽음에서 벗어날 수 있다. 그대의 눈빛이 땅에 떨어질 때, 어떻게 삶과 죽음에서 벗어나겠는가?
   삶과 죽음에서 벗어날 수 있다면, 곧바로 가는 곳을 알 수 있다. 그대의 사대(四大)가 각각 흩어질 때, 어디로 간다고 생각하는가?"

나. 평창(評唱) 및 송(頌)

無門曰. 若能下得此三轉語, 便可以隨處作主, 遇緣卽宗. 其或未然, 麤湌易飽, 細嚼難飢.

만약 이 세 가지 질문에 대해 제대로 답변할 수 있다면, 어디서나 주인이 될 수 있고 만나는 것마다 종지에 딱 들어맞을 것이다. 혹시 그렇지 못하다면 거친 음식을 먹어 배만 부르게 되고, 꼭꼭 씹어 보아도 배고픔을 면하기가 어렵게 된다.

頌曰. 一念普觀無量劫, 無量劫事卽如今. 如今覷破箇一念, 覷破如今覷底人.

무문 스님이 다시 게송으로 말하였다.
 "한 생각 속에 두루 무량겁을 관하니,
 무량겁의 일이 바로 지금의 일이로다.
 지금 한 생각을 꿰뚫어 볼 수 있다면
 보고 있는 그 사람 꿰뚫어 보리."

다. 강론(講論)

인생(人生)에 있어서 참으로 본질적인 질문들이다. 요약하면 이러하다.

첫째, 그대의 성품은 어디에 있는가?
둘째, 죽음이 닥칠 때 어떻게 하겠는가?
셋째, 죽은 뒤에 어디로 가는지 알겠는가?

수행이란 이러한 주제 즉, 생사대사(生死大事)의 일대사(一大事)를 해결하기 위함이다.

생각을 갖고 살아가는 존재(存在)라면 그 누구이든 고민할 수밖에 없는 삶의 숙제이다. 이러한 근본문제 때문에 출가자가 생기고, 눈 밝은 선지식을 찾아 구도행각도 마다하지 않는 것이다. 수행자는 번뇌 망념의 잡초를 헤치고 그윽함을 찾으려고 부단히 정진한다. 그 그윽함의 자리를 본성(本性), 자성(自性), 불성(佛性)이라고 한다. 이러한 성품(性品)을 보는 것을 견성(見性)이라고 하는데, 본다고 함은 직접 확인한다는 의미이다.

중생(衆生)은 본래성불(本來成佛)이다.

자기 성품을 깨달아 본인이 스스로 청정한 부처라는 사실을 확인한다면 생사(生死)의 문제는 저절로 해결된다. 견성성불(見性成佛)은 번뇌 망념의 중생심(衆生心)에서 본래의 청정한 불심(佛心)으로 되돌아가는 것을 말한다.
　'지금 그대의 성품은 어디 있는가!'
　불성(佛性)의 자리를 여기서 당장 확인함은 자기정체성(自己正體性)을 드러내는 일이기도 하다. 그리하면 고(苦)의 대표격인 죽음에서도 벗어날 수 있다. 죽어도 죽는 게 아니다. 번뇌 망념의 속박에서 이미 벗어났는데 죽음인들 무슨 상관이 있겠는가?
　죽음이라는 표현을 쓰지만 살아 있으면서도 분별 작용에 떨어지면 그것 또한 임명종시(臨命終時)이다. 눈빛이 땅에 떨어졌다는 표현이 꼭 맞다. 우리는 수시로 임명종시를 맞는다. 그리고 눈빛이 희미해진다. 우리의 본성은 이러한 위기 상황에서 실참(實參)하는 자각(自覺)을 요구하는 것이다.
　그리하여, 생각이 깨인 사람들은 자기의 본래심(本來心)으로써 지혜로운 생활을 하려고 노력하는 것이다. 이것이 곧 죽음이 닥칠 때 어떻게 해야 하는 것인지를 아는 일이며 죽은 뒤에 어디로 가는지를 아는 일이기도 하다.
　주체적 자각으로 시간, 공간의 주인이 되어 자신의 일에 몰입할 때 그 현실 그대로 진실된 깨달음의 세계가 전개된다.

참으로 한 물건 있어 홀로 드러나(獨有一物常獨露) 담연히 삶과 죽음을 따르지 않는다(湛然不隨於生死).

그 한 물건이 진정 내 것이다.

Case 47
Do Sol's Three Gates

A. Original Case

Seon Master Do-Sol Jong-Yeol created three gates; he asked his disciples,

"1) Having overcome all kinds of thick weeds(hindrances), you seek the profound truth as you devote yourself to realizing self-nature. But tell me, right now, in this moment, where is your true-nature?

2) If you realize self-nature, you are almost free from life and death. But when your life force is seeping into the earth, how can you then escape from life and death?

3) If you can free yourself from life and death, you can realize where you will soon go. But when your four elements disperse, where do you think you will go?"

B. Commentary and Verse

If you can answer these three questions correctly, then

wherever you are, you can be the master, and Seon teaching will be appropriate whatever you encounter. If you can't do that, then the only the act of eating will fill your stomach; even though you chew your food well, it's difficult to appease your hunger.

Ven. Mu Mun said it again with a verse:
> Thoroughly perceiving infinite time in a single thought-
> Infinite time is just this moment.
> If you can see through this moment's thought,
> You see through the one who sees through it.

C. Explanation

These are truly fundamental questions for human beings. In summary:

1) Where is your true-nature?
2) What can you do when death is approaching?
3) Do you know where you will go after you die?

People practice in order to resolve these topics, the 'one great affair' of the 'Great matter of life and death.' This is the homework of life that anyone who has thinking and a so-called existence can't help but be concerned about. People leave society and become monastics because of these issues, and are willing to make pilgrimages in search of a keen-eyed teacher. A practitioner will train ceaselessly, overcoming the weeds(obstructions) of delusory thinking in order to find profundity. This point of profundity is called original-nature, self-nature, and Buddha-nature. Realizing this is 'seeing true-nature' which means that one has directly verified it for oneself.

Sentient beings are originally Buddhas, so when you realize your nature and confirm that you yourself are already a pure and clear Buddha, the matter of life and death is naturally resolved. 'See true-nature and become Buddha' means that one returns to the originally pure and clear Buddha-mind from the ordinary state of delusions and defilements. "Indeed, where is your nature now!" When you realize that your Buddha-nature is right here and now, you reveal your true identity, and so you can even be free from the fundamental suffering of death. Even though you die, it is not death. You have already freed yourself from the fetters of delusions and defilements, but what does that have to do with dying?

We use the word "die," but even while we are still alive, if we get trapped by relative distinctions, we have already reached the moment of death. The expression "life force seeps into the earth" is exactly correct? we often encounter the moment of death, and the light from our eyes, our life force, becomes fainter. In this kind of perilous situation, our original-nature needs us to investigate the truth and awaken ourselves. People who have awakened then strive to lead a wise life with their original minds. This is the realization of both what to do when death is approaching and of where you go after you die. Through one's own self-awakening, you become master of time and space, and when you are absorbed in whatever you are doing, the world of true enlightenment unfolds according to the reality of the situation, just as it is.

There is truly one thing which by itself is clear; it is pure, untainted, and does not follow life and death? this 'one thing' is truly ours.

제 48 칙
乾峯一路(건봉일로)

열반으로 가는 한길

Case48: One Path Leads to Nirvana

가. 본칙(本則)

乾峯和尙, 因僧問, 十方薄伽梵, 一路涅槃門. 未審路頭在甚麼處. 峯拈起拄杖, 劃一劃云, 在者裏. 後僧請益雲門. 門拈起扇子云, 扇子䟦跳上三十三天, 築著帝釋鼻孔. 東海鯉魚, 打一棒雨似盆傾.

한 스님이 건봉(乾峯) 큰스님에게 물었다.

"시방의 모든 부처님들은 한길로 열반의 문에 이르렀다고 합니다. 그런데 그 길이 어디에 있는지 아직 모르겠습니다."

그러자 건봉 큰스님은 주장자를 들어 허공에 한 획을 긋고 일렀다.

"이 안에 있느니라."

뒤에 그 스님이 운문 큰스님에게 자세한 설명을 부탁하였더니, 큰스님은 부채를 집어 들고 이렇게 말했다.

"이 부채가 뛰어올라 33천에 이르러 제석천의 콧구멍을 쑤시고, 다시 동해의 잉어를 치니 한 방에 물동이를 기울인 것처럼 큰 비가 쏟아지는구나."

나. 평창(評唱) 및 송(頌)

無門曰. 一人向深深海底行, 簸土揚塵. 一人於高高山頂立, 白浪滔天. 把定放行, 各出一隻手, 扶竪宗乘. 大似兩箇馳子相撞著. 世上應無直底人. 正眼觀來, 二大老總未識路頭在.

한 사람은 깊고 깊은 바닷속으로 가 흙을 일어 자욱한 먼지를 일으키고, 또 한 사람은 높고 높은 산꼭대기에 서서 하얀 파도를 하늘 끝까지 일으킨다. 쥐는 것과 놓는 것을 뜻대로 하여, 각자 한 손씩 내밀어 선(禪)의 종지를 붙들어 세운 것이다. 마치 두 마리 낙타가 서로 부딪치는 것과 같으니, 세상에서는 이에 대응할 사람이 없도다. 바른 눈으로 살펴보건대, 건봉과 운문 두 노장은 열반으로 가는 길이 어디에 있는지 전혀 모르는구나.

頌曰. 未擧步時先已到, 未動舌時先說了. 直饒著著在機先, 更須知有向上竅.

무문 스님이 다시 게송으로 말하였다.
　　"걸음을 떼기도 전에 벌써 거기에 이르렀고

혀를 움직이기 전에 벌써 다 말해 버렸다.
비록 한 수 한 수 기선을 제압했더라도
다시 향상(向上)의 도리가 있음을 알아야 하리라."

다. 강론(講論)

부처되는 길을 물었더니 한 스님은 허공에 주장자로 한 획을 그었고, 또 한 스님은 부채를 들고 허무맹랑한 얘기나 해댄다. 여기에 대해서 무문 스님은 잘한 짓이 아닌 것처럼 말하는데 그 이유는 향상(向上)의 도리(道理)가 부족하다는 것이다.

본칙이 무문관의 선(禪)에 대한 결론적 의도가 있는 게 분명하다. 강의나 책 서술의 핵심이 처음과 끝에 있음이 통상적인데 본 『무문관』도 예외가 아니다. 화두의 진수 무(無) 자에서 시작하더니 수행의 결론, 부처되는 길에서 막이 내린다.

부처되는 길이 무엇인가?

무분별지의 경계를 넘어 다시 구체적인 차별의 경계인 무분별후득지(無分別後得智)의 경계에 이르는 것을 말한다.

세상살이는 크게 세 가지로 분류할 수 있다.

첫째는 상대적 대립의 경계인데 순전히 업아(業我)의 세계이다.

즉, 유심(有心)으로 살아가면서 가유(假有)에 매여 허덕인다. 차방예토(此方穢土)를 그 공간으로 삼는다. 산은 산이요 물은 물이다.

둘째는 절대적 평등의 경계인데 완전한 무아(無我)의 세계이다. 즉, 무심(無心)으로 살아가면서 진공(眞空)을 자양분으로 삼는다. 현실을 철저히 부정하고 타방정토를 꿈꾼다. 산은 산이 아니요, 물은 물이 아니다.

셋째는 절대적 평등의 경계를 넘어선 구체적 차별의 세상인데 바야흐로 온통 하나로 열린 대아(大我)의 세계이다. 즉, 여여심(如如心)으로 살아가면서 진공묘유(眞空妙有)의 재미를 만끽한다. 그토록 원망하고 부정하였던 현실을 다시 긍정하고 받아들이면서 차방정토(此方淨土) 건설을 책임진다. 다시, 산은 산이요 물은 물이다.

여기 세 번째가 곧 구경(究竟)이요, 완전한 부처의 자리이다.

건봉일로(乾峯一路)!

열반으로 통하는 외통수의 길, 향상의 도리는 눈앞에 명백하게 드러나 있다. 그쪽으로 향하기만 하면 된다. 이미 그곳에 이르렀으니 지도(至道)는 무난(無難)이라 하는 것이다.

Case 48
One Path Leads to Nirvana

A. Original Case

A monk asked Seon Master Geon Bong, "It is written that all the Buddhas of the ten directions have reached the gate to Nirvana by one path. But I still don't know where that path is."

Whereupon Seon Master Geon Bong lifted up his staff, made a stroke in the air, and said,

"It's in here!"

Later the monk asked Seon Master Un Mun for a detailed explanation. The Seon Master picked up his paper fan and said, "This fan jumps up to the thirty-third heaven and picks the nose of Sakra Devanam-Indra; striking the carp of the East Sea, a huge rainstorm pours down, like tilting a water jar."

B. Commentary and Verse

One person goes into the deepest sea, blows on the mud and raises clouds of dust; another one stands on the top of the highest mountain and lifts up white waves to the top of the sky.

This means that one is holding tight, the other is letting go; each one stretches out his hand, holding fast to the Seon teaching. Just like two camels colliding with each other, no one in the world can deal with this. When seen in the correct light, neither of the two old monks Geon Bong or Un Mun know where the path to Nirvana is.

Ven. Mu Mun said it again with a verse:
> Before even a step is taken, you have already arrived;
> Before your tongue even moves, you have said everything.
> Though you may take the initiative every time,
> You should know that there's a higher path.

C. Explanation

When asked about the way to become Buddha, one monk drew a stroke in the air with his staff, the other monk took his paper fan and told an absurd story. Ven. Mu Mun did not praise either because they were lacking a better way.

It's clear that the original case is intended to serve as a

conclusion for the Seon teaching in the Gateless Gate. Usually the main point of a story is placed at the beginning and the end of a lecture or book, and the Gateless Gate is no exception? it begins with the quintessential question "Mu" and finishes with the way to become a Buddha.

What is the way to become a Buddha?

It means that one passes the stage of no relative distinctions, and again reaches the stage of concrete discrimination? the attainment of wisdom after experiencing the lack of relative distinctions. We can broadly classify three ways of living in this world:

The first stage is that of relative conflicts and opposition, which is entirely the realm of the karmic self. That is to say, living one's life with a mind of attachment, and struggling with karmic relationships. The profane world is seen as time and space? the mountain is a mountain, water is water.

The second stage is that of absolute equality, the realm of completely no-self. In other words, as one lives without a mind of attachment, one uses true emptiness as a kind of nourishment; thoroughly denying the present reality, one dreams of the Pure

Land somewhere else. The mountain is not a mountain, water is not water.

The third level is when one transcends even the stage of absolute equality? it's the realm of concrete distinctions, but one which is completely one, where the world of the "greater self" has been opened. That is to say, while living with a mind of true-suchness, one thoroughly enjoys the mystical existence which is true emptiness. To such an extent that as one accepts and reconfirms the present reality which was previously rejected and denied, one becomes responsible for building the Pure Land oneself. Once again, the mountain is a mountain and water is water.

This third stage is complete Buddhahood or enlightenment.

Geon Bong's one path, indeed!

The ultimate, conquering path that leads to Nirvana? this "better" way appears clearly in front of our eyes. It's enough if you only head in that direction? you have already arrived there, the true path of no hindrance.

천일 무문관 청정결사(淸淨結社)

가. 무문관 수행이란?

일체 문 밖 출입을 하지 않으며 바깥세상과는 완전히 담을 쌓는 폐관(閉關) 수행으로 하루 한 끼 먹는 일종식(一種食)을 원칙으로 한다. 공양은 하루 한 끼, 공양간에서 행자를 통해 각 방의 봉창으로 투입함.

수행은 주로 참선이며, 개인이 좋아하는 조사어록을 스승삼아 볼 수 있다. 그리고 사경명상, 절 수행, 자비도량참법 수행 등을 병행할 수 있다.

나. 무문관 청정결사의 의의

무문관 청정결사는 탐욕심, 시기질투심으로 가득찬 사바세계의 모순을 해소하여 청정불국토를 구현하려는 서원에서 무일(無一) 우학 스님이 발기하고 무문관 입방 도반 스님 12명이 함께 하고 있으며 무문관 밖으로는 한국불교대학 大관음사 신도 전체가 재가자로서 후원, 동참하는 결사이다.

한국불교 1700년 역사상 무문관 청정결사는 초유의 일로서 이번 결사의 성과에 따라서 제 2차, 제 3차의 결사도 고려하고 있다.

여기서 결사란 어떤 목적을 가지고 함께 수행하는 모임이란 뜻이다.

다. 무문관 청정결사의 슬로건

[마음 청정, 세상 청정]

무문관 청정결사는 분명 마음의 청정, 육신의 청정은 물론 나아가 사회의 청정, 국토의 청정을 이룰 것이다. 모든 것은 다 나로부터 시작한다는 발상에서 나부터 청정하면 모든 세상이 청정해질 것임을 확신하며 이 결사를 도모하는 것이다. 내 마음이 청정하여지면 온 세상이 청정해짐을 바르게 알아 이번 결사에 적극적으로 동참, 정진할 것을 온 사부대중이 다짐한다.

3대 대승경전 사경명상

라. 무문관 청정결사 기간

2013. 4. 15(음력) ~ 2016. 1. 15(음력)

마. 정진 대중

무문관 입방 대중 12명(대표 無一 우학스님-한국불교대학 大관음사 회주),
한국불교대학 大관음사 신도 전체

바. 무문관 청정 결사의 재가자 수행 과목

(가) 3대 대승경전(법화경, 화엄경, 금강경) 사경명상 - 21권 쓰기
(나) 사경한 글자 수를 고려하여 자기 역량껏 매일 절하기
(다) 매일 금강경 1회 독송(CD를 들으면서)
(라) 참선 하루 1시간

사. 무문관 청정결사의 다짐

무문관 청정결사 기간 동안 온 사부대중은 눈조심, 귀조심,
입조심하며 덜 먹고, 덜 낭비하는 생활을 할 것입니다.
특히, 3대 대승경전을 반드시 사경하겠습니다.
그리고 마음 비우는 오체투지의 절을 하겠습니다.

이는 곧　과거의 참회이며,
　　　　　현재의 보람이며,
　　　　　미래의 성취임을
　　　　　철저히 믿고 완주하겠습니다.

無一 우학 스님

대한불교 조계종 영축총림 통도사에 출가하여 성파 대화상을 은사로 득도하였다. 대학에서 선학(禪學)을 전공하였으며 선방, 토굴, 강원, 무문관에서 참선 등 정통 수행을 체계적으로 닦아왔다. 성우 대율사로부터 비니(毘尼) 정맥을 이었다. 오래전부터 간화선을 한 단계 발전시킨 선관쌍수로써 후학들을 지도하고 있다.
현재는 학교법인 이사장 등 모든 공식 직함을 내려놓고 무문관 3년 수행 정진 중이다.

대표저서

저서는 맨날 고기묵고1~2, 금강경 핵심강의, 새로운 불교공부, 길손여행, 완벽한 참선법, 최상의 기도법, 학습 초발심자경문, 티베트 체험과 달라이라마 친견, 우학스님의 빛깔있는 법문, 불교혁신론 & 포교론, 부처되는 공부, 우학스님의 명상 북다이어리 참 좋은 인연, Soundless Whisper ; Now or Never Forever, 우학스님의 행복 메시지 ; 참 좋은 생각, 좋은 세상 나소서, 하루 한가지 마음공부법, 감사하고 사랑하며, 불교명언명구, 공감, 참좋은세상, 내 인생 최고의 만남 붓, 신심명강설-지혜로운 삶(전2권) 등 200여 권의 저서가 있다.

무문관강론

초판발행	2013. 8. 10
초판 3쇄	2014. 8. 20

저자	無一 우학 스님
영어번역	명행 스님(미국)

펴낸곳	도서출판 좋은인연 book.tvbuddha.org
	편집/ 김현미 손영희 모상미 김규미
	등록/ 제4-88호
	주소/ 대구 남구 봉덕3동 1301-20
	전화/ 053.475.3706 ~ 7

ISBN	978-89-93040-21-0(03220) 25,000원

잘못된 도서는 **구입처에서 교환**해드립니다.
이 책의 저작권은 저자에게 있으며 서면에
의한 저자, 출판사의 허락없이 내용의
일부를 인용, 발췌 및 복제를 금합니다.

우리절 한국불교대학 大관음사
다음카페 불교인드라망/ 홈페이지 한국불교대학
참좋은 병원/ 노인전문요양원 무량수전
참좋은 이서중고등학교/ 참좋은 어린이집,유치원

한국불교대학 大관음사
감포도량 무일선원 무문관